Dispatches from Palestine

Middle East Issues

Series editor: Steve Sherman (Editor, *Middle East International*)

So much coverage of the contemporary Middle East is lost between the immediacy of journalistic reporting and the valuable, but highly specialist, concerns of academic research. Setting out to bridge that gap, Middle East Issues, published in collaboration with *Middle East International*, offers concise, accessible and lively books on the region.

Each title aims to be wide in scope but contemporary in emphasis. Subjects covered will range from major issues such as the peace process and Iraq, to other dynamics such as Islamism in Turkey, the politics of the Gulf, the reform movement in Iran and the new geopolitical alignments in the Caucasus. Middle East Issues is aimed at readers that are interested in – or are becoming interested in – a region whose conflicts and concerns are of immense importance to the rest of the world.

Middle East International is regarded as one of the most informative and influential periodicals covering the Middle East. Further information and subscription rates are available from:

Middle East International
21 Collingham Road
London
SW5 0NU

e-mail: steve@meiuk.u-net.com
101450.3626@compuserve.com
Telephone: 0171 373 5228
Fax: 0171 370 5956

First published 1999 by Pluto Press
345 Archway Road, London N6 5AA
and 22883 Quicksilver Drive, Sterling,
VA 20166–2012, USA

Chapters 1–4 and 6 © *Race & Class*; Chapters 7 and 16 © *Journal of Palestine Studies*; Chapters 8, 13 and 19 © *Al-Ahram Weekly*; Chapters 9 and 21 © *News from Within*; Chapters 10, 14, 15 and 17 © *Middle East International*; Chapter 11 © *Middle East Report*; Chapters 12 and 23 © *Red Pepper*; Chapter 22 © *Independent on Sunday* (South Africa)

British Library Cataloguing in Publication Data
A catalogue record for this book is available from the British Library

ISBN 978 0 7453 1337 5 paperback

Library of Congress Cataloging-in-Publication Data
Usher, Graham, 1958–
    Dispatches from Palestine : the rise and fall of the Oslo peace process / Graham Usher.
        p.   cm.
    ISBN 0–7453–1342–6 (hc.)
    1. Arab–Israeli conflict—1993—Peace. 2. Palestinian Arabs—Politics and government. I. Title.
DS119.76.U83 1999
956.05'3—DC21   99–19670
                                                                                            CIP

Designed and produced for Pluto Press by
Chase Production Services, Chadlington, OX7 3LN
Typeset from disk by Stanford DTP Services, Northampton
Printed on demand by CPI Antony Rowe in the UK and Edwards Bros in the US

Contents

Part 3 Post–Oslo – Decline and Fall
May 1996 to December 1998

Maps

List of Interviewees

Marwan Barghouti is the General Secretary of the Fatah movement in the West Bank, the premier nationalist faction within the PLO. President of Birzeit University Student Council between 1985 and 1987, Barghouti was expelled from the occupied territories in 1987 for membership of Fatah, then an outlawed organisation. He returned to the West Bank in April 1994 and was elected a Palestinian Council member for Ramallah in January 1996.

Yossi Beilin is a Member of Knesset and a leading figure in Israel's Labour Party. As Israel's deputy Foreign Minister, Beilin initiated the Oslo 'secret channel' that led eventually to the PLO-Israeli Declaration of Principles in September 1993. Losing to Ehud Barak for leadership of the Labour Party in June 1997, Beilin has since become the leading advocate in Israel for a unilateral Israeli withdrawal from South Lebanon.

Azmi Bishara is a Palestinian Member of Knesset and leader of the National Democratic Assembly in Israel. A former philosophy lecturer at Birzeit University, Bishara has been active in struggles against Israel's occupation of the West Bank and Gaza and for the political and national rights of the Arab minority in Israel. He is a member of Mutawin – the Palestinian Institute for the study of democracy and author of numerous political and philosophical studies.

Rabbi Aryeh Deri is a Member of Knesset and the General Secretary of Israel's Sephardi List for Tradition or Shas movement. He served as Interior Minister for the governments of Yitzak Shamir and Yitzak Rabin. Currently on charge for corruption (and so prevented from holding any cabinet position), Deri was nevertheless seen as an enormously influential figure in Israel's last government of Binyamin Netanyahu.

Ibrahim Ghoshah is the official spokesman of the Palestinian Islamic Resistance Movement, Hamas. Currently based in Amman, he has been active in Hamas and its forerunner, the Muslim Brotherhood, since the late 1950s. Ghoshah was a member of the Hamas delegation to the 'reconciliation' talks with the PLO in Cairo in October 1995.

Ilan Pappe is one of Israel's 'new historians' whose work has challenged received accounts of Israeli history. A lecturer in Middle Eastern history at Haifa University, Pappe is the author of *The Making of the Arab–Israeli Conflict* (I.B. Taurus, 1994) and several other studies on the Arab-Israeli conflict. He is a founder of the Institute of Peace Research in Israel and a member of the Israeli Communist Party.

Introduction

My first encounter with Palestine was in the summer of 1985 when I spent two months teaching English to Palestinian refugees in the Gaza Strip. On my second day I was given a tour of Jabalyia refugee camp. Picking my way through the warren of sand tracks and breeze-block shelters, I met Achmed Abdallah. In a gesture I soon learned to be customary, he invited me to stay that night in his home. In the neat little 'study' he has chiselled out of his shelter, he relayed to me the story of his life.

Thirteen years later I revisited Achmed as a journalist. I listened again to his story, and published it wherever I could as my contribution to remembering the 50th anniversary of the Palestinian al-Nakba – the catastrophe that, in 1948, delivered the state of Israel for 'the whole Jewish people' and exile to the bulk of the Palestinian people, including those who now reside in Jabalyia.

As I transcribed the tape, I was struck by how little Achmed's reading of his life had changed, despite the momentous events that had passed under the bridge of the intervening years. But I also reflected on my motives for retrieving Achmed's story rather than one of the similar histories I had heard in camps in Gaza, the West Bank, Jordan, Lebanon and Syria. The answer I think was an ill-defined need to return to the original source to place a symmetry on a people and a cause that, for the last 16 years, have become my own.

The currents that swept me to such an identification had none of the usual tributaries. I am not Jewish. I have none of the ties of family, service or travel that bind so many Europeans to the Arab world. Until very recently, I was woefully ignorant of Arab civilisation in general and Palestinian nationalism in particular. Nor – as a committed non-believer – was I enticed by the spectacle of Palestine and Jerusalem as the cradle of the world's three great monotheistic religions. What drew me to Palestine was rather the meaning of an experience and an event.

The first was born of being a teacher in the East End of London in the 1980s. Many of those I taught were the offspring of immigrants who had come in the 1950s and 1960s from the Indian sub-continent and the Caribbean to rebuild Britian's shattered post-war economy. Others were the later arrivals of refugees, asylum-seekers and migrants who had washed up in Britain in flight from the turmoil of their own societies. In classrooms, church halls and living rooms, they narrated their stories with much the same mix of emotion and detachment as Achmed did his, and revealed to me the organic links between the institutional and popular racism they experienced 'here' and the regimes of political oppression and national dislocation they had fled from 'there'.

Many would speak of Palestine. Indeed, of all the issues we discussed, it was Palestine that most exposed the gulf separating their view of the world from 'ours'. For most Europeans, the demand that Palestinians sacrifice all or most of their pre-1948 patrimony by accepting the state of Israel was but a negligible part of the atonement for the incomparable crime done to the Jewish people by the Nazis and their allies. It troubled very few of us that the penitence was to be paid by a people who had played no role in the genocide.

But, for the refugees in my classroom, Palestine was the emblem of their own dispossession. For them, the PLO's quest for a homeland chimed with their own aspirations of liberation, independence and return. As for Israel, that was merely proof of the enduring fact of colonialism in what was supposedly a post-colonial world. Palestine thus became for me not simply one cause among others, but the prism that threw into relief the context, bitterness and violence of all those other causes espoused by my Kurdish, Iranian, Sri Lankan and Chilean students. It lent light to their experience and shade to my experience of them.

The event was Israel's 1982 invasion of Lebanon. Like most interested observers, I was initially stunned by the sheer scale of the carnage – a toll of 18,000 Palestinian and Lebanese dead in less than five months of hostilities, according to Lebanese statistics. But I was also outraged by Israel's purpose.

'Israel invaded Lebanon in order to kill an idea,' wrote the Lebanese journalist, Salim Nassib, in August 1982, 'the idea of the existence of the Palestinian people.' In pursuit of that end, Israel revealed itself a state capable not only of inflicting extraordinary suffering on another people, but of inducing amnesia in its own – a defence mechanism only partially broken in September 1982 when some 350,000 Israelis took to the streets to protest at their government's complicity in the massacre of 2,750 Palestinians in Beirut's Sabra and Shatila camps.

It was to give flesh to the 'idea' that, over the next three years, I embarked on the road that led to Gaza. It turned out to be one of the most formative events of my life.

On the one hand, it was my first experience of a third world. In Gaza, the fine print of statistics to do with infant mortality, malnutrition and population density became the real and plain misery of barefoot children, overcrowded classrooms and open sewers that flowed beside the makeshift domiciles of a people who had fled their homes in 1948 and had been 'beached' in Gaza ever since.

It also revealed the apartheid that stood at the core of Israel's rule in the occupied territories. I remember one bumpy ride that took us via a dirt road on the coast to the electrified fence of Gaza's Kfar Darom settlement. On the perimeter were sand dunes strewn with garbage and women and children sorting the cucumber crop. Inside there were ashphalt roads, lawn sprinklers and a tennis court. Believing we were a Jewish delegation down from a Kibbutz, a settler told us that the main problems facing Kfar Darom were 'the salinity of the soil, the insects and the Arabs – in that order'.

On the other hand, Gaza utterly changed my perception of Palestinians. Like most of my generation, I had been inculcated with PLO and Israeli stereotypes of Palestinians as freedom fighters or 'terrorists', depending which side of the page you read. Prior to 1985, perhaps my main image had been of videotaped but faceless guerrillas scampering from one Beirut sidestreet to the next in lonely defiance of the Israeli army. In Gaza, the tape shrivelled up to reveal the physiognomy of a people and a society, and my identification with them became all the stronger for it.

During those two months – usually under an ancient palm tree that arched the yard of the school where we lived – I listened to ordinary people tell of extraordinary lives. They described how the social structures of their villages in pre-1948 Palestine had become transplanted to the urban sprawl of the camps. Due to their jobs across the Green Line, many spoke fluent Hebrew and displayed a deep knowledge of the flaws (and merits) of the state 'the Jews' had built for themselves. Armed with this peculiar intimacy, they would argue the worth – with us and between themselves – of the competing political strands out of which the PLO's modern brand of nationalism was woven.

In all this, there was much that I found alien, even disagreeable. But there was much I held in common. Out of the experience of exile and occupation – and nurtured by their nationalism – I came across a people who had been forced to live by unspoken codes of community, solidarity and self-sacrifice. As a child of the working-class movement, these were my values. And fresh from a society that embodied their obverse in Thatcherism, my encounter with them again in Gaza lent a kind of moral familiarity to my support of the Palestinian cause. In London, 'Palestine' had been the key to another world. In Gaza, it enabled me to see more clearly the ethical bases of my own.

Out of that motivation above all others, I have been returning ever since. In 1989 – during the *intifada* – I went with a delegation of British teachers and students to publicise Israel's collective punishment policy of school and university closures. In 1991, I took up the offer of a friend to work again as an English teacher in Gaza. I expected to stay for a year or so and perhaps write the occasional article for whatever publication would take me.

Seven years later, I was still there. I remained partly out of the desire to write. But another, deeper reason was to do with the moment. Arriving in Gaza on the back of the Gulf war but before the Madrid Peace Conference, I was privileged to be on hand during one of those rare periods in which history breaks cover to become a lived, contemporary experience.

Not that I was so prescient at the time. In August 1993, I acted on a hunch when I asked the then deputy editor of *Middle East International*, Steve Sherman, whether he would be interested in regular copy from Gaza. A month later, the Oslo accords were signed, and the copy flowed to *MEI* and various other publications. I soon abandoned teaching and whatever plans I had to return to London. I became a journalist.

I give this map of my route to Palestine as the background to the articles in this book. In a precise sense, it explains where they came from and what, for many readers, will be seen as their obvious bias. A cursory read from the first piece to the last makes pretty clear where my political and moral sympathies lie. Nor is there any attempt to hide the fact that this is the work of an anti-Zionist writer.

For me Zionism remains a colonialist ideology, if a peculiar one. Israel has undoubtably created a haven for persecuted Jewish minorities. But, because of its original settler and later messianic ambition, it has done so by either dispersing the Palestinians from a land it claims is exclusively its own or by concentrating those who remain into ever contracting cantons. This essentially apartheid logic is as true today as when the state was founded, whether the terrain is inside Israel, the occupied territories or the countries that host the Palestinian diaspora. And until this supremacism is overcome I cannot see how Israelis and Palestinians can coexist as equals, whether together as citizens or separately as sovereignties.

Yet if today I am no more forgiving, I am I think a little wiser. I understand now for instance that only the Israelis can rid themselves of their ethnocentrism. Nor will the change be anything other than a long, attritional process. For Zionism still explains both Israel's internal coherence as a society and why the notion of an exclusively Jewish state will always be experienced by the peoples of the region as an imperial, foreign and running wound.

It took me a while to reach that conclusion. For a long time I believed that an inclusive, non-sectarian and democratic nationalism could in the end include both Palestinians and Israeli Jews. I was never an advocate of a resolution by force of arms. But I did hanker after the old dream of a democratic, secular Palestine from the river to the sea.

I don't think I believe that any longer. This is not simply because Palestinian nationalism has its own tendency to sectarianism and exclusivity. It is more because I have come to realise that the ties of persecution, religion and ethnicity by which the modern Israeli identity is bound are long and tenacious. For better or worse, Israeli Jews are today a nation, 'forged' (in the words of one their most trenchant and best informed Palestinian critics) 'out of the Hebrew language, the army, the special Israeli experience and the Jews' own aspiration to have a state'. That state exists and is called Israel.

By the same criteria, the Palestinians too are a nation, a fact that even old rejectionists like Ariel Sharon and Henry Kissinger have recognised. Thus the old goal of 'killing the idea' of Israel or Palestine – for either side – has gone or at least been weakened.

But – as these pages make clear – mutual recognition has not meant reconciliation. At root, the conflict remains the claim of two peoples for one territory. And the conflict continues – even if masked in the name of the Oslo peace process – because Israel has yet to decide whether reconciliation is to be through two states or one or, indeed, whether reconciliation is to be sought at all.

Whatever my political biases, I have tried to be true to certain journalistic principles. First, I have tried to listen to my sources so that it is their story that is being told rather than my own. For me, this should be a tenet of journalism everywhere, even if one notably unfashionable at present. But on the question of Israel–Palestine it is essential. For the conflict is also one of contending narratives: what for Jews is the 'liberation' is for Palestinians the 'catastrophe'; what for Palestinians is a natural right of return is for many Israeli Jews the threat of extinction. Each narrative has its voice and its terms, and is comprehensible within them – whether I listen to Sheikh Ahmad Yassin's 'story' in Gaza or Salah Tamari's in Bethlehem or Aryeh Deri's in Jerusalem.

Far more than its textual commitments, Oslo was a process driven by events. As someone who witnessed most of them, I always aimed to capture the mood of their moment, in all its ambiguity. Thus, in September 1993, I tried to convey the doubt that tempered Palestinian jubilation around the signing of the Oslo accords. In May 1994, I wanted to grasp the melancholy joy that accompanied the first troops of the returning Palestinian Liberation Army. And, in September 1996, I felt compelled to show the fear of the Palestinians' realisation that, in the absence of a negotiated settlement, the fight for the occupied territories would no longer be between stones and tear gas, but between Kalashnikovs and helicopter gunships.

Finally, I have always believed that journalism at its best acquires the rank of what John Pilger has called 'contemporary history' – when it explains the making of an event as well as its ephemeral significance or 'news value'. The longer analytical pieces in this collection were thus written out of the need to 'think aloud' about the social and political processes that turned the 'children of the intifada' into the often brutal foot soldiers of the Palestinian Authority's intelligence forces; or about the causes and the circumstances that explained not only the rise but also the appeal of Hamas in Gaza or Hizbollah in Lebanon or Shas in Israel. The same need accounts for the space given here to interviews with activists, thinkers and politicians from both sides of the divide. For all, my questions were prompted less by the hunt for a scoop than by the iniquisitive, 'Where did this come from?', 'Where is this going?' and, above all, 'What does this mean?'

Which is not to say my goal was the disinterested pursuit of knowledge. It was always – and unapologetically – to aid the Palestinians in their struggle, if not for absolute justice, then for the maximum of attainable justice that the facts of Israel and Israelis will allow. Nor was the motivation anything other than political, in the sense that politics for me means a morality in practice. The reason is self evident. If history is written by its winners, then journalists who side with the losers should write in the faith that the last, in the end, shall be first. Until that rendezvous with victory is come, our job is to bear witness and to give voice – for 'the struggle of people against power is the struggle of memory against forgetting'.

London, December 1998

Part 1

Oslo One – Gaza/Jericho First
September 1993 to September 1995

f

Preface

Known colloquially as 'Gaza/Jericho First', Oslo's preamble was rocked by crises and events that first derailed the timetable and then determined the content of the Declaration of Principles (DOP), signed in Washington on 13 September 1993.

The initial negotiations on the DOP were immediately snarled by Israel and the PLO's conflicting interpretations over the substance of Palestinian self-rule. No sooner had agreement been reached – largely due to Yassir Arafat acceding to the Israeli version – than did the Jewish settler and Israeli army doctor Baruch Goldstein kill 29 Palestinians at prayer at Hebron's Ibrahimi mosque on 25 February 1994. The massacre not only expedited Arafat and the Palestinian Authority's arrival in Gaza and Jericho in May and July 1994, but also the first wave of Hamas suicide operations inside Israel. The simmering tensions between Arafat and his Islamist opponents exploded on 18 November 1994, when Palestinian police shot dead 14 Palestinians outside Gaza's Palestine mosque. This confrontation laid the bases for an increasingly authoritarian Palestinian regime as Arafat sought to quell Hamas in line with Israel's security-led template for Palestinian self-government.

The focus of the five pieces in this section is less on these events than on the circumstances and motivations that produced the DOP. 'Why Gaza says yes, mostly' argues that an Israeli consensus had emerged in the early 1990s for a move from direct military rule over the Palestinians in the occupied territories to more indirect or neo-colonial forms of domination. This was particularly so in the Gaza Strip. The brutal closure and repression policies applied there from April 1993 prepared the ground for the new dispensation endorsed by Oslo.

The principal reason for the new consensus was the *intifada*, and Israel's failure – despite six years of ruthless and collective punishment – to crush it militarily. By April 1993, the occupied territories were hovering on the brink of an anti-colonial war, with military forms of resistance replacing the uprising's earlier modes of mass protest and civil disobedience. Nor did it escape Israel's notice that the armed struggle was being led not by the PLO but by Hamas

Palestinian Autonomous Area –
Gaza Strip 1994

Ele Sinay Crossing

Erez Crossing

Mediterranean Sea

Gaza City

Nahal Oz Crossing

Karni Crossing

Netzarim

ISRAEL

Kfar Darom

Katif Bloc

Kissufim Crossing

Khan Yunis

Rafah

Sufa Crossing

EGYPT

Rafah Terminal

International Passage

Kerem Shalom Crossing

▦	Israeli settlement area.	0 2 4 kilometers
☐	Palestinian autonomous area.	0 1 2 miles
—	The Delimiting Line.	
- - -	The Security Perimeter (Palestinian police responsible for security between the security perimeter and the delimiting line of the Gaza Strip.)	
☐	Military installation area.	
═══	Roads patrolled by Israel (Lateral road).	
■	"Yellow area" (Israel responsible for security. Palestinians responsible for civil affairs, except for settlement areas.)	

Source: Agreement on the Gaza Strip and the Jericho Area.

– whose orgins, evolution and policies are described in 'What kind of nation? The rise of Hamas in the occupied territories'.

Ending the *intifada* was not the only factor driving Israel to change the *status quo ante* in the West Bank and Gaza. In 'An Israeli Peace', Israeli historian, Ilan Pappe, argues that with the Tunis-based PLO Israel found a Palestinian interlocutor ready to accept a negotiated settlement on Israel's terms. These were to gain a Palestinian covenant for Israel's long-held ambition to decouple what Pappe calls the '1948 issues' (refugees, Jerusalem and withdrawal), non-negotiable as far as Israel was concerned, from the '1967 issues' (settlements, borders and the prospect of a demilitarised Palestinian state), where some form of accommodation could be sought.

Speaking in 1995, Pappe was also prescient about Israel's regional objectives with Oslo. These were less a 'New Middle East' based on open borders and an integrated market than the old Middle East, but now with Israel as an accepted military party to the region's geo-political alliances.

The argument is amplified in 'Palestine: the economic fist in the political glove'. Based on economic relations blooded in Gaza prior to Oslo, the article describes how after its signing Israel moved openly to neo-colonial rather than direct forms of control of the economic resources of the occupied territories. The upshot envisaged is an apartheid solution in which greater economic integration is combined with demographic and political separation.

'Jabalyia and the meaning of return', reflects on the contending notions of 'return' in Palestinian nationalism. Prompted by the arrival of Palestinian Liberation Army units in Gaza and Jericho in May 1994, the conclusion drawn is that any two-state solution means an abandonment of a right of return to a specific locale in favour of the right of return to a polity called Palestine.

The first four of these articles were published in shorter versions in various magazines, but received their final treatment in *Race & Class*, the quarterly journal of the Institute of Race Relations. Written in May 1994, 'Jabalyia and the meaning of return' gets its first airing with this volume.

1

Why Gaza Says Yes, Mostly

Sunday, 12 September 1993: 27th year of the Israeli occupation; 70th month of the uprising; the day before Rabin and Arafat meet in Washington to sign the Oslo accords; the night before the peace ... A convoy of trucks, loaded up with hundreds of youths waving gigantic Palestinian flags, slowly wends its way through Gaza's Rimal quarter to the city's main square. Women lean out of balconies shrieking ululations of joy, while, on the street, men dance the *dabka* between snarled, honking cars and to a din of deafening drums. Bemused Israeli soldiers try to make sense of it all. One, outside Gaza Central Prison, sits astride a wall, his helmet in his hands. In peace – as in war – Gaza eludes his understanding. The crowd, uncontrollable now, surges into the square, gripped by a wave-like movement that drives it on. Everywhere there are pictures of Abu Ammar (Yassir Arafat), and a single, resounding chant, 'Gaza, Gaza, Jericho first; and then Jerusalem'.

A boy – no more than 14 – grins at me. 'Hamas', he says, 'is finished'. Another of about the same age shakes his head in disgust, 'They have forgotten Palestine.' He pulls his bicycle on to the road and rides away, an outcast from the feast. Then a father strides up to me, a son and two daughters straggling behind him in tow. He shakes my hand furiously. I don't know him but gregariousness in Gaza is as ingrained as resistance. 'What about the peace? What do you think?' I reply, honestly, that I don't know. 'It's good', he says. We watch a group of about a dozen guys gather round an Israeli soldier who chats to them in Arabic. The father lifts the youngest daughter on to his shoulder and kisses her on the forehead. 'It's good,' he insists, 'because of the girl.'

The Conditions for Withdrawal

At the beginning of April 1993, Israeli PM Yitzak Rabin sealed off the West Bank and Gaza Strip 'until further notice', in response to some of the highest levels of inter-Israeli–Palestinian violence seen since the *intifada* erupted in 1987. In March alone, 15 Israelis and 28 Palestinians had been killed. And the Israelis, leaders and people alike, were scared, not just in the occupied territories but of them – in West Jerusalem, Jaffa and Ashkelon.

An editorial in the daily of *Yediot Aharonot* on 29 March encapsulated the fear: 'If the present wave of violence continues it will only be a matter of time before an overall confrontation breaks out and the balance of force between the IDF and the stabbers will be brought into play. Again the Palestinians will be the ones to pay the price.' The next day Rabin threw an iron curtain across the territories and announced 'tough new measures' to 'take Gaza out of Tel Aviv'. 'It is better', he said, 'for the Arabs not to be swarming around here.'

Even by the bloody annals of the occupation, these 'measures' were without precedent in their ferocity. During the next two months, IDF foot patrols, sometimes 40 deep, trawled through Gaza with the express remit of 'reclaiming the towns and camps from masked gunmen', while 'search operations' – deploying anti-tank missiles, explosive charges and helicopters – blew up scores of houses, displacing hundreds of families, on the hunch that in them might or might not reside 'terrorists'. Undercover units – special IDF groups who masquerade as Palestinians – infiltrated deep into camps and villages to dredge out and usually take out 'intifada activists'. Across the Strip, observation posts were set up with 'open fire' regulations so relaxed that, in the words of the human rights monitoring group Middle East Watch, they underwrote 'a licence to kill'. To take one instance from hundreds: in less than three days after a new observation post had been installed in Khan Younis in south Gaza, five Palestinians had been shot dead and a further 250 injured.

When asked about this massive increase in Palestinian casualties, the IDF Chief of Southern Command, General Vilnai, explained: 'We introduced new parameters in the Gaza Strip and the local population didn't like it. They replied with stones, and in our response – in which all standing orders were followed – dozens were wounded by precise fire.' What these 'standing orders' meant on the ground was spelled out by an Israeli border police officer in an interview in the newspaper *Maariv*: 'If you see someone holding a cinderblock, Molotov cocktail or an iron bar, you shoot him without making any bones about the matter. There is no longer a procedure for apprehending a suspect.'

The upshot of this savage new turn in Israel's counter-insurgency operations is given eloquent testimony in dossiers compiled by Palestinian, Israeli and international human rights organisations. Between February and May 1993 – i.e. the months immediately preceding and following the closure – 67 Palestinians were killed by the IDF in the Gaza Strip alone, including 29 in May, making it the bloodiest month of the uprising. A staggering 1,522 were wounded, of whom 474 were children, with 98 per cent of their injuries coming from live ammunition. Ten 'search operations' were carried out, leaving 450 permanently homeless or, as one local expressed it, 'refugees from refugee camps', and costing in damage to property something to the tune of $50 million. In the meantime, Palestinians were beaten, their houses raided, their localities curfewed, with such monotony that most lawyers and human rights researchers simply gave up counting. At the time of writing – as peace dawns – there are 12,000 Palestinians in Israeli prisons and detention camps, two thirds of whom are from Gaza, with most of these rounded up during the last year.

If Gazans have lived through 'sheer hell' these last six months, the political message rammed home by the terror has not been lost on them either. It was delivered by a senior IDF source cited in the *Jerusalem Post* on 16 April: 'We fully realise this closure cannot be a permanent solution, but it did have a profound psychological effect on those under closure. It shattered their illusions that terrorism will simply cause us to abandon the territories without any word of agreement or arrangement. They should realise that they will get absolutely nothing without negotiations.'

In other words, the territories – via the political and military oppression wrought and veiled by the closure – were to be held hostage until and unless Palestinians came round to Israel's way of thinking at the peace talks. As for human rights abuses, extra-judicial executions, the enduring illegality of occupation, these were to be so many bargaining chips. 'You [the Palestinians] want to solve the problem', said Rabin in April. 'The place to do that is around the negotiating table. So it is permissible for me to keep the territories closed as long as possible.'

By May 1993, Rabin pronounced himself satisfied with the 'security situation', adding that 'separation' of the territories from 'sovereign Israel' would now be 'indefinite'. Attacks on Israelis inside the Green Line were down to a trickle, even though armed actions on the IDF within the occupied territories continued undimmed, with 58 such assaults in Gaza in August alone. At about the same time, Rabin signalled that he was ready to do a deal on an 'interim settlement being applied first in Gaza'. He did not have to wait long. Delivered through the canny midwifery of Norway's Foreign Minister Jurgen Holst and Israeli Foreign Minister Shimon Peres, Arafat himself came up with 'Gaza/Jericho First'. The rest is history

– recognition of the PLO, peace accords, a World Bank bail-out and handshakes on the White House lawn.

But the victor is Rabin. He has managed to translate Israel's near hysteria of March 1993 into a mandate for his government to extricate itself from Gaza on its own terms. Sure, 'a strong Palestinian police force' can have Gaza's refugee camps, and the PLO can run a few municipal services. But, on the crucial issues of land, settlements and sovereignty, Rabin, as he repeated *ad nauseum* in the Knesset debates on the agreement in September, has 'budged not an inch'. What 'Gaza/Jericho First' amounts to is a truncated version of autonomy in Gaza and Jericho first. And autonomy for the 'Arab residents of the territories' is what Rabin's Labour Party has been advocating – and what the PLO had historically rejected – ever since it was broached at Camp David in September 1978. As Israeli journalist Ze'ev Schiff put it – writing presciently in *Ha'aretz* on 2 April 1993 – 'What is actually going on in Gaza now is a battle over the conditions of withdrawal.'

At a Crossroads

The day after the news broke on Gaza/Jericho first, Azzam Ahmed Hassan, a 17-year-old from Gaza's Nuseirat refugee camp, was killed by an IDF undercover unit. It was, locals said, 'a typical operation'. The boy was trying to enforce a strike called by Palestinian rejectionist factions against the eleventh round of peace talks in Washington. A Mercedes taxi with Gaza number plates drove up alongside him. Three soldiers dressed as Arabs got out and shot him in the chest. They then strip-searched him for weapons, and dumped the body in the trunk of the taxi.

Four hours later, I am drinking coffee with a Palestinian pharmacist whose shop lies adjacent to the square where the killing took place. How does he feel about the agreement? 'Look, I hate curfews, the killings, the occupation. I hate what I myself have become.' About the killing earlier in the day he simply shrugs his shoulders. 'Most of the people in the camps are with the agreement', he says. 'They want the army to go.'

His hunches are right. According to numerous opinion polls published since the signing of the accord, a solid 66 per cent of Gaza supports it. Given what they have just been through – coupled with an economic siege brought on by the closure that has sent unemployment soaring in the camps to nearly 60 per cent – this is hardly surprising. 'Anything,' people say here, '*anything*, is better than what went before.'

Yet there has been a curious ambivalence, a kind of schizophrenia, about the Strip in the months since 13 September. Palestinian flags fly from almost every rooftop, while portraits of Arafat are slung across everything from telegraph poles to desktops. The welcoming ceremonies staged to greet the first batch of 617 Palestinian prisoners released by the agreement, including 274 from Gaza, were felt and moving, especially for ex-internees such as Salim Zerai, captured by Israeli forces 23 years ago 'in a boat off Haifa', and Naima el-Helo, imprisoned for a total of eight years, who has 'paid the price' of her freedom also with the loss of a hand and the sight of one eye.

At the same time, a quiet rage smoulders, periodically exploding into the ugliest of forms. In the wake of the agreement, Gaza saw a spate of suicide missions in which Palestinians wired up with explosives threw themselves at sundry IDF installations. There has been an upsurge in so-called 'collaborator killings', in which Palestinians have killed other Palestinians not just for the treason of 'working for the enemy', but also for alleged 'social' crimes like drug-taking, adultery and theft. A new 17,000 strong Palestinian police force is waiting in the wings, instructed, under the terms of the agreement, to 'work closely' with Israeli intelligence and security forces to maintain 'law and order' in the 'autonomous enclaves'. And, most ominiously of all, the last two months have witnessed the assassinations of three major PLO figures in the Strip, with the word on the street that the perpetrators are from 'inside the Palestinian house' rather than *agents provocateurs* trying to sow mischief outside it.

Viscerally and psychologically, Gazans, like Palestinians everywhere, are at a crossroads. They could go either way. In a series of articles in the Palestinian press, former Palestinian delegation head Haidar Abd al-Shafi, who hails from Gaza and is viewed by many as embodying the conscience of Palestinian nationalism, has said: 'I tell you plainly the negotiations are not worth fighting about. The critical issue is transforming our society. Only when we achieve this will we be in a position of strength. We must accept nothing less than democracy and a united Palestinian front.'

Amen to that. If the agreement creates enough political and civic space for Palestinians to set about renewing their institutions, democratising their life, mobilising around issues of national and social justice, then, maybe, something can be salvaged. If, on the other hand, the agreement augurs only an apartheid of separate political development shackled by Israeli economic domination – the *sine qua non* of autonomy – and the camps are torn down only to be replaced by ghettos, and the ghettos become the turf of rival militias, then, 'God forbid', says Abd al-Shafi, 'We may cease to exist as a people.'

Gaza Accepts

I ended my visit to Nuseirat at the house of Abu Musa. He is not the sort of Palestinian in Gaza usually courted by Western journalists, being neither a bearded Islamist nor a stone throwing youth. He is a fisherman and he is old – 60 years. He has lived under the British, the Egyptians and the Israelis. He comes from Magdal, now Ashkelon, and 'lost everything' when Israel was established in 1948. Like many of his generation, he forged his national identity through work and education, paying for three of his brothers to go through university in Europe and the Gulf countries. His skin has the consistency of cracked leather, but he has the kindest eyes you will ever see. How does he feel about 'Gaza/Jericho First'?

'I feel like a man who has lost a million dollars and been given ten.' He pauses for a moment, then leans over to touch my arm. 'But, you see, I lost the million dollars a long time ago. So I will keep the ten. We cannot go on the way we are. I accept, I accept, I accept. After so much bloodshed, I accept. But, please, don't ask me how I feel.'

Gaza, September/October 1993; *Race & Class*, January–March 1994

2

What Kind of Nation? The Rise of Hamas[1] in the Occupied Territories

In December 1992, the Izzadin el-Qassam brigade – the military wing of the Palestinian Islamic Resistance Movement, Hamas – launched a series of guerrilla actions in the West Bank and Gaza that claimed the lives of six Israeli soldiers in as many days. The spectacular success of these operations – together with the fear they aroused in Israeli society – prompted the Rabin government to summarily expel 415 alleged 'Islamic fundamentalists' to the hills of South Lebanon and inaugurated the worst period of Israeli repression in the occupied territories, certainly since the outbreak of the *intifada* in 1987 and arguably since Israel's occupation in 1967.[2]

Hamas's actions also impressed on the Israeli government and people alike the political urgency of extracting themselves from the 'quagmire' of Gaza, in Rabin's words, of 'getting Gaza out of Tel Aviv'. The solution – cultivated in secret Israeli/PLO negotiations during the course of 1993 – was the idea of Israel's partial military withdrawal from Gaza and the West Bank town of Jericho as a prelude to a fully-fledged peace agreement, a remedy that would eventually underpin the Israeli/PLO Declaration of Principles (DOP) signed in Washington in September of that year.

If Hamas had done nothing else, these military operations and their dramatic political fall-out would have ensured it at least a footnote in the annals of the Israeli/Palestinian conflict. But Hamas is much more than its military arm. But what is it? What are its origins? And what kind of challenge does its essentially modern banner of political Islam mount to PLO nationalism?

From Culturalist Politics ...

Hamas first appeared publicly in February 1988 as 'a wing of the Muslim Brotherhood [MB] in Palestine'.[3] Under the stewardship of its 'spiritual guide', Sheikh Ahmad Yassin, a specifically Palestinian MB had emerged in the occupied territories in the 1970s as a culturalist and social movement whose primary aim was the

18

'founding of the Islamic personality'.[4] In political terms, this entailed an abstention from all forms of anti-occupation activity, prioritising instead a cultural struggle against the PLO's 'atheist' commitment to secular nationalism.

Lubricated by Saudi money, in Gaza especially the MB built an impressive social infrastructure, by 1986 controlling 40 per cent of Gaza's mosques and its single Islamic University, which, with 7,000 students, was then the largest in the territories.[5] These advances were facilitated not only by the internal crises that had rocked the PLO after its 1982 military defeat in Lebanon. They were also encouraged by the Israeli occupation authorities, who viewed the rise of political Islam as a useful tool for fomenting dissension within Palestinian nationalism. 'We extend some financial aid to Islamic groups via mosques and religious schools in order to help create a force that would stand against the leftist forces which support the PLO', acknowledged the Military Governor of Gaza, General Segev, in 1986.[6]

When the intifada erupted, the MB was posed with a dilemma: either forgo its *de facto* accommodation with the occupation or lose the Palestinian street, where legitimacy was born less of piety than national resistance. After initial hesitation,[7] it resolved the contradiction through the formation of Hamas, an Islamist movement whose goal was national liberation.

In August 1988, the MB published the Covenant of the Islamic Resistance Movement, spelling out 'who Hamas is and what it represents'. Essentially a political manifesto – it mirrors in its format the PLO's founding National Charter – the Covenant is a pastiche of the MB's socially puritanical version of Islam, an accomodation to PLO nationalism and a rehash of Euro-centric anti-semitism. Territorial nationalism – once adjured by the MB as 'idolatry'[8] – is now 'a function of religious belief', while the distinction made by the PLO between anti-Zionism and anti-semitism becomes so obscured that the Jews are held responsible not just for Israel and the 'murder of the prophets', but also for 'the Second World War' and 'the League of Nations'. But the legacy of the MB's pre-intifada social agenda persists, with a swipe at 'secularism as completely contradictory to religious ideology'.

Hamas pledged 'unity with our PLO brothers' during the uprising's early years. But on the street it organised independently of the PLO's tribune in the territories, the Unified National Leadership (UNL), issuing its own leaflets, following its own calendar of strike days and refusing to acknowledge the sole representative status of the PLO.[9] Hamas's actions also continued to be largely culturalist in thrust, imbuing the uprising with an Islamist flavour, rather than with a political or military strategy. Its principal activism in this period was less national struggle than a vicious social offensive against all manifestations of 'un-Islamic behaviour', especially in Gaza where women were forced to wear the headscarf as a sign of both modesty and nationalist rectitude.[10] The UNL's defensive, apologetic response to this campaign was to cost them dear among the crucial contituencies of women, youth and Christian Palestinians.[11]

Despite the vitriol of its propaganda against Jews as the 'sons of apes and swine', Hamas's relations with the occupation authorities remained essentially quietist, with the army 'never interfering with Hamas strike days'.[12] Israel's then Defence Minister, Yitzak Rabin, met such prominent Islamist figures as Mahmoud Zahar and Ibrahim Yazouri for 'talks' in the summer of 1988.[13] It wasn't until June 1989, on discovery that Hamas guerrillas were behind the kidnap and killing of two Israeli soldiers,[14] that the IDF finally declared the movement illegal. This was a year and a half after the uprising's outbreak, and nearly one year after Israel's banning of all nationalist (e.g. PLO/UNL) popular committees. Until then, the Israeli mindset *vis-à-vis* the Islamists was one that stubbornly mistook a socially conservative movement for a politically conservative one.[15]

... to Political Culture

By the close of the 1980s, Hamas could claim to have become an integral part of the Palestinian scene, regularly polling second only to Arafat's Fatah movement in professional and student elections across the territories. But it was not a hegemonic or even counter-hegemonic force at this stage. Rather, Hamas's tack was less to politically oppose the PLO than to ignore its existence.[16]

Two events were to undercut such apoliticism, propelling Hamas to increasingly challenge the PLO's claim of sole representative of the Palestinian people and thereby transforming Islamism in the occupied territories from a culturalist politics to the advocacy of an alternative political culture for the liberation of Palestine.

The first was the Palestine National Council's (PNC) decision in 1988 to recognise Israel as defined by its pre-1967 borders and formally adopt 'two states' as the solution to the Israeli/Palestinian conflict. This, Hamas deemed, was sacrilege, since 'Palestine, from the river to the sea, is a holy trust afforded to Muslims by God.'

The second event was the US-brokered peace plan for the Israeli/Arab conflict in the wake of the 1991 Gulf war. 'We will confront the (Madrid) Conference', railed Hamas leader, Ibrahim Ghoshah, 'and we will do that by escalating the uprising in the occupied territories.'[17]

In response to the PLO's eventual endorsement of the Madrid founded peace process, Hamas vowed 'a full return to the military option' and demanded '40 to 50 per cent representation on all PLO bodies'. These were demands that invited, and got, rejection.[18] The PLO countered by accusing Hamas of 'being the plaything of Israel and the US and of intending to replace the PLO as leader of the Palestinian movement'.[19] The period of tenuous unity between Palestine's nationalist and Islamist wings, one that by and large had held during the uprising, was over. The Israelis blew on the flames by choosing this time to arrest several hundred Hamas supporters and by sentencing Yassin to life imprisonment for his alleged involvement in Islamist inspired 'terrorism'.[20]

In late 1991, in open defiance of the PLO leadership, Hamas mounted a series of ominously well supported actions against Madrid, shutting down Gaza with three consecutive days of strikes and exposing just how frail was the nationalist consensus behind the Madrid formula. Subsequent events served only to confirm this, marked by rising popular frustration at the lack of political progress at the negotiating table and, on the ground, by factional tension and tit-for-tat strikes which succeeded only in divesting the intifada of what was left of its mass appeal. The degeneration reached its nadir in July 1992 with street battles in Gaza between Fatah and Hamas supporters that left over 100 injured and three dead.

At the time, political wisdom had it that with the 'July clashes' Hamas lost the street; when it came to the crunch, Palestinians were nationalist first and Islamist second.[21] Yet this was only part of the story. Hamas were driven into open confrontation with Fatah not only because of Madrid, but also because of the election in June 1992 of a Labour Government pledged to 'make peace with the Palestinians within nine months' – a prospect Hamas viewed with trepidation as undercutting the 'rejectionist' basis of its support.

Hamas's fully-fledged turn to armed struggle in December 1992 was thus not so much based on any strategic vision *vis-à-vis* how to revive the intifada. Rather, it was a belated attempt to rescue Hamas's credibility within Palestinian public opinion – a public that was growing weary of the sacrifices entailed by the uprising as well as of such 'negative phenomena' associated with the 'fundamental-ists' as a rising toll of internecine 'collaborator' killings and a stifling social puritanism.[22] Having failed to wrest legitimacy from Fatah on the street, Hamas instead tried to appropriate its nationalist legacy of armed struggle against Israel and, in upping the military ante, stymie Rabin's plans for autonomy.

In the run-up to the DOP, Hamas could look back on the intifada as a period of sustained activism in which it had made considerable inroads into the PLO's hegemony on the social, political and military fronts. For the first time in the occupied territories, Palestinian nationalism was faced with an indigenous, authentic and mass opposition completely outside its sway. In the aftermath of the expulsions, an opinion poll showed that 16.6 per cent of Palestinians in Gaza and 10.5 per cent in the West Bank held that 'the Islamic Movement rather than the PLO represented them'.[23] Like other radical Islamist currents in the Middle East, Hamas had become a barometer of political discontent, nurtured, in this case, by a divided national leadership and by an immobilising Madrid formula that had stubbornly refused to bring peace.

Oslo

With the signing of the DOP or Oslo accords in September 1993, there was a sense that Hamas's days as a counter-hegemonic force were numbered. Oslo – so the argument ran – would not only restore the PLO's standing as the 'sole legitimate representative of the Palestinian people'. More importantly, the international funds pledged to underwrite the autonomy would replenish the PLO's empty coffers and so lubricate the networks of support and patronage through which legitimacy could be consolidated.

Yet, in the period since Oslo, Hamas has established itself as the single largest political opposition in Palestinian society. It has done this through cleverly calibrated tactics of guerrilla warfare, political alliances and a pragmatic social agenda. But the aim is not so much the destruction of self-rule[24] as the flexible pursuance of a long-held Islamist strategy in the occupied territories – namely, the assertion of an Islamist culture for Palestinian civil society.

The Gun

In 1989, former Israeli army General Aharon Yariv paid a back-handed compliment to two decades of Palestinian armed struggle. 'The PLO', he said, 'understand that the aim of any military operation is political, and that the success of such operations should be measured in political terms.'[25]

A like logic drove Hamas's military policy after Oslo. The political aim was less to scupper the DOP completely than to stall the pace of its implementation. The longer the delay of the dividends of peace in the territories, the Islamists figured, the greater the PLO's loss of support and legitimacy. It was an accurate prognosis.

Actions such as Hamas's ambush in December 1993 of Colonel Mintz, coordinator of the IDF's undercover units in Gaza, or General Security Service (GSS) operative, Noam Cohen, killed by one of his own informers in the West Bank in February 1994, generated huge political kudos on the Palestinian street. They also put the fear of death into the Israeli military establishment. On the Mintz assassination, army sources were quoted to the effect that in terms of professionalism Fatah 'had achieved nothing remotely resembling it during the 26 years [*sic*] of its existence'.[26]

Yet if the military targets were Israeli, Hamas's political sights were fixed firmly on the PLO leadership, and particularly Arafat. Given the loathing with which most Palestinians view the GSS and undercover squads, no Palestinian leader could possibly condemn the killing of a Mintz or Cohen, and none did. Arafat's dilemma was that whereas for the Israelis silence was tantamount to collusion, for Palestinians any public disavowal implied collaboration. The PLO leader was thus damned if he did speak and damned if he didn't.

A similar logic obtained with Hamas's actions after the Hebron massacre in February 1994, especially its revived penchant for hitting Israeli civilians inside the Green Line.[27] In April of that year, a West Bank Palestinian rammed a car full of explosives into a crowded bus station in the Israeli town of Afula, killing eight and wounding 40 others. In a statement claiming responsibility, Hamas said that ending the attacks was 'conditional on Israeli settlers quickly leaving the West Bank and Gaza' – a sentiment with which polls showed 88 per cent of Palestinians in the territories concurred. But if killing soldiers and settlers compromised Arafat, killing Israeli civilians 'inside sovereign Israel'[28] lit the fire beneath Rabin.

In a survey published in January 1994, 70 per cent of Israelis said they would consider 'Palestinian autonomy a failure if terrorists continue to murder Jews'. Domestic opinion compelled a gesture from the Israeli PM after every Hamas attack, usually the rote demand that Arafat curb 'fundamentalist terror'. The problem for Rabin was that he knew that the PLO leader was ultimately powerless to stop Hamas, not just because his Palestinian Authority (PA) with its 'strong police force' had yet to be installed, but mainly because such impotence was written into the Oslo agreement. There it states categorically that Israel retains responsibility for the 'external security' of the 'autonomous areas', in other words, for Israel and the Israelis. Hamas, of course, knew this too. 'If Hamas launched an attack against Israelis in Gaza during the autonomy, this would undoubtably cause problems for the PLO leadership', said one Islamist. 'But what if Hamas were to hit Israelis in Tel Aviv? What has the PLO to do with the protection of Tel Aviv?'[29]

Rabin was thus repeatedly pushed into using collective sanctions against Palestinians whose sum political effect was to shore up Hamas rejectionism at the expense of the PLO's awkward conciliation. He would close off the West Bank and Gaza, round up hundreds of 'Hamas suspects'[30] and launch massive punitive raids against Palestinian communities to dredge out and often take out 'Muslim extremists'. Yet each successive crackdown not only chipped away at the PLO leader's support in the territories; it undermined Rabin's own conviction that 'only Arafat' could govern the self-rule.[31]

The upshot of Hamas's military policy after Oslo was perhaps best encapsulated by Israeli journalist, Danny Rubinstein. 'Hamas's terrorist activities contain two main political messages. The first – to Arafat and the PLO – is do not dare ignore us; the second – to the state of Israel – is that negotiations with the PLO do not constitute the final word and that Hamas must also be taken into account.'[32]

The Olive Branch

Hamas's military policy since Oslo has been a considered one of spectacular strikes designed to pack the maximum political punch. A similar foresight has marked its handling of relations with the PLO, and especially Fatah. However rejectionist its public face against Oslo, Hamas's stance *vis-à-vis* the other PLO factions after its passing has been essentially conciliatory, signalling that the Islamists are fully cognizant of the new political realities thrown up by self-rule.

In January 1994, Hamas announced its formal enlistment in the Palestinian Forces Alliance (PFA), a Damascus-based coalition of ten Palestinian movements opposed to Oslo and including the PLO's Popular and Democratic Fronts. Hamas had in fact been in negotiations with the Fronts since Oslo, but these had snagged on wrangles over the weight of each's representation in the alliance.[33] Inside the territories, however, Hamas's main motive for joining this unprecedented nationalist-Islamist bloc was opportunist.

On the one hand, the Islamists worked with the PLO rejectionists to notch up such notable victories as Birzeit University's 1993 Student Council elections when a Fatah-led coalition lost out to an anti-Oslo one.[34] On the other, Hamas ditched the Fronts whenever it saw no electoral need for them – as for the Engineers' Association elections in Gaza in February 1994, where Hamas stood with Islamic Jihad to score a tie with pro-Oslo nationalists. Needless to say, both Bir Zeit and the Engineers had historically been bastions of Fatah.

Participation in the PFA also allowed Hamas to drop some of the more offensive (or unpopular) features of its social agenda in the name of Palestinian unity. The months after Oslo witnessed a visible relaxation of Hamas's strictures against un-Islamic behaviour – such as Palestinian women going about unveiled or families going to the beach 'at a time of national suffering and martyrdom' – in favour of a more pragmatic line maximising political rather than sectarian support. It was, of course, supremely ironic that in their desire to avoid 'giving Arafat cover', the Fronts gave cover to the Islamists, ideologically the greatest foe of the PLO's Marxist factions.

But for most Palestinians in the territories the main fear born of the DOP was not so much the jockeying of the Damascus-led rejectionists than that its implementation would lead to civic strife between Fatah and Hamas. A deft mix of clear political direction and discipline on the part of both leaderships in the period between the signing of the DOP and the installation of the PA kept this nightmare scenario largely at bay.

In September 1993, Fatah and Hamas prisoners signed a pact banning inter-Palestinian violence to resolve political disagreements over Oslo. Hamas leader, Aziz Rantisi, declared that the job of Islamists was 'to fight against any confrontation between supporters and opponents of the PLO–Israeli agreement'. Apart from a couple of skirmishes at street level, this line of peaceful coexistence was adhered to, even in relation to potentially explosive issues such as the fate of collaborators and the role of the Palestinian police.

Hamas repeatedly warned the PLO in its self-rule negotiations with Israel not to amnesty collaborators in exchange for promises to release Palestinian prisoners. But Yassin also acknowledged that once a 'Palestinian state or autonomy is established under Arafat ... the residents ... will be forbidden to harm others'.[35] A like approach held *vis-à-vis* the Palestinian police. In October 1993 – after an ambush near a Gaza settlement in which two Izzadin el-Qassam guerrillas, dressed as Israelis, killed two IDF reservists – Hamas released a video vowing peace with the police 'unless they raise their guns against us'. On the eve of the police's entry into Gaza and

Jericho, even this vaguely menacing tone had become moderated to the point of fraternity. 'We welcome the Palestinian security forces as brothers', said Yazouri, in May 1994.[36]

The new conciliationism was perhaps most evident in Hamas's shifting perceptions of the centrality of the PLO to Palestinian politics, nationalist and Islamist alike. Whereas historically Palestinian Islamism had evolved as a reaction to the PLO's secular nationalism, after Oslo Hamas was at pains to impress the patriotism of its opposition. 'It would not be in the Palestinian interest to have the PLO fall apart' over the DOP, said Islamist intellectual, Bassam Jarrar.[37] Rantisi mused that Hamas sought not the 'downfall of the PLO' but rather that its 'structure and shape be redefined on a democratic basis'.[38]

The Ballot Box

From the moment Arafat shook Rabin's hand most Islamists understood that the DOP was politically irreversible. 'We can't stand up and say to people we want the occupation to stay. That would be irrational. You have to be realistic or the current will move you aside', said Islamist journalist Khalid Amayreh.[39] The issue for Hamas was what was going to be its place in the self-rule, and particularly its stance towards the elections for the PA.

According to the PFA, the line was to have no truck with 'any elections or bodies to be established in compliance with the Gaza/Jericho accord'. But it was clear from the outset that Hamas was hardly going to be bound by this. 'Islamists are divided between those supporting participation [in elections] and those opposing it', said Yassin in November 1993, but, 'I consider it better to participate than to abstain, providing that the (autonomy) council be empowered with legislative privileges.' Participation would 'reassert the strength of the Islamist presence ... and prevent it losing ground because of its isolation'.[40] But Hamas's representative in Jordan and on the PFA, Ibrahim Ghoshah, was more hard-line, insisting that Hamas would not participate in 'any elections associated with autonomy'.[41]

In the period since Oslo, Hamas's position on the PA elections has swung between these two poles, suggesting a rigorous debate within the movement between the 'pragmatists', who seek some sort of accommodation with the PA, and the 'rejectionists', who do not. The crux of the argument is clear. While many Hamas supporters view any participation in the self-rule as lending 'the DOP a credibility it does not have',[42] others point to the electoral successes

Islamists have scored since Oslo not just at Birzeit and in Gaza, but in an array of professional and student associations across the occupied territories.[43] If they were to participate in the self-rule elections, they argue, they would almost certainly not defeat Fatah, but they would be the strongest opposition party. The unprecedented political and social leverage this would give them would be one the PA would have to accommodate or ignore at its peril.

Upon the installation of the PA in July 1994, Hamas's public stance on elections struck a compromise between its pragmatic and rejectionist trends, and has been most clearly articulated by Jarrar and its Gaza spokesperson, Mahmoud Zahar. Both stated that while Hamas would not initially participate in elections 'born of the DOP', it would stand for institutions of 'Palestinian public interest' such as municipalities and the professional bodies.[44] Other Islamists have mooted that their eventual participation in the PA is conditional on the extent of the independent legislative powers it enjoys. Either posture, however, suggests a role in the self-rule that is at once oppositional but loyal or at least not mutinous.

A New Politics?

In April 1994 – one month before a 10,000-strong Palestinian police force rolled into Gaza and Jericho – Fatah's and Hamas's military wings in Gaza signed an accord of non-belligerence. The two dominant strains of Palestinian nationalism promised a moratorium on collaborator killings, an end to all 'defamatory campaigns' between them and the cutting back of separately called strike days 'to lighten the economic burden of our people'.

While Palestinians in the territories breathed a collective sigh of relief, news of the pact sent Israeli leaders (to borrow Rabin's parlance) 'spinning like propellers', enraged that the liaison had made no mention of Hamas's armed attacks, let alone any commitment to end them. 'It is out of the question', thundered Rabin, 'that the PLO should even think of achieving cooperation [with Hamas] on the basis of attacking Israelis.'

These outpourings may have been necessary government PR, but they were also disingenuous. Not only had individual Israelis like the army's Chief of Staff, Ammon Shahak, long foreseen that finally Hamas would have no option but to join the autonomy; the Israeli government flew numerous kites enticing it to do so.

Shortly after the Fatah/Hamas pact was announced, IDF Commander Doron Almog met with Hamas leader Muhsein Abu Ata to discuss the Israeli–PLO agreement and the new Fatah–Hamas *modus vivendi*.[45] At around the same time, Israeli Foreign Minister Shimon Peres floated the idea that his government would 'sit down with Hamas' and release its prisoners if it renounced violence and started 'down the road to negotiations'.

For PLO activists in the territories the meaning of the Fatah/Hamas agreement was transparent – Hamas, finally and publically, had accepted the DOP as fact and were about to set out their store for the new politics it augured.

An Islamist Nation ...?

But what does Hamas want? This is not such an easy question, since political Islam in Palestine, like the Islamist resurgence elsewhere in the region, is homogeneous neither in its constituencies nor in its aims.

The bulk of Hamas's support in the territories is drawn from socially conservative sectors for whom the ideology of 'secular nationalism' remains an apology for the rank materialism, corruption and moral permissiveness of the region's ruling regimes.[46] Such strata are the legatees of the MB's old culturalist tradition. For them, the chief attraction of Islamism lies still in its austere moral code, with its stress on pious conduct and application of Islamic values and law to all civic spheres.

Thus for Bassam Jarrar the conditions governing Hamas's role in the autonomy are not so much the incendiary political questions of Israeli settlements and Jerusalem as of the PA allowing Palestinian civil society to function 'in a democratic way' and that all school curricula be grounded on 'Islamic civilisation'.[47]

If there is a red line, it resides in the Islamists' insistence that there remain a total separation between the territories' existing Islamic courts, which cover laws pertaining to personal status such as marriage, inheritance and divorce, and the PA's new Justice Ministry, which (it is assumed) will follow secular law. For Hamas, the preservation and consolidation of religious law or the *Sharia* over this private sphere of civil society and, with it, the social repro-duction of the patriarchal Palestinian family as the 'basic unit' of Palestinian society,[48] affords perhaps the greatest potential prize of the autonomy. It ensures, says Jarrar, 'the guarantee of Palestinians' human rights as Muslims'.[49]

But these demands have now to be accommodated with more overtly nationalist slogans. Due its turn to active national struggle in the intifada, Hamas succeeded in drawing under its wing increasing numbers of younger and more militant elements of Palestinian society.[50] For these generations Islam means not just the *Sharia*, but also national liberation from Israeli occupation.[51] Hamas's message for them is enshrined less in the sage wisdom of figures like Yassin than in the exemplary military actions of Islamic Jihad and Hizbollah, the daring operations of Izzadin el-Qassam and the heroic martyrdom of fighters like Imad Akel.[52]

The presence of this younger constituency in Hamas signals not the eclipse of nationalist ideology – which was the original aim of modern Islamism – but its transformation, imbuing it rather with a religious soul of 'spiritual and community release'[53] that secularism is felt to palpably lack. If, in other words, Hamas had to ideologically accommodate to nationalism by fact of the intifada, it did so by 'reinventing' for it an Islamist tradition that is now experienced – especially among those generations politically forged by the uprising – as an integral part of Palestinian national identity.[54]

... or a Nationalist Islam?

Whether this mix of social conservatism and radical nationalism can be contained within one movement under the changed conditions of autonomy is the dilemma Hamas now faces.

Unlike most of the PLO factions,[55] Hamas operates politically as a broad alliance whose line at any point is determined by consensus. On the eve of the PA's entry into Gaza and Jericho, the consensus was revised in an 'important official statement' issued by the head of Hamas's Political Department, Musa Abu Marzuq.

Hamas, he said, would offer a 'ceasefire [*hodna*][56] with the occupation' if Israel withdrew to its 1967 borders, disarmed all settlers as a prelude to dismantling all settlements, released Palestinian prisoners and permitted elections to a 'sovereign' body that would represent all Palestinians and possess the authority to 'define Palestinian self-determination' (including the legislative power to repeal or at least modify the DOP).

Israel, of course, would reject any 'truce' under these conditions. But this was not the point. Rather, Hamas was not only highlighting the gross deficiences of the DOP (which in its textual committments guarantees none of these demands), but making a pitch for mainstream Palestinian opinion, since the references to 'The 1967 borders' and 'settlements' indicated its *de facto*, if not *de jure*, recognition of Israel, and so placed its politics in the centre of contemporary Palestinian nationalist discourse.[57]

Marzuq's statement brought murmurings of disquiet among Hamas's more militant cadres, but it was ambiguous enough to appease moderates and rejectionists alike. For Islamists like Khalid Amayreh the new line intimated Hamas's eventual reversion to its 'ideological fundamentals by placing more emphasis on its eternal bedrock theme – Islam is the solution – and less on its ultimate theo-political objective, the complete liberation of Palestine and the establishment of an Islamic state'.[58] In this scenario, the attitude to Israel – as evinced by leading Islamist figures like Sheikh Ahmad Bitawi – becomes pragmatic to the point of defeatist. 'The Islamic tendency has reached the conclusion', he said in April 1994, 'that it is no longer possible to halt the [DOP] negotiations, since the US, which rules our region, is pushing towards [their] completion. But the negotiations with Israel must grant the Palestinians minimal rights, such as the 1967 borders, and at this time they will be satisfied with that. The continuation of the solution of the Palestinian problem will be in the hands of future generations.'[59]

Another leading Hamas figure said that for mainstream Islamism in the occupied territories there is now 'only one taboo, and that is the recognition of Israel ... anything else is permissible'.

But for Islamists who identify with the Izzadin el-Qassam tendency Marzuq's statement meant what it said – that the national, including military, struggle would continue unless and until Israel fulfilled 'Palestinians' minimal rights' of withdrawal, prisoner releases and sovereignty.

It is clear that if Hamas wants to return to its 'ideological fundamentals' it will have to establish some kind of working rapprochement with the PA. But it is also clear that no rapprochement is going to be feasible – none at any rate that would survive the long reach of Israel's (and now, ominously, the PA's) security forces – without a commitment from the Islamists to end the armed struggle, both within the autonomous areas and inside Israel. Figures like Jarrar say only that 'Hamas will cease military operations when it sees it to be in its best interest to do so.'[60] But the debate among Islamists hinges on the timing of 'best interest'.[61] The pragmatists say it should be now, to foreclose any 'fractricidal' conflict with the PA. The rejectionists say it should be on realisation of Israel's military withdrawal from the West Bank and Gaza.

In October 1994 – in response to a crackdown on Hamas supporters by both Israel and the PA – Izzadin el-Qassam unleashed the worst onslaught on Israeli civilian and military targets of its five year history. Three separate operations – a random gun attack in West Jerusalem, the kidnap and killing of an Israeli soldier near

Ramallah and a bomb planted on an autobus in downtown Tel Aviv – left a toll of 25 Israelis dead and over 50 injured. The demands that accompanied these actions were nationalist rather than Islamist in sweep: to the Israelis, that it immediately release 200 Palestinian prisoners, including Yassin; and to the PA, that it cease supplying 'information ... on our *Mujahedin* (Islamic fighters) ... to the Zionist intelligence and occupation authorities'.

These actions brought PA–Hamas relations in Gaza to the very brink of civil war, stretching the Islamist consensus to breaking point.[62] In the wake of the Tel Aviv bombing, Amayreh said that the action 'would be detrimental to Hamas and its popularity' and that 'some people identified with Hamas will distance themselves from the perpetrators'.[63] But a Hamas leader in Gaza, Sheikh Ahmed Bahar, justified the operations as 'legitimate ... as long as the occupation continues'.[64]

Perhaps the only solution – one that is currently under intense discussion in Islamist circles – is the formation of an Islamist political party for the changed circumstances of autonomy. This would be affiliated to Hamas and would enjoy the same quasi-independent relations with it as Hamas originally had with the MB. While the party would focus on promulgating 'Islamic values' for all civic spheres, Hamas's military arm would be kept in reserve, able, in Mahmoud Zahar's words, to pursue its 'own independent policy and strategy'.[65]

Yet – as another Hamas leader, Ismail Haniyeh, implies – even this 'independence' would have to be rationalised. 'I think the movement will carry out military operations only in response to blatant Israeli aggression against our people, and the scale of the attacks will be determined by the level of popular support for such a strategy. A political party is crucial for dealing with the new situation,' if Hamas is to accommodate to the dual challenge of 'resisting the occupation, but avoiding a showdown with the PA'.[66]

Conclusion

In the short term, Hamas's metamorphosis into a loyal opposition in the autonomy may be the best-case scenario: not just to ensure its own political survival, but ironically because a genuinely independent opposition is sorely needed if the PLO is to pull through what is increasingly being recognised as its midnight hour.[67] But this will come at a price, probably the Islamists' augmented influence in the legal and cultural spheres of Palestinian civil society.[68] The alternative, Hamas's continuation as an active military organisation, is liable to provoke, at best, an extremely authoritarian form of self-government or, at worst, civil war.

But in the long term the prospect of an emergent Islamist political culture in the occupied territories carries many risks for the Palestinian national struggle and holds no promise for its historic claims of self-determination and authentic de-colonisation.

Like other varients of political Islam, Hamas represents an apparent conundrum. On the one hand, it is an entirely modernist political movement, deploying mass modes of mobilisation, propaganda and social organisation to propagate its ideology, and garnering for itself a deserved reputation of financial probity, community service and military prowess.[69] On the other, its primitive and prohibitive interpretation of Islam can meet none of the political, social and economic challenges raised by the struggle for self-determination.[70] More dangerously, its eventual hegemony would bequeath a vision of Palestinian national identity that it is anti-democratic, sectarian and racist.

In the opinion of Palestinian political analyst and PLO member Jamil Hilal, it is a vision that would ultimately corrode the very foundations of contemporary Palestinian nationalism. Hamas's rejection of secularism, implicit contempt for 'territorial' nationalism and ideological transformation of the Palestinian/Israeli conflict into an eschatological struggle between Islam (representing Good) and Jews (representing Evil),[71] threatens precisely that modernist political and cultural identity that, says Hilal, 'has been one of the strongest and most militant tools in Palestinians' fight against Zionist sectarian ideology ... as well as one of the strongest safeguards against attempts to assimilate, dominate and settle Palestinians in the diaspora'.[72]

If Hamas commands support among Palestinians, this is not because of any mass turn to faith on their part. Rather, it is the fruit of two interrelated crises of PLO nationalist ideology and practice. On the one hand, a political crisis of representation, aggravated by an increasingly unaccountable, autocratic and inadequate national leadership. On the other, an ideological crisis over the social and political agenda and content of any future Palestinian polity. The rise of Hamas in the occupied territories can only be understood in relation to the organisational, ideological and political degeneration of the PLO. Hamas's 'growth has fed first and foremost on the crisis of the Palestinian national movement', says Hilal. 'It could not have prospered without the political discontent that had been spreading among ever-widening sectors of Palestinians in the occupied territories and diaspora.'[73]

Hamas's nationalism is one that reveals itself via an Islamist discourse and practice.[74] But it remains a moralistic, ahistorical and ultimately sectarian nationalism, gutted of any progressive social and political kernel. It is not – as Hamas's ubiquitous but archaic slogans would have it – that the mass of Palestinians genuinely believe 'killing Jews is as an act of worship'[75] or 'Islam is the solution'. It is rather that such sentiments have popular, and populist, resonance because they raise the hidden, cardinal yet unanswered questions of Palestinian nationalism in its post-Oslo phase: What kind of peace? And if not an Islamic nation, what kind of nation?

Gaza/Jerusalem, June 1995; *Race & Class*, October–December 1995

3

An Israeli Peace: an Interview with Ilan Pappe

Ilan Pappe, a lecturer in the department of Middle Eastern history at Haifa University, is known in Israel as one of the new 'revisionist' historians who have challenged received accounts of Israeli historiography. The author of *The Making of the Arab–Israeli Conflict* (I.B. Tauris, 1994), he is also the founder and head of the Institute of Peace Research in Israel.

What is the significance of Oslo for Israel and Zionism?

Well, as a historian, the best answer would be it's soon to say. But provisionally we can at least say that Oslo has opened up a number of options.

The chief significance, and probably the only genuinely irreversible part of Oslo, is the mutual recognition between the PLO and Israel. It has humanised the two parties to the conflict. This is not to say that there will no longer be a bloody conflict. But the context in which the conflict is waged is different. It has made any peace agreement easier to accomplish for future generations, even though I doubt whether Oslo itself can deliver such an agreement. The only way it could now be reversed in fact is if the PLO were to disappear and a new Palestinian movement replaced it.

The problem is what does mutual recognition incur, politically? And it is this that is so difficult to answer, because there are various possibilities.

First, there is the optimistic scenario, which remains prevalent among sections of the Israeli Zionist left. This says that through recognition we have irreversibly began a process of de-colonisation, by which is meant Israel's withdrawal from the West Bank and Gaza. De-colonisation is typically painful, slow and violent, but, once begun, its end is inevitable: the final, historical separation of the two peoples culminating in the establishment of a Palestinian state in the West Bank and Gaza. Among elements of the non-Zionist Israeli left, there is an even more optimistic reading (at least if you are a non-Zionist Israeli) that says recognition will inevitably lead to a non-Jewish or non-Zionist Israel, either in the form of a democratic secular state in the whole of Palestine or an Israel that will be a state for all its citizens, rather than a Jewish state.

The other, pessimistic scenario heard on the left in Israel is argued most forcibly by critical Palestinians like Edward Said. This says that through Oslo and recognition Israel has succeeded in replacing one form of occupation with another – the bantustan option. By separating from Gaza and parts of the West Bank, and by importing foreign workers to replace Palestinian workers in Israel, Israel becomes a country without a problem, since for Israelis like Rabin the cause of violence is the demographic mix of Palestinians and Israelis. His (and their) analysis doesn't really get much beyond that. In exchange, Israel not only rids itself of 'terror'; it garners huge international benefits. Its reputation becomes restored in the West after the battering it took in the intifada. And it opens the way for peace with the Arab world. And, since Oslo, Israel has realised a peace treaty with Jordan and started quiet, semi-official relations with North African countries and even certain Gulf states.

My own analysis is less interested in whether these scenarios are right or wrong but in the historical processes Oslo may release. I happen to think Said is right about the Israeli government's intentions and I share most of his criticisms of the agreement. But I'm a historian, and for a historian the distinction must always be made between what a government desires and what it gets. I believe that Rabin with Oslo has opened a Pandora's Box. He thinks it's a box of perfumes; but I think a better analogy is the Dutch story about the little boy who removes his finger from the hole in the dam. He may have unleashed a flood. I say this not only because history has a habit of producing consequences that cannot be foreseen; but also because of the peculiar formula that underwrites the Oslo agreement.

The Oslo agreement is a wholly Israeli formula. There is nothing Palestinian in it. Here I would disagree with Palestinian critics like Said. He says Oslo is an American peace. It isn't: it's an Israeli peace.

But it's an ingenious formula. The Israeli negotiators behind Oslo looked at the contending Israeli and Palestinian positions. And the main predicament for them was how to reach a deal that wouldn't reopen the unresolved questions related to the 1948 war. There is an absolute Israeli consensus on this. All wings of the Israeli Labour Party are willing to discuss the territories occupied in 1967. Even Likud accepts that the *status quo ante* in the 1967 occupied territories is not a given and is prepared to offer some version of Palestinian autonomy there. But the consensus for the Israeli political mainstream, both Labour and Likud alike, is that 1948 is off-limits.

Now the PLO position, at least prior to Oslo, was the precise opposite. Historically, it had always argued that the Israeli/Palestinian conflict did not start in 1967, but fundamentally in 1948. The PLO's *raison d'être* was to represent the Palestinian refugee community that emerged from the 1948 war. The three historical PLO demands were: a Palestinian state, the right of return and Jerusalem as a Palestinian capital. All of these have their roots in the 1948 conflict rather than in the 1967 conflict. Now, for sure, since 1967 other demands have emerged, such as the removal of Jewish settlements in the West Bank and Gaza. But this was never a cardinal issue for the PLO, even after 1967, neither in its Jordanian, Beirut or even Tunis periods. It was, of course, the main issue for the Palestinian leadership in the occupied territories, but not of the PLO 'outside'. For the latter, the main issues were those embodied in its constituency – the Palestinian refugees from 1948, and later from 1967, in the diaspora.

So you see the problem: how to find a bridge between one side that was only prepared to talk about the 1967 occupied territories and the other side which was mandated, by virtue of its constituency, to talk about 1948. The solution, as far as the Israeli negotiators were concerned, was Oslo. If you read the Declaration of Principles, it says that for two years neither the PLO nor Israel will negotiate on issues pertaining to 1948. It is only after this 'interim period' that matters such as Jerusalem, refugees, settlements and borders will be addressed in the final status negotiations.

Now this, for the PLO, was not such a big problem: by and large it was prepared to defer these issues. The problem is an unstated Israeli condition in the Oslo agreement which you will not find in its text, but let us say in its spirit. For Israel, the interim stage is not merely a waiting period to separate 1967 issues from 1948 issues: it's a probation. So, for the Israelis, the PLO can only get to the final status negotiations to the extent that it safeguards Israel's security concerns during the interim period. If it fails to do so, Gaza/Jericho First becomes Gaza/Jericho last.

Now this is an almost impossible condition for the PLO to fulfil. Think about it. Arafat returns to Palestine. What is he going to say? Is he going to talk about the weather? He has to at least refer to statehood, Jerusalem and refugees, if he is to carry the Palestinians with him. But for Israel these issues are taboo. Every time Arafat opens his mouth Israel accuses him of breaking the spirit of Oslo and immediately puts the brakes on the process, because the interim period is a probation and the PLO leader isn't behaving himself.

But there was another reason why Arafat was forced to address the 1948 issues. And this was Israel's actions on the ground. For sure, Rabin hasn't raised the issue of Jerusalem in the talks; he has merely continued to settle Jews in Jerusalem. He hasn't talked about settlements; but his government has proceeded to thicken settlements in the West Bank. He hasn't referred to the 1948 refugees, except to say that there is absolutely no possibility of their repatriation. This is what I mean by Oslo being a wholly Israeli formula: it embodies the immense imbalance of power between the two sides. Israel can do what it wants during the interim period; Arafat cannot even say what he wants.

But this carries its own contradictions. Through the interim period – and precisely through the return of Arafat and elements of the PLO – Israel has allowed the creation of a new reality which is wholly unpredictable, and which, I think, accounts for the optimistic/pessimistic confusion of the Israeli left. Arafat in Gaza and Jericho has established a mechanism, over which he has control. It's a limited control for sure; but he has powers of patronage, of salaries, of prestige, the rudiments, if you like, of a bureacratic mini-state. This may bear little resemblance to the national aspirations of the Palestinian people, but it is a form of power.

But it is a wholly unstable form of power. And this is Israel's dilemma. Should the Oslo process remain stuck, will Arafat remain content being head of a bureaucracy oiled by five or six secret security services? Maybe he will but, then again, maybe he won't. If he does, then he is confirming Said's vision of perpetuating the occupation on Israel's behalf. But, should this be so, what is going to be the reaction on the Palestinian street to a 'final' peace agreement with Israel that does not include refugees in the diaspora, does not include the Palestinian citizens of Israel, does not include Palestinians who live in Jerusalem and, most probably, does not include Palestinians who live in what Israel deems are vital settlement areas in the West Bank? And who will lead this discontent, assuming that Arafat cannot contain it? Will it be Hamas or a new leftist nationalist opposition? Nobody can predict what will happen, least of all the Israelis. Which is why I say Rabin has opened a Pandora's Box.

So to return to your original question: what does Oslo mean for Zionism? I believe that it contains all the potential of being a break-through in Israeli/Palestinian relations, but not because the Israeli architects of Oslo want it to be. But rather because, despite their best efforts, Oslo is raising all those issues of 1948 that it was designed to avoid. Rabin was sold the deal on condition that he and Israel would keep a firm grip on the wheel – Israel wanted rid of Gaza anyway, Jericho is not important, and it's no big deal if Palestinians control tourism in Jenin and Bethlehem. He can stop Oslo any time he wants, his advisers assure him. But of course he can't. He may have a firm grip on the wheel but history is a slippery road.

The same contradictions, by the way, will face Likud, should it be elected. Likud is happy to play an aggressively nationalist card while in opposition. But, ideologically, they occupy the same Zionist mainstream as Labour. After all, Oslo is a good deal for Israel, and Likud is the party that gave back the whole of the Sinai to Egypt. Labour never had the guts to do this.

But how does Oslo raise the 1948 issues?

Most Palestinians in the occupied territories saw Oslo as the beginning of a process that would lead to a fair and just solution of their cause, which of course included matters like refugees, Jerusalem and statehood. Even the most ardent Palestinian supporters of Oslo did not accept Gaza and Jericho as better than nothing at all. This is something most Israelis simply fail to understand. For Israel, Oslo is a modular scale – plus one is better than zero. We will give the Palestinians as much as we can, says Rabin, but if they don't get everything, it doesn't matter – they are happier than they were before.

Of course, nothing could be further from the truth. In Oslo, Palestinians saw eventual statehood, and should these revived expectations be dashed then really a whirlwind could be released that will sweep not only Oslo but Arafat, the PLO and everything else from the scene. In this sense, a future historian may say that Oslo succeeded only in provoking a new resurgence of Palestinian nationalism, this time laden with a strong Islamist content, dragging Israel into a situation worse or at least no better than what preceded it. So beware of any categorical judgements about Oslo, at least on the Israeli side. All Israelis – whether for or against – are wholly uncertain about what they have done.

Given this 'uncertainty', and as a way out of the impasse, would you be in favour of going directly to the final status talks now, in effect scrapping the Oslo formula? Has the time come to open, once and for all, the 1948 issues?

Yes. If Israel and the PLO started to negotiate now a comprehensive settlement on these issues, I have absolutely no doubt that Oslo will have marked a turning point in Israeli/Palestinian relations. If you ask me whether this is going to happen, I'm less optimistic.

From 1948 onwards, these issues have been avoided. At times, this led to a partial peace, but more often it exacerbated the conflict. Now it's true that whenever a comprehensive peace has been attempted it has failed, whether it was the Lussanne Conference in 1949 or the Geneva Conferences in the 1970s or the Madrid Conference in 1991. But today any PLO/Israeli agreement is tantamount to a comprehensive settlement; it no longer requires an international forum. I am not minimising the Lebanese and Syrian 'tracks' here, but everybody knows that the root of the conflict is the Palestinian question.

I'm pessimistic because I don't believe that Rabin government is capable of taking such a step. Having started Oslo, they are divided about what they want from it, which manifests itself as political hesitancy and indecisiveness. But, should a new coalition government be elected that is committed to a comprehensive settlement, then for sure we are entering a significant phase. Would such a coalition have popular support? My answer is that such coalition had popular support in 1992. After all, Rabin was elected not on the basis of the Oslo accords, but on the basis of his pledge to make peace with the Palestinians. What Oslo has demonstrated – largely by its failure – is that peace has to be comprehensive.

If we moved to the final status issues now, two gains would be made immediately. First, Arafat would be able to command a genuine Palestinian constituency for it, embracing everyone from nationalists like Abd al-Shafi and Said to the rejectionists of the PFLP/DFLP and even the moderate or pragmatic wing of Hamas. Second, for most Israelis peace really does translate as personal security. And perhaps the gravest flaw of the Oslo formula is that, because it is predicated on a slow, incremental and probationary progress, it is extremely easy to sabotage. All you need really do is plant a bomb somewhere and everything stops for six months. For groups genuinely opposed to peace, whether Israeli or Palestinian, Oslo is a train waiting to be derailed.

What does Israel want out of Oslo regionally? Does it mark a strategic decision to become part of the Middle East environment?

No, not in my opinion. Most Israelis have no desire to integrate into the Middle East. Israelis, by and large, define themselves as belonging to a Westernised, European society and culture very different from the countries that neighbour them. Whether in fact they are this is of course an entirely different question. But most of them think they are.

So who are they? Talking about Israelis in general is as dangerous as talking about Palestinians or Islam in general. First of all, the ruling Israeli elite, whether in the political sphere or in the cultural sphere, has no desire to integrate into the Middle East other than on a purely economic basis. I wouldn't even call it economic integration. The Israeli power elite – whether political, economic or military – views the whole Middle East region as a kind of precarious jungle. In this jungle, you need certain political alliances in order to counter other alliances. In building these alliances, of course you can make a lot of profits, you can act as a bridge between the Arab and European economies, but the driving force is the military-political alliance, not the profits.

A good indicator of the mentality of Israel's ruling elite is Shimon Peres. In his new book, he basically repackages the classical Zionist idea. And this, by his lights, is an entirely benevolent idea. It says to the Arabs, 'Look, we are far more advanced than you are, far more modernised, so you can only benefit from us. We are the shining sun in the region: stay away from us and you remain in the cold; come close, and you will get at least some of the heat.'

In economic–strategic terms, he is saying that Israel no longer wants a belligerent relation with the Arabs. It no longer seeks any more territories; in fact, it is willing to cede certain territories. It doesn't want war, it wants strong economic ties with the Arab world, it wants Israeli tourists to be able to travel anywhere they want. But what does Peres really want? He wants Israel to be part of the European Union. It's incredible. Look at his book. It's called *The New Middle East*, and its main conclusion is that it's high time that Europe allowed Israel to join the Union as a full member! This typifies the Israeli ruling mentality perfectly.

Peres' *New Middle East* is a marriage of Israeli know-how with an Arab workforce. He sincerely, if naively, believes that this marriage can be mutually beneficial rather than exploitative. But of course it can't; it will be domineering and exploitative. Which is why so many Arab leaders – including those most sympathetic to Israel – are so wary of Peres' vision.

On a cultural level, you only have to talk to intellectuals like Amos Oz, who, as you know, is fully committed to peace with the Arabs. Does he identify with Arab culture? No way. Israel is a European culture, he says, a liberal democracy, while the Arabs are something else, we have nothing in common with them. This is not to say that many Israelis don't see their cultural roots and ethnic identity in the Arab world. Of course they do. But this is not the same thing as them wanting to fuse with the wider Arab environment. Most do not. They regard the European, 'higher' culture offered by Israel as superior.

This, I believe, is the central contradiction in the vision of Peres and others like him. A genuine integration with the Arab world presupposes the de-Zionisation of Israeli society. Now this, in the end, may be inevitable. Nationalism at the moment is running on a high tide but, like all tides, it is likely to ebb, to be replaced perhaps by ethnicity or some mutant of ethnic nationalism. And Israeli nationalism of course is not immune from this, especially as the Sephardi and non-Jewish sectors of Israeli society increase in size and power relative to the European or Ashkenazi sectors.

But this is for the future. It certainly has nothing to do with the Oslo accords. On the contrary, most Israelis welcomed Oslo not as marking their integration with the Arab world but as inaugurating their peaceful (as opposed to their belligerent) segregation from it. In this scenario, peace signals not so much reconciliation as a better economic life, the diversification from military to non-military production, increased business opportunities not just in the Arab countries but, more importantly, in Europe. Peace – if it holds – harbours Israel's final arrival at the place where Herzl always wanted us to be: a sun-splashed Venice, in the Middle East, but not of it.

Haifa, July 1995; *Race & Class*, October–December 1995

4

Palestine: the Economic Fist in the Political Glove

In an article in the Israeli daily *Ha'aretz*,[1] Israeli political analyst, Meron Benvenisti, argues that the 'success' of the PLO/Israeli peace agreement was only made possible by its 'deliberate ambiguity'. In the Declaration of Principles (DOP) signed in Washington on 13 September 1993, he says, can be read two mutually exclusive political visions. For the PLO, the DOP is 'the first step' in the 'theory of stages' by which 'a national authority will be established in any area of liberated Palestine'. For the Israeli government, however, the DOP is the final political realisation of former Defence Minister and architect of the 1967 occupation, Moshe Dayan; a classic 'functional compromise' strategy, where Palestinians of the occupied territories are granted 'administrative authority within municipal boundaries', while the Israelis keep a firm grip on all matters pertaining to security and the territories' resources.

Hence, says Benvenisti, the symbolically explosive nature of the 'border question' in the current PLO/Israeli negotiations on implementing self rule, and why its resolution or otherwise 'may even determine whether the agreement is implemented'. Control of border crossings pits the two conflicting visions against each other and forces them out of ambiguity and into the cold, clear air. If the PLO, however emblematically, wrest some kind of authority over borders, then what they have signed with the DOP is the rudiments of an international entity, or sovereignty in its incipient stage. For the Israelis, 'owning the fence' strikes at the very meaning of self-rule which, by their lights, is and must remain a wholly 'internal arrangement'. 'Control of external security', Israeli Foreign Minister Shimon Peres told President Mitterand in Paris on 16 December 1993, 'is the most important difference between autonomy and an independent Palestinian state'.[2]

Benvenisti probably overplays his hand a little. One should not underestimate both the PLO and Israel's facility for resolving one ambiguity by substituting it for another. Yet he is right to point out the essentially political nature of the dispute, with both sides waging a war of attrition to extract from the DOP entirely different scenarios for self-rule.

This is something that cannot be said about the economic debates so far thrown up by the agreement. Unlike the fraught issues of borders, settlements, refugees and even the size of Jericho, the future of the Palestinian economy during the 'interim phase of self-rule' is bathed in the rare light of PLO/Israeli unanimity. On his return from Paris, Peres let it be known that 'the Palestinians agree with us today on creating a market economy, an open economy with no borders, with free movement of goods and trade between the two of us',[3] while chief of the PLO delegation Nabil Sha'th, on the eve of the Washington signing, gushed that the DOP means 'a full peace with Israel, with totally open borders' which will 'create with Israel an economic community for the whole Middle East'.[4]

'Open borders', 'a Middle East economic community' and the like are politically loaded terms that, since 13 September, have been, in both Israeli and PLO discourses, voided of all political content. Yet the DOP is primarily an economic document. Two thirds of it is devoted to describing the functions of eight PLO/Israeli 'liaison committees' whose job it is to harness, in Sha'th's words, a degree of 'mutual economic interest that exceeds any agreement signed between the two states' (*sic*).[5] A less charitable interpretation has described the DOP thus: 'It's political divorce and economic marriage. The Palestinians have negotiated a partnership with the Israelis for developing their own economic affairs'.[6] Whatever the PLO has signed in the DOP, the strategic question of Palestine's future economic relations with Israel lies, or should lie, at the heart of any Palestinian political vision for statehood.

Palestinian critics of the agreement base their critique less on the economic stipulations adumbrated by the DOP – for these are so nebulous as to be 'almost vacuous' – than on the rosy vistas sketched by people like Sha'th and Peres. Perhaps the most trenchant advocate of this line is the head of Gaza's Economic Development Group, Salah Abd al-Shafi. Neither an apologist for the agreement nor an 'ideological rejectionist' of it, Abd al-Shafi counts himself among a growing band of Palestinian intellectuals (like his father, former Palestinian delegation head, Haidar Abd al-Shafi, Edward Said, Mahmoud Darwish and others) who view the DOP as both politically irreversible and, in Mouin Rabbani's words, 'deeply flawed and potentially fatal to Palestinian national aspirations'.[7]

If Abd al-Shafi agrees with Sha'th that the *sine qua non* of Israel's new relationship with the occupied territories will be 'totally open borders' rather than military subjugation, this for him spells not so much 'reconciliation and cooperation' as Palestine's final and 'absolute incorporation into the Israeli economy' and, with it, the vanquishing of 'any notion of developing a genuinely independent Palestinian economic sector'.[8]

Gaza's New Economic Arrangment

The DOP sets the political seal of approval on a new economic dispensation that the Israelis have assiduously been carving out in Gaza for the last three years and which, with the agreement, they now plan to extend to the occupied territories as a whole. The 'new arrangement' had its germ in a series of reports on the Gazan economy written in the early 1990s by Israeli economist Erza Sadan, described by the Israeli press as 'a champion of Greater Israel in his politics, but a neo-liberal when it comes to economics'.[9]

In the wake of the Gulf war, Israel's perceived 'security need' was to staunch the flow of Palestinian labour across the Green Line, running at the time at around 30,000 to 40,000 workers from Gaza and about 100,000 from the occupied territories as a whole. However, Sadan's remit was not so much to lessen Gaza's chronic dependency on the Israeli economy as,[10] in Abd al-Shafi's words, 'to restructure the relations of that dependency ... The means of this dependency were not, as had been the case historically during the occupation, via a daily migration of mass Palestinian labour into Israel. Rather, the new vehicle was a system of sub-contracting between Palestinian capital and sectors of Israeli capital.'

In terms of labour, the Israelis have clearly been successful in their desires. By the time of the peace agreement, the number of Palestinian workers from Gaza entering Israel on any day was down to 20,000. Abd al-Shafi lists three other spheres of the Gazan economy where the new arrangement has also taken hold. 'In August 1991, the military governor issued order 1055 which aims to encourage investment in the Gaza Strip. Generally speaking, this liberalised the licensing of firms so that it became much easier for Palestinians to engage in investment activity.'

In practice, however, licences were granted selectively to Palestinian outfits whose trade was entirely dependent on Israeli contractors. Nor did the move open up competition with Israel. 'While such [newly licensed] Palestinian firms may threaten certain unviable companies in Israel,' says Abd al-Shafi, 'they certainly cannot challenge entire sectors, given the difference in scale between the two economies.' On the contrary, as Palestinian economist Adel Samara points out, what the new relationship actually portends is 'the swallowing of the economies of the Palestinian cantons' (like the Gaza Strip) 'and converting them into components of the Israeli economy, but with an Arab face'.[11]

In addition, since 1991, Israel has imposed a number of punitive measures on Gaza's agricultural sector, whose economic effect has been to thwart its traditional citrus and vegetable production in favour of the manufacture of ornamentals or flowers. Citrus is the single biggest income earner of all economic activities in the Gaza Strip, with export routes to Europe and the Gulf countries. As a result of Israeli confiscations, however, the amount of arable citrus land in Gaza has shrunk from 75,000 to 53,000 dunams. But Israel's purpose here is not merely territorial. Rather, it is to decouple Gaza's trade with other economies, the better to lock it firmly into Israel's own. According to the head of the Strip's Citrus Producers Union, Hashem Shawa, of the 9,000 tonnes of citrus harvested in Gaza in 1993, '90 percent was sold to Israeli juice factories' and at a captive price so cheap that it 'hardly covered the farmers' production costs'.[12]

A further means of 'deepening dependency', says Abd al-Shafi, is to encourage single crop sectors like flowers. 'Israel is a major exporter of flowers to Europe, but production costs are high in Israel because Israeli labour is expensive. So, by shifting production to the Strip, the Israelis reduce substantially their labour costs while maintaining their market share in Europe because – it goes without saying – all of the export routes open to Gaza's flowers are in the hands of Israeli contractors.'

While the Strip's agricultural base has, in Sadan's parlance, been 'encouraged' to 'degenerate',[13] 140 industrialised greenhouses have been constructed in the last 18 months whose output is wholly geared to ornamentals. 'In addition', says Abd al-Shafi, 'our strawberry yield is now totally dependent on exclusive export to Israel.' All the signs are, with the agreement, this will be Israel's agrarian game plan for the occupied territories as a whole. At the economic committee talks held in Paris in October 1993, for example, Israeli negotiators signalled that Israel was 'ready' to lift prohibitive tax burdens on Palestinian agricultural producers and, on 16 December, Peres announced that his government 'would ultimately end its 26 year ban on allowing Palestinians to freely export their farm produce to Israel'.[14]

Finally, the Israelis have set about establishing what Sadan calls 'industrial parks' throughout the Gaza Strip. These parks are modelled on similar projects set up in countries like Taiwan and Mexico.[15] As Abd al-Shafi says:

They amount to pockets of infrastructure surrounded by deserts of underdevelopment. Sadan said that because the task of developing an economic infrastructure for the whole of the occupied territories would cost billions, Israel should instead concentrate on providing business facilities like electrification and telecommunications for industry alone, sited on small parks. These parks would be made up of small Palestinian and Israeli sub-contracting firms which would be umbilically tied to the Israeli economy. Remember that Sadan was writing before Gaza/Jericho First and before the arrival on the scene of the World Bank, whose infrastructural prescriptions for the occupied territories, by the way, fit him like a glove.

Israel has just opened Gaza's first industrial park in the Beit Hanoun district, is busy constructing another and has laid plans for a third. There are similar moves afoot, says Abd al-Shafi, to establish a 'network of parks' in the West Bank.

Unlevel Playing Fields and Closed Borders

Against this backdrop, the PLO leadership's zealous embrace of the 'free market' appears not only uncritical but catastrophic, especially if, in the words of PLO executive member Yasser Abed Rabbo, the new Palestinian entity 'wants to forge the strongest possible economic links with Jordan and our Arab surroundings'.[16] Abd al-Shafi explains why:

> If the new Palestinian authority wants to pursue a policy of genuine, or even partial, disengagement from the Israeli economy, it will have to offer Palestinian farmers, businessmen and sub-contractors a real economic alternative. But if, as certain PLO and Israeli economists insist, this is going to be left to the free market, then this class will obviously choose the Israelis. First, because the mutual relations are already established and, second, because, come the peace, Israeli contractors can guarantee them authentic export markets.

A like argument obtains with the PLO's currently unproblematic commitment to 'open borders' which, as Abd al-Shafi warns, in reality will be open for the Israelis to penetrate Arab markets but closed to Palestinians to trade in any market other than Israel's. Only now, under 'self-rule', the 'veto' will not be imposed by military diktat but, rather, through economic imperative:

If there is one point that unites all shades of Israeli political opinion about the agreement, it is that there must be open borders between Israel and the new Palestinian entity. While direct taxation can be in the hands of the PLO authority, say the Israelis, indirect taxation or VAT will have to be standardised. But if Palestinians are made to buy and sell at Israeli prices, we may as well forget Jordan or any other Arab market for that matter. And this trade disadvantage would be reinforced, not lessened, if, in the wake of the agreement, there is peace and economic normalisation between Israel and the Arabs. Gaza, for example, simply cannot compete with an economy that in terms of GNP is currently ten times its own size. As with most free markets, this is not a level playing field.

If Abd al-Shafi's prognoses sound unduly alarmist to those who follow Israel and the PLO's largely Panglossian vision of the economy under self-rule, they nevertheless strike a chord among Israel's business community. According to Israeli journalist Asher Davidi, the consensus among Israel's capitalist class is that the DOP marks the beginning of 'a transition from colonialism to neo-colonialism'[17] in Israel's economic dealings with the occupied territories. The tableux Abd al-Shafi paints on sub-contracting, agriculture, tax standardisation, industry and labour are enthusiastically endorsed by Israel's manufacturers and financiers and represent 'positions that are acceptable to the Rabin government'. 'Israel's policy is clear', says Davidi. 'As Lieutenant-Colonel Hilel Sheinfeld, Israel's coordinator of operations in the territories, put it, the declared goal of his work is to integrate the economy of the occupied territories into the Israeli economy.'[18]

The political form of 'integration' is ultimately less significant than its economic prize. 'It's not important whether there will be a Palestinian state, autonomy or a Palestinian-Jordanian federation', says President of Israel's Industrialists' Association Dov Lautman. 'The economic borders between Israel and the territories must remain open.'[19]

If the PLO leadership really has given up on any economic self determination, then, in Edward Said's words, 'most Palestinians in the territories, economically speaking, will almost certainly remain where they are'.[20] Abd al-Shafi agrees. He predicts two distinct economic phases for the interim period of self-rule. In the short term (for 'security reasons'), Israel will maintain the economic siege of the West Bank and Gaza, sustaining thereby a vast 'reserve pool of cheap labour' on which both 'Palestinian and Israeli sub-contractors can draw at minimal cost' and through which the 'new economic arrangement' can be consolidated.[21] In the long term, if there is 'peace', the blockade will be quietly lifted, which means that 'between 100,000 and 120,000 Palestinian workers' will still have to go for work inside the Green Line. In the first phase, structural unemployment rates in Gaza will stick at their current averages of 40 per cent overall and 60 per cent in the refugee camps.[22] In the second, the rate would decrease to around 20 per cent. This, Israeli army analysts inform us, is 'entirely manageable from a security point of view'. But, in both phases, says Abd al-Shafi, 'we will be working for Israel. Maybe now we will be working for them in Gaza and the West Bank rather more than in Tel Aviv or Ashkelon or Beersheva. But we will be working for them nonetheless.'

Should Abd al-Shafi's forewarnings be anywhere near the mark, then Palestinian debates on the economy under self-rule will have to move away from the finer points of how best to stake out 'coalitions between Israeli and Palestinian capital', and on to, as Adel Samara puts it, more mundane and 'class' matters like 'labour, wages, rights and safety'.[23] Otherwise, for the mass of Palestinians in the occupied territories, the understanding is likely to dawn that, as Edward Said once said, 'much more important than having a state is the kind of state it is'.[24]

Gaza, January 1994; *Race & Class*, July–September 1994

5

Jabalyia and the Meaning of Return

It is early morning on Saturday 14 May 1994 and the news on the wire is that the IDF have evacuated Jabalyia. Our initial reaction is of disbelief. If there had been one constant about Israel's agonisingly slow pull-out from Gaza, it was that the Strip's largest refugee camp – given its size, history and symbolism – would be the last to be 'transferred'. The army's chief spokesperson in Gaza had told us as much the week before. The army gone? Impossible. Like many things in Gaza these last few weeks, it is something we feel we have to confirm with our own eyes.

The Tower

On the main drag into Jabalyia, we drive into a mêlée of honking cars, shouting street vendors and thousands of Palestinians stalking a wary pilgrimage between the camp's warren of breeze-block shelters and garbage tips. Like them, we are consumed by one vision.

From the camp's centre – as always – rises the IDF's notorious 40-metre-high watch tower, still topped by its gaudy orange look-out nest. But whereas yesterday an Israeli flag flew above its eyrie of machine guns, today a vast Palestinian flag vanquishes them. From the tower's tangle of scaffold, girder and wire hang hundreds of Palestinian youths, like bees round a honeycomb. From the tumult, someone fires round after round of Kalashnikov into the blue, liberated sky.

Think about the meaning of this for Palestinians. It was here – seven years ago – that thousands gathered to mourn the 'accidental' killing of four of their kin by an Israeli truck and, in the ensuing riots, gave birth to the intifada. Here that the principal agents of the uprising were transformed by Israel's 27-year-old occupation from a dispossessed peasantry into a dispossessed but enraged proletariat, forged by the 'dirty work' of Israel's factories and the modern, secularist nationalism of the PLO. Here that foreign journalists, delegations and dignitaries were brought to peer through the tower's perimeter fence to be told, by local and soldier alike, that Jabalyia is

Israel's Soweto and the reason why one day the IDF would have to get out.

Here, finally, where you see the plain misery of a system of colonial rule which has forced over 60,000 people into a living area of less than 1.5 square kilometres, giving Jabalyia a higher population density than Manhatten but without, the locals tell you, 'the skyscrapers'.

'Yes', says a Palestinian friend as we stand at the tower's base. 'They've gone.'

The Major's Story

Inside the old barracks, Palestinians pick over the detritus of occupation. A boy clutches ammunition shells in one hand and makes a V-for-victory salute with the other. Men, women, children sift the sandy floors prospecting for scrap, fittings, wire – anything, basically, they can lay their hands on. 'They left nothing,' says one in disgust, 'not even doormats.'

On the whitewashed walls, there is already a weird *pentimento* of Israeli army notices overladen with freshly daubed Palestinian graffiti. 'Welcome to the Palestinian police', scrawls one message, while beneath it, in Hebrew, can be made out the edict, 'Soldier! Improve your appearance!'

We're ushered into a couple of shabby, blacked-out army shelters. 'Interrogation cells', says my guide, who lives in Jabalyia. 'I spent two nights in here.'

Slouched in one of the corners, surrounded by vegetable offal and cans of Coca-Cola, I get my first close-up view of the Palestinian police. He is black, very young, dressed in khaki and a green beret, and utterly exhausted. He tells us that he has spent the last 48 hours travelling, setting out from a Palestinian Liberation Army camp in Sudan, then mustering at Rafah and finally bussed to Jabalyia. He is nervous, a little fazed by the locals who fire off questions about his origins, family and purpose while feeding him an endless supply of tea and cigarettes.

An officer with grey hair shakes us by the hand. He is Samir el-Kwaji, a major in the police. So when did the Israelis leave?

'They transferred authority to us between 2 and 3 a.m. last night. We didn't see the Israeli flag being taken down. There were only about 15 Israeli soldiers left when we arrived. Their Commanding Officer just said to us *'Ahlan wa salan'* ['Welcome'] and *'Salam'* ['Goodbye']. Then they picked up their things, marched out and that was that.'

Some guys have gathered to hear the major's story, and nod at its veracity. One is angry.

'Last night the army shot and wounded two youths for breaking curfew', he says. 'It was their goodbye gift to us, so we wanted to organise a little farewell party for them. We were thinking as soon as they start to dismantle the tower, we'll let them know just how much we've appreciated their stay. But they went without taking it down!' He sinks into a gloomy reverie. 'Even at the end, they had to outsmart us ...'

I want to know more about the major.

'I am originally from Magdal [now the Israeli town of Ashkelon] where my family had land, but was expelled in 1948. I was one year old. This is the first time I've set foot in Palestine since then, even though I have a brother in Gaza. For the last ten years I've served with the PLA in Sudan, and before that, Lebanon, Beirut battalion. I'm not going to tell you if I saw action against the Israelis in Lebanon. When there's peace, there'll be no more secrets between us. But we are only at the first step. Anyway,' he adds, 'the Israelis already know all there is to know about us'.

Will he be able to police Gaza?

'I am confident we can do the job expected of us', he says.

The Meaning of Return

Whatever else the police may or may not do, their very presence in Gaza has put into symbolic fact the Palestinian right to return. This 'miracle' – as Mahmoud Darwish once described the coming home of any Palestinian from exile – augurs not just a new political reality for Palestinians in the occupied territories, but also a disturbing national emotion, at once liberatory and tragic. On the morning of Jabalyia's 'liberation', head of its clinic, Mohammed Abu Salama, called the returning officers 'our children from the diaspora'. Others refer to them as 'brothers', surrogates for their lost sons and fighters, as the first tentative ingathering of the dispersed Palestinian family.

This discovered sense of filiality manifests itself as a restrained intimacy, and is the more poignant for it. In Gaza's Deir el Balah – where the first police were encamped – families have 'adopted' an officer, invite him to their homes, point out the 'good places' to buy clothes or get a haircut. In Gaza Town, crowds gather to watch the police direct traffic with the rapt attention of children at a circus. In Rafah, families stream to the new Police HQ on the off-chance that a son or cousin may be among the returnees.

Yet the return is also a reunion of strangers. In Khan Younis, an old woman greets a smartly uniformed officer with the salutation, '*Ag'nabi!*' ('Foreigner'). The officer is so angry that he bursts into tears.

For Palestinians, whether from inside or the diaspora, 'return' is inextricably bound up with a fiercely imagined national conscious-ness. What unites and defines them, wrote Edward Said in *The Question of Palestine*, is not how or from where they fled, but rather that 'they are entitled to return'.

But 'return', like any idea, undergoes changes, depending on the different circumstances and histories of its reception. For the police officers suddenly decanted in Gaza – many of them boys who have spent their entire lives in Yemen, Libya, Sudan – return is to an abstract entity, a future polity that will give them rights of citizenship and patrimony and end the 'absurd journey of exile'.

For Palestinian refugees in Gaza, on the other hand, return is to a concrete locale, a domicile across the Green Line whose tangible memory has been kept alive for 45 years in camps that bear the names and offspring of the 450 or so Palestinian villages that were destroyed when Israel was established in 1948. Or, as an old woman said to me on that morning in Jabalyia, 'I am happy that our Palestinian brothers are returning. But when will we return?'

If sadness danced with joy in Jabalyia at the sight of the Palestinian police, it is because their symbolic reality – with their uniforms and guns – has answered that question. 'The first battalions of our new government', as one Gazan put it, signifies the victory of an essentially modern, ideological notion of nationalism over an older, geographical one – a victory, in the eyes of Gaza's refugees, of politics over justice.

From now on the battle for Palestine will be over passports, stamps, flags and, of course, territory, but not over the specific places of Faluga, Magdal, Barbara or the myriad other communities on Israel's southern coastal shelf from which Jabalyia's refugees derive. And this is so whether the frontiers of the new Palestinian entity are, as many fear, merely cantons in the territories or, as most hope, the West Bank and Gaza with Jerusalem as their capital or, as all dream, Palestine from the river to the sea. It is so because Palestinian police are in Jabalyia and because Faluga, Magdal, Barbara are no more, and can never be again.

Gaza, May 1994

Part 2

Oslo Two – Oslo's High Tide
September 1995 to May 1996

Preface

This section spans the intense period from the signing of the Oslo interim agreement on 28 September 1995 to Israel's 14th elections on 29 May, which, against all odds, brought to power a Likud-coalition government led by Binyamin Netanyahu.

For Israelis, the period was triggered and overshadowed by the assassination of Prime Minister Yitzak Rabin by Yeshiva student Yigal Amir in Tel Aviv on 4 November 1995 – an act that revealed to all just how deep were the schisms over the meaning of Jewish identity in contemporary Israel.

For Palestinians, the period witnessed both Oslo's high tide, with Israel's military redeployment from six West Bank cities between November and December 1995 and elections to the new Palestinian Council on 20 January 1996, and its most ominous denouement, with a wave of Islamist-inspired suicide operations in Israel in February–March 1996 followed by draconian domestic repression by the PA and increased external control of the new Palestinian entity by Israel.

The articles included in this section cover all these events, but also look beyond them. In 'Bantustanisation or binationalism?', Palestinian analyst and now Member of Knesset, Azmi Bishara, argues that Oslo not only brought about the organisational demise of the PLO. It also put paid to the idea of a solution based on two states for two peoples. In their stead, Bishara calls for a revamped national movement based on democratic institutions and a new vision of binationalism, in which the two nations that now inhabit Israel/Palestine coexist within one political entity.

Less radically, 'Outsider in: a profile of Salah Tamari' explores the changes Oslo wrought in mainsteam Palestinian political thinking. Following the trail of a candidate amid the excitement of the Palestinians' first ever election campaign, it documents the dissension the poll caused in Arafat's Fatah movement and the realisation – in Tamari's case at least – that the Palestinians' 'unfinished struggle' can no longer be waged in the name of 'the armed struggle and the *intifada*' but rather on a programme of national and democratic reconstruction.

Areas of National Priority — 1997

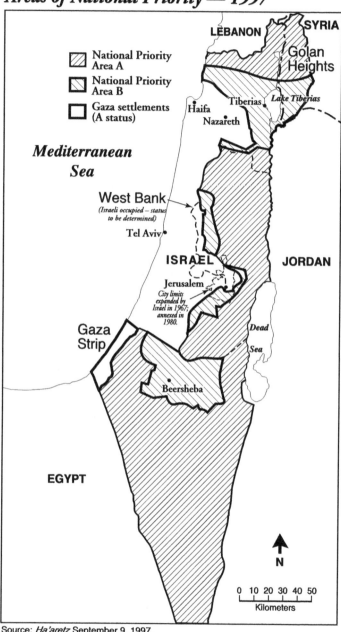

Source: *Ha'aretz* September 9, 1997.

The antithesis of this hope is described in 'The politics of internal security: the PA's new intelligence forces'. This traces the means through which Israel and Arafat transformed the remnants of Fatah and the PLO's former military cadre into the shock troops of the PA's myriad security forces. Wedded to Israel not only by the terms of Oslo but also by common political and economic interest, the article argues that the security forces' aim is less to protect their own people than to implement Israel's military and territorial agenda in the occupied territories – above all, by quelling all domestic opposition to Oslo.

The next three articles highlight the effect of these transformations in three different arenas. 'The politics of atrocity' looks at Hamas's return to suicide operations in Israel in the spring of 1996. It suggests that the motivation behind them was not to destroy Oslo or avenge Israel's assassination of the Hamas 'engineer' Yahiya Ayyash. Rather, it was the bitter outcome of an internal struggle within Hamas over whether the future of Islamism in the occupied territories should be one of loyal opposition within the PA or of a military resistance outside and against it.

'The Charter and the future of Palestinian politics' investigates the polarities set up between the newly elected Palestinian Legislative Council (PLC) and the old structures of the PLO. Focusing on the debates over whether to amend the Palestine National Charter, it predicts that the future locus of any opposition to the PA's authoritarianism will be found less in the old PLO factions than in new democratic institutions built in the occupied territories, the PLC chief among them. But it also argues – if a comprehensive Palestinian national movement is to be revived – that such institutions will have to find new ways of representing and linking with the bulk of the Palestinian people in the diaspora.

The third article – 'Closures, cantons and the Palestinian Covenant' – details the new, indirect military control Israel intended with Oslo and realised in the wake of the suicide operations. Devolving responsibility for the control of the Palestinian population centres to the PA, Israel moved quickly to tighten its strategic and demographic grip on the territory that surrounded them. It was this cantonised reality – set in place by the Labour government – that Netanyahu inherited and consolidated following his election win.

The last two pieces take a closer look at those elections. 'The Palestinians in Israel' analyses the impact of Oslo on the one in five Israeli citizens who are Palestinian. It suggests that 'peace' has inaugurated a shift away from overtly nationalist politics to the struggle for civic and equal rights as Arab citizens within Israel. The last piece follows Shimon Peres' doomed attempts to win the elections he had called in the aftermath of Rabin's assassination. It also anticipates Israel's 'coalition of outcasts' that would, on 29 May, give Netanyahu his victory – the newly empowered constituencies of Russian immigrants, Orthodox Jews and the Sephardi poor.

'Bantustanisation or binationalism?' was published in *Race & Class*, while the version here of 'The politics of internal security: the PA's new intelligence forces' received its first outing in the *Journal of Palestine Studies*. 'Outsider in' and 'Shimon Peres – a fourth time loser' were published in Egypt's *al-Ahram Weekly*. 'The politics of atrocity', 'The Charter and the future of Palestinian politics', 'Closures, cantons and the Palestinian Covenant' and 'The Palestinians in Israel' were published respectively in *News from Within, Middle East International, Middle East Report* and *Red Pepper*.

6

Bantustanisation or Binationalism? An Interview with Azmi Bishara

Azmi Bishara, a Palestinian who is an Israeli citizen, has long been involved in the struggles of the Arab minority in Israel and against the occupation in the West Bank and Gaza. He has also been active on the Israeli left. A lecturer in philosophy at Birzeit University, he writes regularly in both the Israeli and Arabic press in Israel and the occupied territories.

You have said that, with Oslo, Israel recognised the PLO without recognising its goal of national liberation. What, then, remains of PLO nationalism?

From the end of the 1970s, the nationalism of the PLO was a nationalism in transition – in transition from a liberationist project to a statist project.

Then, of course, a lot of things happened. There was the PLO's military defeat in Lebanon. There was the rise to prominence of the national movement in the occupied territories, especially in the *intifada*. There was the collapse of the Soviet Union and with it the remnants of Arab nationalism in the region. There was the end of the old 'cold' world order and also the old 'Arab world' order.

All of these factors had been the political and regional preconditions for the PLO's project for statehood. It was only after these material preconditions had collapsed that Israel felt able to recognise the PLO. In fact, through recognition Israel rescued the PLO, gave it a *raison d'être*. After the Gulf war, the destiny of the PLO had appeared clear. It was a disintegrating bureaucracy in Tunis without money. Its only aim was survival, its only claim was that it represented the Palestinians. Israel's recognition reconferred on the PLO the international status it had steadily lost since 1982 and particularly after the Gulf war.

Now it is true that the *intifada* partially arrested this decline, especially during its first two years when it was a genuinely popular uprising. It enabled the PLO to disguise the terrible defeat of 1982.

But really this was only at the level of public relations. As the existential conditions for statehood crumbled with the changes in the international and regional balance of power, the PLO's international status crumbled with them. By 1992, it had gone, whatever the temporary gains of the *intifada*.

The *intifada*, in other words, did not and could not change this adverse balance of power. What the *intifada* posed was a problem, above all to the Israelis. Prior to the *intifada*, Israel had maintained a *de facto status quo* in the occupied territories which boiled down to two 'Noes' – no withdrawal and no annexation. The *intifada* came along and added another 'No' – no withdrawal, no annexation but no *status quo ante* either. This was the new reality Israel had to face.

If we combine all these factors – the weakness of the PLO, the adverse change in the international and local balance of power and the meaning of the *intifada* – then we have the context for Israel's brilliant chess move of 13 September 1993, in other words, for Oslo.

What does Oslo do? It inaugurates a process which sustains Israel's historic position of no withdrawal from and no annexation of the occupied territories, but addresses the problem of no *status quo ante* – which the *intifada* had posed – by bringing in the PLO to solve it on Israel's behalf. This is the essence of autonomy.

So how would you define the Palestinian entity that is taking shape in Gaza and the West Bank?

The Palestinian autonomy can only be defined negatively. It is a reality that is neither Israeli withdrawal nor annexation. So what is it? It is the creature we have slowly coming to life in Gaza and the West Bank. It is an Israeli creation that has its seeds in the Camp David accords of 1978. Then, too, Israel had been posed with a dilemma. When Begin was elected in 1977, he had advocated annexation of the territories, but he quickly drew back from it. For one very good reason. Annexation would mean the transformation of Israel into a binational state, because annexation would have entailed Israeli citizenship for the Palestinians in the West Bank and Gaza. Begin saw this. But his solution wasn't withdrawal. He suggested a demographic rather than territorial compromise: autonomy for Palestinians in the occupied territories – autonomy, that is, for non-citizens.

Now autonomy for non-citizens is a wholly unique formulation. It represents a political alternative both to a separate Palestinian state and to equality for all citizens in Israel, or to the bases of a binational state. The main problem facing Begin had been the PLO.

It had rejected Camp David. Yet, without it, there was no Palestinian representative able or willing to take responsibility for autonomy in the occupied territories. Again, for very good reasons, since autonomy means a form of Israeli control where Palestinians agree to define and police themselves as non-citizens. It was in this period that the idea of the PLO being the sole legitimate representative of Palestinian people became so holy. It was an idea that undermined all Israeli attempts to create a Palestinian alternative to the PLO in the occupied territories, such as the Village Leagues in the early 1980s. It was an idea that Israel invaded Lebanon to liquidate by liquidating the PLO's political and military infrastructure there. It was an idea the *intifada* temporarily revived but, by the nineties, was, let us say, becoming exhausted.

With Oslo, the PLO accepted the role of being Israel's chosen Palestinian representative for the autonomy. The only difference from the original Camp David formulation was that Israel now also accepted Arafat and the PLO as its chosen representative.

So to return to your first question. Given Oslo and what it means, what remains of PLO nationalism? My answer is that it has passed away. To speak of it now is an anachronism. For sure, there is the symbolic continuity, the biological cord, represented by the person of Yassir Arafat. But that is all he is – a body and a symbol. Nothing remains from the pre-Oslo PLO in the post-Oslo PLO. Even in terms of personnel – with the exception of Arafat – the PLO's historic leadership is either dead or in the diaspora.

Secondly, the PLO historically was the movement of the exiles. The origins of the PLO are to be found in Gaza, Lebanon and Kuwait, or in precisely those places where Palestinians didn't have passports. In the West Bank, Palestinians had and have Jordanian citizenship. Prior to 1967, West Bank Palestinians were active in *Baathist*, Communist, Nationalist parties in Jordan. But the PLO was always the expression of the Palestinian refugees.

Now the Israeli condition number one in Oslo is that the Palestinian question no longer refers to the refugees of the diaspora: it refers exclusively to Palestinians in the West Bank and Gaza. So the historical base of the PLO is not on Oslo's agenda. This is what I mean: what we have in the West Bank and Gaza is no longer even in remotest sense the PLO. It is Arafat and something called the Palestinian Authority.

But the PLO factions still operate in the occupied territories?

Do they? I think what we are witnessing now is the collapse of Palestinian political society in the occupied territories. If you look at all the PLO factions, you will see an exodus of members from them. The old Palestinian political map is changing. This is particularly evident among the PLO's opposition factions like the PFLP and DFLP. And its meaning is clear: these factions are still functioning as though the PLO exists, and it doesn't. And unless they adapt to the changed circumstances brought about by Oslo they are going to disappear from the scene.

But their disappearance from Palestinian politics would, in my opinion, be genuinely catastrophic. Because, without them, the vacuum is going to be filled by two alternatives. First, we will see – are seeing – the revival of the traditional tribal structures of Palestinian society, or what is known as the *hamula* or extended family structures. Such a trend is wholly regressive. There are many criticisms that can be made of the PLO factions: they were often corrupt, always undemocratic; but they were a modern mode of political organisation. They broke the traditional, backward, *hamula* structures of Palestinian society.

There are already very clear signs that the PA – since it is not the PLO – is reviving the old *hamula* structures to serve as its main political ally in the autonomy. Its other ally, and this is the second alternative, is the institutional transformation of the PLO's remnants into the PA's police and security services. These are going to be the two bases of the PA and both are wholly reactionary bases.

If, in other words, a nationalist progressive force does not emerge in the autonomy, we are going to be left with an archaic despotism coupled with an Islamist opposition. This is not our inevitable destiny. But, if we are to avoid it, the PLO's leftist factions must start to become realistic.

How do you counter the argument that the very fact of having a PA in the West Bank and Gaza will release a dynamic towards statehood that will prove irreversible? That you are being premature in writing off the potential of Palestinian nationalism?

Let's look at the actual situation, without predictions. Let's try and define what is this autonomy in Gaza, and what are Israel's intentions in extending it to the West Bank, at least for the next couple of years.

To look at the second point first. Israel has made it clear that it wants to generalise the Gaza model to the West Bank, regardless of how big or small the areas of autonomy will be. So what is the Gaza model? The Gaza model is a bantustan. Gaza, currently, is a 'place' that lacks sovereignty and at the same time is not a part of Israel. It's neither one thing nor the other. Its people do not have right of entry to Gaza's neighbouring countries. In this respect, they are even more restricted than in the bantustans of South Africa, where at least you could travel to work. The main aim of the PA's security forces in Gaza is not the security of its inhabitants but the security of the colonial country. Gaza is an entity that is totally separate from yet totally dependent on Israel, politically and economically. It is a bantustan with one gate that can be opened and closed any time Israel chooses.

And Gaza is the model for the West Bank. Look at what Israel is doing on the ground. It is investing millions of dollars for an infrastructure of roads that will link up most of the Jewish settlements and fragment the Palestinian 'areas' into so many townships. At the end of the day, we can call these townships a state if we wish. We can call Arafat 'emperor' if we wish. But the reality is bantustanisation.

Let's say Israel extends this model to five or six areas in the West Bank. Where is the basis for statehood? It resides only in the fact that there will be one PA for all these bantustans.

Now, when the Israeli and Palestinian negotiators sit down to negotiate the final status, they are going to be the same negotiators who negotiated the bantustans. They are going to operate according to the same imbalance of power. If we add that by that time Israel may also have peace treaties with all the frontline Arab states, where is the incentive for Israeli withdrawal? The aim of autonomy is separation without withdrawal, and it's realisable. Why would the Israelis throw it away?

This would suggest that the room for manoeuvre of the Palestinian opposition forces is going to be extremely limited. And yet you strongly advocate that all Palestinian forces should participate in any upcoming elections to the PA?

The main problem facing the opposition forces – by which I mean the progressive, leftist and secularist forces in Palestinian politics – is that since Oslo they have been locked into a peculiar duality of thinking. This thinking has two poles. If you say that Oslo is a reality that is not going to be reversed, this – according to the opposition – means somehow you agree to it. To oppose Oslo is thus to pretend – and to act – as though it does not exist. The third option – that Oslo exists and the opposition's role is to criticise it – simply does not figure in the opposition's discourse. It's a kind of mythological thinking that swings between what should be and what shouldn't be, but suppresses what is.

The sole position of the opposition since Oslo has been 'down with Oslo'. There was no other position. Yet it was also clear (including to the opposition) that not only was Oslo here to stay, but also that its reality was far stronger than Camp David had ever been. With Camp David, the PLO was against it, all of the Arab world (with the exception of Egypt) was against it and half of the international community was against it. With Oslo, the PLO is for it, most of the Arab world is for it and all of the international community is for it. You can say you are against Oslo, that it's a bad agreement, but you cannot pretend it doesn't exist.

The question now is not 'Oslo: Yes or No?' The question rather is 'Oslo, now what?' This is the question the people want addressed by their leaders. The PA can't answer it, because the PA is no longer the PLO. And the opposition can't answer it because they have yet to realise that the demise of the PLO is also their demise. They have to acknowledge this. They have to admit that they too were complicit in a structure of politics that led to Oslo, no less than Arafat.

But self-criticism that is not accompanied by constructive criticism as to what now should be done ceases to be self-criticism; it becomes self-destruction. This is what is happening to the PLO opposition. But we cannot allow it to happen.

So what are the left's options? First, let us describe the options it doesn't have. It no longer has the option of armed struggle, especially if and when Syria accepts peace with Israel. Then even the Lebanese/Israeli border will be quiet. It no longer has the option of 'reviving' the *intifada*. Anyone who calls for reviving the *intifada* today demonstrates only his or her utter divorce from the current reality of the occupied territories, which is that of an exhausted people, a weary people.

This leaves the struggle for elections. I do not mean here the 'debate' as to whether one should or should not participate in elections, because by participating you grant 'legitimacy' to Oslo. This is a luxurious debate, as though Oslo's legitimacy depended on the left's participation in it.

Participation is vital because the issue of elections is going to dominate Palestinian society for the next six months. It is the only vehicle for raising political issues that Oslo has left us. If the leftist forces abstain, they are in effect abstaining from this political debate. This is not to say that the left has to accept the terms of the elections. It is not even to preclude the option of boycotting the elections. But, if you boycott them, boycott them from within, from inside the political discourse around elections. Use the mobilising potential inherent in elections to critique Oslo, so that a vote for you is a vote against Oslo. Because, politically, a 60 per cent vote for Arafat is different to a 90 per cent vote for Arafat.

But there is another reason why elections are important. The political debate raised by elections would allow us to 'think aloud' with the people. And one of the things we should start to think aloud about is whether a Palestinian state is any longer a viable aim for achieving Palestinian self-determination. And, if it isn't, what are the options? I can only see two.

First, the Jordanian option in which what is left of Palestine integrates with the larger Jordanian sovereignty and so, in that way, returns to the Arab world. Second, in the struggle against Oslo's bantustans, we pose as their alternative not statehood, but a binational state for the whole of Israel/Palestine.

Why is the option of Palestinian statehood *passé*? Because a Palestinian state that is the sum total of its collective bantustans will never be able to solve the refugee question. Confederation with Jordan could solve the problem, and so could a binational state in Israel/Palestine because both would have the territorial depth and the sovereignty to absorb the refugees.

An isolated Palestinian 'state' in the West Bank and Gaza would always be under Israeli military hegemony, which would mean, should it accept this role, entering into junior partnership with Israel against other Arab countries or, should it refuse this role, being subject to an Israeli/Jordan alliance against it. It would be a 'victim' state, prone to Israeli manipulation and/or military threat.

These are new directions for the national struggle that we should now seriously start to discuss, if we are to get beyond Oslo.

What would be the bases of this new national struggle? For example, do you foresee the demand for, say, a binational state emerging out of a future struggle against the bantustans? And, if so, is the Palestinian struggle now essentially an anti-aparthied struggle?

Yes and no. First of all, we have to be clear what we mean by binationalism. When elements of the Israeli left say they want a binational state, they envisage a state for Jews and its other citizens. This is not the basis of a binational state. It is the basis of a confessional state, along the lines of Lebanon.

By binationalism, I mean a new political orientation of the national struggle that is for equality between Jews and Arabs and against separation, both for the Arab citizens of Israel and for Palestinians in the occupied territories.

Now, without doubt, there will resistance to this, especially among Israelis. After all, they are the victors. Why should they give up their national privileges? We will have to implant in both the Palestinian and Israeli democratic forces what I call binationalist values over narrowly nationalist values. We will have to point out to the Israeli left that its current slogan of separation – in the context of Oslo – is actually a racist slogan: it legitimises Israel's ongoing domination of another people; it legitimises the idea that Palestinians are a demographic threat. In its stead, we must propagate political programmes that emphasise the genuinely binational values of equality, reciprocity and coexistence.

Among the Palestinians, I think there is less resistance to the idea of binationalism. The PLO's original demand was for a democratic, secular state in the whole of Palestine. There was also a period – in the seventies – when it advocated a binational state. Now, admittedly, the PLO never gave much thought to what these slogans would mean in practice. But my point is that the demand for a separate, exclusively Palestinian state in the West Bank and Gaza is still a very young demand in Palestinian political thinking. It is not so sacred. And, in the wake of Oslo, I believe that more and more Palestinians will see that they have everything to gain from adopting a genuinely binationalist programme.

As for Israelis, it will force them to address the meaning and challenge of equality. Why? Because the bantustanisation option may defer resolution of the Palestinian question, but it cannot, in the end, be the resolution. A historical compromise between the two peoples will still have to be made, and one that is something more than a mere reflection of the existing balance of power.

Jerusalem, July 1995; *Race & Class*, October–December 1995

7

The Politics of Internal Security: the PA's New Intelligence Services

With the signing of the Israeli–Palestinian interim agreement ('Oslo II'),[1] it has become clear that future realisation of a peace settlement between Israel and Palestinians no longer hinges on international legality.[2] Increasingly, it rests on a definition of 'peace' which translates as unconditional security for the Israelis and conditional security for Palestinians.[3] The overarching concept of Israel's security is operative in the new agreement, deciding not just the pace of the expanding self-rule but, very likely, its eventual geo-political shape.[4] It is also a definition with which the present Palestinian leadership has acquiesced, whether tactically (as its adherents claim) or strategically (as its opponents accuse).[5]

The subordination of the Palestinians inherent in Oslo II is underlined by a depth of cooperation between Israeli and PA security forces in the West Bank far greater than anything seen in Gaza and Jericho. With the new agreement, PA security forces are obligated to 'act systematically against all expressions of' (Palestinian) 'violence and terror', 'arrest and prosecute' (Palestinian) 'individuals suspected of perpetuating acts of violence and terror' and 'cooperate in the exchange of information as well as coordinate policies and activities' with the Israeli security services. But they are not 'in any circumstances' allowed to arrest or place in custody Israelis, despite the latter having the right of movement throughout the West Bank and Gaza, including within the 'autonomous enclaves'. Should an Israeli be questioned by the police in these areas, it will be the 'Israeli side' of a 'joint patrol' that does the talking.[6]

In its scope, powers and actual or intended infrastructure,[7] Oslo II perpetuates for Oslo's interim period Israel's security hegemony over the West Bank and Gaza. This hegemony is based less on a recognition by Israel and the PLO of 'mutual legitimate and political rights', as expressed in the preamble of Oslo I, than on an older Israeli formula of military 'supremacy and subordination'[8] determined by the massively imbalanced distribution of military and territorial resources held by Israel over the PA. It follows – at least for the current PA leadership – that any political and territorial movement towards Palestinians' historic goals of statehood and self-determination can only occur within the confines of such hegemony rather than through active resistance against it.[9] The PA's principle and determining alliance in the interim period is going to be security-led, and with Israel.

As such, the crucial Palestinian agency in Oslo's coming phase will be neither the PLO nor the new Palestinian Council nor any new political parties thrown up by the forthcoming Palestinian elections. Rather, it will be the Palestinian police whose job, stipulated by Oslo, is to guarantee Palestinian 'public order' and the PA's various intelligence services whose vague remit, unstipulated by Oslo, covers 'internal security'.[10]

The Security Forces

The establishment of a 'strong police force' is one of the few unequivocal powers the PA is granted in the original Oslo agreement of September 1993. In the Cairo Agreement signed in May 1994, the ceiling of security personnel the PA was permitted to recruit for Gaza and Jericho was 9,000. With Oslo II, the ceiling for the West Bank was set at 12,000. In both agreements it is stated that the Palestinian police will 'constitute the only Palestinian security force' and will have four operational divisions – civil, public security, emergency and intelligence. These prescriptions, however, are on paper, with neither the PA nor Israel nor representatives of the international community in any way bound by them. In December 1994, an official working for the UN's special coordinator in the occupied territories – one of whose tasks was 'coordinating' the allocation of donor money for police salaries – stated that the number of security personnel on the PA's payroll had swelled to 13,000. In August 1995 – the eve of Oslo II's signing – the PA's Head of Police in Gaza, Nasser Yusuf, said before the UN's Local Aid Coordinating Committee (LACC) that salaried police officers under the PA in Gaza and Jericho numbered 22,000. Given Taba's additional commitments, this means a police force for the interim period in the West Bank and Gaza in excess of 30,000, a figure both PA and Israeli officials take as given. This too is likely to be fluid. In June 1995, the Head of Civil Police in Gaza City, Ghazi Jabali, mooted the PA would eventually require a police force of 'around 40,000' for the autonomy.

The chief beneficiary of this inflation has been the PA's intelligence division or, more precisely, divisions. According to available information, the various intelligence forces include:

(a) The General Intelligence Service (GIS): the 'official' PA intelligence agency, headed by Brigadier General Amin al-Hindi. Israeli sources estimate its current strength in the West Bank and Gaza to be around '1,000 agents'.[11]

(b) The Preventive Security Force (PSF) headed by Colonel Jibril Rajoub in Jericho and Colonel Mohammed Dahlan in Gaza. By common assent this is the largest of the PA's intelligence forces, though precise figures are impossible to get. The Israeli monitoring group, Peace Watch, says according to 'information it has obtained' (presumably from Israeli intelligence sources) the PSF currently has '2,000 salaried agents' in the West Bank and at least the same number in Gaza but probably more. What is confirmed by both Israeli and Palestinian sources is that the PSF has staff and offices not just in Gaza and Jericho, but in at least eight other West Bank locations, including East Jerusalem.[12]

(c) The Presidential Guard (PG)/Force 17 headed by Colonel Feisal Abu Shirah in Gaza and Colonel Ikhmat Barakat in Jericho. It is unclear whether PG/Force 17 is actually one agency or two, since it is composed of new Palestinian recruits from the West Bank and Gaza as well as from Fatah's old diasporal Force 17, whose specific task was to protect the PLO leader. Peace Watch says the force/forces have 'several hundred' members. Palestinian sources say these are mainly concentrated in Nablus and in the north of the West Bank, with PG officers taking a direct hand in preparations for the 'civic' policing of these areas via the recruitment and training of new municipal police forces.

(d) The Special Security Force (SSF) headed by General Abu Yusuf al-Wahidi. This is the smallest of the services – Peace Watch estimates its present strength at 'a few dozen policemen' – but with the murkiest of remits. Formally authorised to protect Arafat during his visits to Jericho, Palestinian sources say its actual function may be to gather intelligence on and monitor the PA's other security services. It is currently based in Jericho, but is expected to radiate once redeployment in the West Bank gets underway.

According to the Palestinian human rights organisation, Al-Haq, there are also smaller forces such as the PA's Military Police (MP), Navy Police (NP) and Disciplinary Police (DP). But it is unclear whether these constitute separate forces, with their own command and structure, or whether they are subsumed under the larger intelligence services. There is also Fatah and its military wing in the occupied territories, the Fatah Hawks, which, in November 1994, was publically reactivated by Arafat to 'work with the forces of the PA ... to protect this land'.[13]

Amorphousness and Murky Remits

The most ominous feature of these forces is their number and amorphousness. 'There is no terms of reference for any of the services', says Khalid Bitrawi, a Palestinian lawyer at Al-Haq. Given this lack of an 'overarching structure', he says, it is impossible to define their different roles and responsibilities. It is a difficulty shared by the services' commanders.

In December 1994, the PSF's Gaza chief, Mohammed Dahlan, described his service tautologically as 'an organ of the PA which deals with preventive security issues pertaining to the PA'.[14] Yet the PSF's chief in Jericho, Jibril Rajoub, has repeatedly stated that the PSF is 'an extension of Fatah in accordance with the new reality of the PA'.[15] These two functions are not the same. Fatah is a political movement that derives its legitimacy from the PLO. The PSF is a quasi-state body entrusted with enforcing 'preventive security'. Apart from these statements by Dahlan and Rajoub, no other PA definition of the PSF's role exists.

More alarmingly, none of these agencies technically exist according to the Oslo agreements or the PA, despite being armed and resourced by the latter, tacitly recognised by Israel and at least partially paid for by the donor countries under their various international umbrellas. They are in a precise legal sense lawless and boundless both in the occupied territories and the autonomous areas.

They exist, however, as a reality on the Palestinian street. In Gaza and Jericho, they work alongside the official Palestinian police. In the West Bank – aside from the now legal if faded Palestinian flag – their presence embodies the most tangible proof of the PA's imminent arrival. Together they comprise a clandestine force that could have a personnel strength as high as 9,000. And their activities have been documented with increasing concern over the last year by Palestinian, Israeli and international human rights bodies,[16] and by the Israeli and, to a much lesser extent, Palestinian and international media. Broadly speaking, the various forces appear to have three main tasks.

First, they are police forces. From the moment the Oslo agreement was signed – and even more so after the PA was established in May 1994 – PSF/Fatah operatives assumed the role of a *de facto* civic police throughout the occupied territories, activated to fill the 'law and order' vacuum created by the *intifada* as well as that anticipated ahead of Israel's military redeployment.[17] Palestinian and Israeli human rights groups – as well as eyewitness testimony – have amassed scores of cases where PSF agents or Fatah activists (or Fatah activists claiming to be PSF agents) have intervened in Palestinian communities, whether 'autonomous' or occupied, to fight crime, solve clan or family disputes and mete out punishment to those accused of 'moral offences' such as drug-taking and prostitution. In Gaza and Jericho, these actions occur in the shadow of the PA's jurisdiction; in the West Bank, often in the name of Fatah. In both areas they are happening illegally and beyond any reach of judicial scrutiny.

Second, the PSF especially appears to have assumed powers to solve the 'unfinished business' of Palestinian collaborators. According to the Cairo Agreement, Palestinians working for the Israeli General Security Service (GSS) prior to the Oslo accords were to have been granted amnesty or, in certain cases, given Israeli citizenship to enable them to move inside the Green Line. Numbers of collaborators working for Israel at any one time are murky, though one Israeli human rights worker says he has 'reliable information' that around 5,000 collaborators were on the GSS's payroll at the time of the Oslo agreement. If family members are included as well as those Palestinians who passed on occasional intelligence in exchange for GSS 'favours', then the collaborator population in the occupied territories before Oslo may well have been as large as 30,000.

Despite the 'amnesty' pledge in the Cairo Agreement, the PA's public stance *vis-à-vis* collaboration, both past and present, is that the guilty will be punished as traitors. Israel has granted a small number of 'big' collaborators citizenship, but is clearly not going to absorb them all. The upshot is a legal black hole that serves both Israel and the PA's interests.

On arrival in Gaza and Jericho, the Palestinian police began a sweep of Palestinians from those areas suspected of collaborating. A similar campaign was launched in the West Bank by the PSF/Fatah, though here suspects were abducted either to secret locations or to Jericho. Since, by virtue of Cairo's amnesty clause, these suspects of collaboration cannot be charged with it, they cannot be arrested; they are simply taken and detained at varying length without warrant.[18] The sweeps have continued in the West Bank and Gaza ever since. Their purpose appears to be not just punitive, but intimidatory.

Abandoned by their former GSS employers, ex-collaborators surrender themselves to the PSF as a way of gaining mitigation. Some are imprisoned, others tortured and around five have 'died' while in PA custody. Some, however, are 'turned', not in the classical sense of becoming 'double-agents', but in the more mundane sense of becoming employees of the PSF rather than of the GSS. In this way, an unspecified number of ex-collaborators have been absorbed into the PSF. In return – and as the price for their amnesty – they offer the intelligence they possess.[19] This is an especially valuable asset given the PA's intelligence agencies' third and most critical function.

This involves the internal surveillance of Palestinian political opposition to Oslo. How the labour is divided between the various intelligence services in performing this task is obscure, but the crucial agency appears to be the PSF. This is not just due to its size, but more so to its political and social composition. Drawn almost exclusively from inside the occupied territories, the PSF is made up overwhelmingly of young Fatah activists who won their political spurs during the intifada as prison leaders, youth activists or as 'fighters' in Fatah's military wings, the Fatah Hawks in Gaza and the Black Panthers in the West Bank.

Dahlan had been the Gaza leader of Fatah's *Shabiba* (youth) movement prior to his expulsion by Israel in 1988. Rajoub had spent 16 years in Israeli prisons and been an established Fatah leader before he too was expelled by Israel in 1988. Both men exude enormous street credibility, and not just among Fatah supporters.[20] Unlike the 'outside' PLO cadres, they know Israel and the Israelis, and the occupied territories and 'inside' Palestinians, like the backs of their hands. A fact which for at least certain sectors of Israel's security establishment is perceived as a major asset.

Israeli Connections

In January 1994, Rajoub and Dahlan met in Rome with the former head of the GSS, Ya'acov Peri, and the IDF's then deputy (now full) Chief of Staff, Amnon Shahak, to sort out the modalities of their future roles in the autonomy. The meeting did not reach any formal accord but rather 'an understanding'.[21] This boiled down to a *modus vivendi* where, in return for intelligence on the Palestinian opposition and particularly the Islamist Hamas and Islamic Jihad movements, the GSS and the IDF would grant Dahlan and Rajoub a free hand to create a *de facto* police force throughout the West Bank and Gaza, both before and during Israel's redeployment from these areas.[22] The so-called 'Rome Agreement' does not formally exist, but it is operative, a fact admitted by Yitzak Rabin himself. On 18 September 1994 – in reply to a question in the Israeli cabinet and a full year before Israel's West Bank redeployment commenced – the late Israeli PM stated that PA security personnel operated throughout the West Bank, with 'Israel's knowledge and in cooperation with Israel's security forces to safeguard Israel's security interests'. The red line was that this would not be tolerated in 'sovereign' East Jerusalem.[23]

The extent to which the PSF has kept to its side of the bargain since the Rome rendezvous has caused dissensions within Israel's security establishment, with the GSS broadly 'impressed' with Dahlan and Rajoub's cooperation but the Border Police and elements of the IDF less so. But that there has been 'coordination' of intelligence between the Israeli and Palestinian security services is indisputable.

On 11 October 1994, Hamas guerillas announced that they had abducted an Israeli conscript, Nachshon Wachsman, whose ransom would be the release of 200 Palestinian and Arab prisoners. Five days later, Wachsman and three of his kidnappers were killed after a botched IDF rescue attempt in the West Bank village of Biet Nabala, where the soldier was held hostage. It was, say Israeli sources, largely on the basis of information passed by the PSF to the GSS that led the army to its quarry.[24] In August 1995, Israel closed off Gaza for nearly a week on the grounds that a 'wanted' Hamas activist, Wa'il Nasser, was 'at large' there. On 18 August he was arrested by the Palestinian police, after street battles between them and local Palestinians had left over 30 injured. In September 1995 the GSS supplied information to the PSF that two PFLP members, Yusuf and Shahar Ra'i, were 'wanted' in connection with the killing of two Israelis in the West Bank and were hiding out in Jericho. Within 48 hours, the two had been arrested by the Palestinian police and sentenced to twelve years imprisonment for 'incitement against the peace process'.

The GSS understood that it would not look good on the Palestinian street for the PA and the PSF to go public on such liaisons. But the Border Police and elements of IDF – as articulated by Police Minister, Moshe Shahal – wanted just this, the overt extradition by the PA of Palestinian suspects into Israeli custody.[25] Rajoub refused, and Dahlan stated in an Israeli newspaper that under 'no circumstances would the PA ever extradite Palestinians to Israel'. In retaliation, the army closed off Jericho. After six days, the siege was lifted, quietly, with the Ra'i brothers staying put in Jericho. In this turf war, the GSS's post-Oslo policy of 'internal security' won out over the Border Police and the IDF's pre-Oslo mentality of military might. Its essence was summed up by one of the GSS's closest allies in the Israeli government, Environment Minister Yossi Sarid. 'After all,' he said, as long as 'Palestinian killers sit in jail for twelve years, it is not so important which jail'.[26]

Patronage, Rivalries and Keeping the Opposition in Line

Given the internal security bent of both the Cairo and Oslo II agreements, a strong and massive Palestinian intelligence force is an indispensible condition for the Oslo-inspired peace process. It is not so much tolerated by the Israeli government as Israel's absolute precondition for any Palestinian movement toward 'self-rule'. Creating 'a reality whereby internal Palestinian security will be in the Palestinians' hands'[27] was, after all, Rabin's main motive for backing the Oslo formula in the first place. He was candid about his reasons. 'The Palestinians will be better at it than we were,' he said in September 1993, 'because they will allow no appeals to the Supreme Court and will prevent the Israeli Association of Civil Rights from criticising the conditions there by denying it access to the area. They will rule by their own methods, freeing, and this is most important, the Israeli army soldiers from having to do what they will do.'[28]

But that there should be a multiplicity of PA intelligence agencies rather a single unitary force has less to do with Israeli prescriptions. It relates rather to the internal and patrimonal dynamics of PLO politics or, more precisely, to the way Arafat has mediated those dynamics into the 'new reality' of the PA. He rules, as Rabin would put it, 'by his own methods.' And Arafat's methods require a proliferation rather than concentration of forces.

First, a myriad of forces gives Arafat an enormous scope for political patronage. Since their initial disbandment in September 1993, former cadres from Fatah's Hawk and Panther wings in the occupied territories have been steadily absorbed into the PSF and other intelligence forces, making an increasingly nominal distinction between Fatah's old military wing and the PA. This served a precise political purpose. Had these cadres felt excluded from the spoils of self-government, they could have formed an oppositional constituency to it. Their absorption into PSF and other agencies not only pays them a wage, it affords them a political and social status commensurate with their former role of fighters.

The same logic holds with Arafat's incorporation of the PLO's old diasporal military forces into the PA's new security structures. In the Cairo Agreement, it was agreed that up to 7,000 of the PA's 9,000 allotment of police could be recruited from abroad, with most brought in from Palestinian Liberation Army (PLA) units stationed in Egypt, Jordan, Sudan, Yemen, Iraq and Algeria. With the interim agreement, says Nasser Yusuf, 5,000 exiles will be included in the 12,000 new recruits, with nearly half returning from what remains of Arafat's loyalist Fatah constituency in Lebanon. These forces have been mainly dispersed throughout the PA's police and intelligence services, with the leaders among them becoming the services' latest 'generals' and 'colonels'. This not only pays them, too, a wage and affords them a status commensurate with their former leadership roles. It also works to erode any lingering political opposition such figures may harbour towards Oslo.

Second, the absence of a clear chain of command means that the various forces do not operate as an army or police force. They are rather horizontal forces or militias, of indeterminate strength, with no hierarchy. This is almost certainly deliberate on Arafat's part. It rehearses one of his oldest methods of rule, tried and tested in Jordan, Lebanon and Tunis, and described by one Israeli journalist as 'one boss but a thousand franchises'.[29]

Because there is no hierarchy, the various forces compete and conflict with each other for the spoils of political, social and economic power in the self rule. In the run-up to Israel's redeployment in Nablus and the north West Bank, there have been intermittent turf wars between Fatah cadres belonging to the PG and those aligned with the PSF, with the PG generally representing the concerns of Nablus's residents and Rajoub's operatives being stronger in the refugee camps, villages and Nablus's poorer quarters such as the Casbah.[30] In Gaza, the fault-line appears to be more between the old 'inside' Fatah leadership – represented by figures like the PSF's deputy leader, Rashid Shback, and PG/Force 17 leader, Sami Abu Samhandana[31] – and 'newcomer' police officials like Ghazi Jabali. These tensions sometimes turn violent, especially over what many Gazans see as Jabali's over-zealous attempts to arrest Fatah activists wanted by the IDF for 'extradition'.[32]

In all disputes it is Arafat who acts as arbiter. This, too, serves a political end. By allowing tensions to simmer between the various forces, he fragments them and forestalls any alternative centres of power from coalescing. This is an absolutely crucial political task, and not just because of the dissensions Oslo threw up in Fatah. More importantly, such tactics weld together the divergent class, regional and generational constituencies from which Fatah's 'non-ideological' brand of nationalism has evolved. If Fatah and Arafat are to keep their hegemonic position in the self-rule, these contending forces must somehow be kept under at least a loose form of unitary command. That command is Arafat. In fighting over the 'franchise', the Fatah leader ensures that 'his' forces – and the constituencies they articulate – are not fighting over the 'boss', nor over the politics and interests he may at any one time espouse.

Finally, the profusion of security forces has enabled Arafat maximum leverage in his dealings with Oslo's Palestinian dissidents, since it enables him to alternate between being the 'good cop' and 'bad cop' against them. This has been especially valuable with the Islamists. Unlike with Oslo's PLO opposition, Arafat cannot bring to bear his enormous powers of financial and political patronage to keep the Islamists in line, since Hamas and Islamic Jihad are not dependent on them. Hamas particularly represents a mass, indigenous and authentic political constituency in the occupied territories by virtue of its own finances, structures, organisation and, above all, ideology.[33] It is because Hamas represents an independent force outside the PA and the PLO's sway that it is perceived as the main internal threat[34] – the most difficult of all Arafat's opponents to 'tame'.

From the outset of the PA, there were major divergences between the security forces over how best to deal with Hamas. For Dahlan and Rajoub – and the PSF generally – Islamist fighters were 'patriots', who could only be won over to the self-rule through 'dialogue' and political co-option.[35] For Jabali and Yusuf, Hamas were 'agents' of foreign powers bent on wrecking Oslo at all costs.[36] The Islamists had therefore to be crushed or at least massively intimidated.

These divergences on occasion broke out as semi-public rows. In August 1994, Hamas guerrillas killed one Israeli and injured five others in an ambush near Gaza's Gush Qatif Jewish settlement. The Palestinian police, under order from Yusuf, arrested 20 of Hamas's front-rank political leadership. Dahlan stepped in and had them released. 'The political leadership should identify a clear-cut policy on how to deal with the armed opposition elements and use of weapons', railed a furious Yusuf.[37] But the political leadership (i.e. Arafat) hedged, seemingly indifferent to these internecine security tussles.[38] But he hedged no longer after Friday 18 November 1994, when 14 Palestinians were shot dead by the Palestinian police during clashes in Gaza. After 'Black Friday' – the gravest challenge to the PLO leader's authority since he returned to Gaza and Jericho – Arafat decided that force would, after all, be needed with the Islamists. But the agency to administer it would not be the official (and largely 'outsider' led) Palestinian police, whose lack of legitimacy and power on the Palestinian street was made patently obvious by the events of 'Black Friday'. It would be Fatah, particularly its 'inside' cadre, and its 'extension', the PSF. 'We have been very patient with Hamas and Islamic Jihad', said a PSF operative in November 1994. 'From now on they should know that there is only one authority'.

In the year since, this message appears to have sunk in. Under pressure from the Israelis – but also to get the message across – Arafat has on occasion used the stick with the Islamists, dispatching his official police to round up scores of 'Hamas suspects' after every military operation against Israeli targets, regardless of whether such actions were launched from inside Gaza/Jericho or elsewhere. But he has also dangled the carrot, quietly mandating 'inside' Fatah civilian leaders like Hisham Abdl Raziq and Marwan Barghouti to cultivate a dialogue with Hamas's political leadership in the West Bank and Gaza.

In September 1995, this leadership announced that it had a 'draft agreement' with the PA in which Hamas would 'cease all military actions in and from the PA areas' and would 'respect all agreements (i.e. Oslo, Cairo and Taba) reached between the PLO and Israel'.[39] In return, the PA would grant Hamas an independent political role in the autonomy, perhaps through the launching of an Islamist party or list to contest the PA elections. If Hamas holds to its commitments in the agreement, Arafat will hold to his, since his aim has never been to eliminate Hamas altogether. Rather, he wants Hamas domesticated to accept his – but only his – authority. The September draft agreement, if kept, amounts to that acceptance.

The Harvest of the Security Culture

Such methods undoubtably demonstrate Arafat's prowess as a faction fighter. Whether the same qualities are those required of a leader who can marshal and mobilise the resources of the Palestinian people for the immense task of building a state is another matter. But the safe answer is no.

The PA's massive centralisation of political power in the hands of one man and one faction, as well as its disportionate emphasis on 'internal security', augurs rather the emergence of a wholly dependent and authoritarian Palestinian entity. The prospects this has for the economic, legal and moral spheres of Palestinian society are stark for the interim period and, for Palestinians' historic claims to self-determination and return, probably mortal.

First of all, there is the economic cost. At the time of the Cairo Agreement, the World Bank estimated that the annual budget for a 9,000-strong police force would be $180 million.[40] A police force three times this size will therefore cost over $500 million a year. Coupled with a PA civil bureaucracy of 27,000 employees, the idea the PA can financially cover such non-productive sectors out of locally generated revenue – as well as run much needed social services – is wholly imaginary. It has not been able to in Gaza and Jericho and will not be able to in the West Bank. What such an inflated public sector (in which nearly 70 per cent of all jobs are security-related) actually portends is an interim period every bit as economically dependent and politically conditioned by donor money as was its Gaza/Jericho preamble. Very simply, the PA does not need a 30,000 strong police force to facilitate the economic, social and political development of its 2.6 million people. A police force of this size is only needed to keep the lid on a people in the absence of such development.

Second, there is the legal cost to Palestinians' political, civil and human rights under autonomy. From the moment of their arrival, the various PA security forces' attitude to these rights has been *ad hoc* at best and abusive at worst, but in all cases ungoverned by due process. Between October 1994 and February 1995, PA security forces in Gaza undertook no less than five mass arrest sweeps, rounding up hundreds of Palestinians on 'suspicion' of belonging to either the PLO or Islamist opposition, but 'without judicial warrant or sanction and contrary to the rule of law'.[41] In February 1995, Arafat personally authorised the setting up of 'special state security courts'. These are independent of any civilian judiciary system, allow secret evidence, brook no appeal procedures and are 'judged' by PLO military personnel appointed by the PA. Verdicts are the prerogative of Arafat, who – says the PA's attorney-general – has sole power to 'confirm, ease or stiffen' any sentence passed by the 'courts'.[42] In the period since, over 30 Palestinians have been tried and sentenced by them. One Palestinian has been executed.

These political violations are amplified by civic ones, as the PA's security forces have asserted their own brand of 'crime prevention' and 'law and order'. In its recent report on the PSF,[43] B'tselem gathers testimony from 13 Palestinians who charge the agency with 'illegal abduction', 'arrest without warrant', 'detention for lengthy periods without judicial scrutiny', 'refusing legal representation', 'refusing family visits', and the use of 'harsh torture techniques such as beatings, painful tying-up, threats, humiliation, sleep deprivation, and the withholding of medical treatment.' And this is in the West Bank, before the formal arrival of the PA. In Gaza, there are now no fewer than 17 prisons and detention centres run either by the police or one or other of the intelligence forces.[44] There is, says one Palestinian lawyer, 'little or no coordination between them'. Legal access to prisoners is 'not regular' and, in certain centres, non-existent.

Yet it is the effect such 'securitisation' has had on the political and moral content of Palestinian culture that, in the long run, may exert the greatest toll. The emergence of an increasingly authoritarian PA has contributed to a process of de-politicisation of Palestinian society in which many of its ablest members have 'collectively withdrawn', reverting to individualistic or clan-based (rather than political) solutions for their needs and aspirations. This is not only regressive in itself. It is erosive of the essentially modernist and political national Palestinian identity that the PLO, via its factions and for all their faults, had brought into being.[45] And it is fatal for any future Palestinian strategy of national resistance and independence, especially for the bulk of the Palestinian nation left adrift (and unrepresented) in the diaspora.

What the PA's politics of internal security actually betrays is a culture of defeat. This is not just due to the fact that the current Palestinian political leadership has and is lowering Palestinians' national claims to a series of disaggregated parts of the West Bank and Gaza. More corrosively, it is born out of an obsessive ethos of 'national security' and 'national interest' that, once their political and ideological content is unpacked, turn out to be no more than the practical implementation of Israel's territorial and military ambitions in the occupied territories.

Jerusalem, October 1995; *Journal of Palestine Studies*, Winter 1996

8

Outsider In: a Profile of Palestinian Council Candidate Salah Tamari

It is a cold January night in Betier, a small village east of Bethlehem. Around 100 men and boys (women tend not to attend political meetings in Palestine's villages) are squeezed into a tiny youth club – a room equipped only with plastic chairs and a single billiard table. The fluorescent light picks up the men's unfurling breath, but also their rapt attention. They have come to listen to one of the 31 candidates contesting the four seats allocated to the Bethlehem area on the new Palestinian Council.

He is Salah Tamari, an independent candidate but many feel is the front-runner for one of the two Muslim seats assigned to Bethlehem. His biography encapsulates why.

Tamari was born in Bethlehem in 1941 to a large Beduin clan. But since 1965 his personal history has been inseparable from that of the Palestinian national struggle. In 1965, he joined Yassir Arafat's Fatah movement, a decision that 'disrupted' his studies in English Literature at Cairo's Ain-Shams University. He fought the Israelis during the six day war and again in 1968 at Karameh in Jordan, a battle which for many in the Arab world signalled the arrival of Fatah's guerrillas as the leading force in the Palestinian revolution. After the 'Black September' debacle in Jordan, Tamari became a commander in the PLO's militias in Lebanon, resisting the Israeli invasions in 1979 and 1982.

He was imprisoned by Israel in its notorious Ansar jail in occupied south Lebanon, where he gained international renown as the eloquent and charismatic spokesperson for the jail's Palestinian, Lebanese and Arab detainees. Released in 1984, he spent the dark years of the PLO's Tunis exile as a 'roving emissary' for the Palestinian national movement in Tunisia, Algeria and Washington. Israel finally allowed Tamari to return to Bethlehem in August 1994, 'one month after the Chairman', he says. Like Arafat, it was the first time he had set foot on Palestinian soil in 27 years. Commitment to the national struggle counts for a lot in the Palestinian elections. Tamari has that commitment in bucketfuls.

But the emphasis of his campaign is not on the past. 'In crossing the Allenby bridge I knew I wasn't only covering a geographical distance', he says, 'but crossing from one era into another.'

Unlike many of the PLO returnees, Tamari didn't take up a post in the Palestinian Authority's (PA) new political or security structures. He threw himself rather into what he calls mass work, particularly among the young. 'I started scout troupes in the Eastern villages. They are now 2,000 strong. They are poorly equipped, but their voluntary participation in building schools, roads and kindergartens marks a qualitative step forward in consciousness.'

It is a political intervention that Tamari sees as absolutely critical given the changed political realities thrown up by Oslo. 'We must redirect the anger of our youth that has accumulated under occupation into constructive channels. Their anger is just, and I share it. But there are ways to resist other than by destroying our society in the name of armed struggle and the *intifada*.'

The same stress on self-reliance and pragmatic political change is evident at Tamari's campaign rallies. 'The question is not whether one is for Oslo or against it', he says at one meeting. 'The question is how we confront it. Oslo itself is an unfinished struggle. We still have to fight over issues like settlements, the refugees and Jerusalem.'

At another meeting in el-Duha near Bethlehem, villagers present Tamari with a petition of grievances, such as their need for a proper waste water system. Tamari's response is sympathetic but blunt. 'Look, I know your problems are severe,' he says, 'but they are not as severe as the problems of the refugees in Gaza or of those villages in the West Bank that still lack electricity. The PA must have priorities; it can make no promises.'

Such honesty goes down well in el-Duha, although it is impossible to say whether it will garner Tamari extra votes. Other questions, however, are more difficult to field.

For the people of Bethlehem – and for many Palestinians across the occupied territories – Tamari is Fatah. Why, then, is he not running on the official Fatah list for Bethlehem?

The answer is complicated. In the run-up to the elections, Fatah in Bethlehem held primaries to select their four nominations. Tamari headed the poll. After the decision by Hamas and the PLO opposition factions to boycott the elections, however, Arafat and Fatah's Central Committee decided that the official list should not be party based, but rather a 'national coalition'. In Bethlehem, the official Fatah list is headed by George Hazbon, a respected Christian and trade union activist, but whose political affiliation is the old Palestine Communist Party rather than Fatah.

Tamari's decision to run as an independent was made largely in protest at this lack of internal democracy inside his own movement. 'The official Fatah list is one thing and Fatah is another', he says. 'But, let's be clear, I am Fatah. The conflict is between who the grassroots want to represent them and who the leadership wants to represent it.'

After a day of hard campaigning, Tamari sips sweet tea in a makeshift office covered in election posters and abuzz with young Fatah activists. Whether talking of Oslo or of Fatah, for him the main issue in the elections is the same. 'The most important thing is credibility. There is a fine line between dreams and illusions. But it is important to think aloud with the people, to be honest about what is possible and what is not. Candidates often understimate the intelligence and sensitivities of our people', he says with a weary smile.

Bethlehem, January 1996; *Al-Ahram English Weekly*, January 1996

9

The Politics of Atrocity

On 25 February 1996 – two years to the day since Baruch Goldstein shot dead 29 Palestinians in Hebron's Ibrahimi mosque – two Hamas inspired suicide bombers claimed a like toll of Israeli victims, once more pitching the Oslo peace process into crisis.

The first blast – in a crowded Egged bus in central Jerusalem – left 26 dead and 55 wounded, 19 critically. The second – at a junction near Ashkelon known as a hitch-hiking base for Israeli soldiers – left two dead and 35 injured. Both assaults were claimed by a previously unknown Hamas affiliate, the Yahiya Ayyash Units, 'in revenge' for the almost certainly Israeli-sponsored assassination of Ayyash in Gaza in January. Taken together, the assaults amounted to the worst atrocity against Israeli civilians since the Oslo accords were signed in 1993. And Israel's response was brutal and swift.

Israel reimposed a blanket closure on the West Bank and Gaza that might endure (according to Housing Minister Binyamin Ben-Eliezer) 'for a year'. Israeli PM Shimon Peres ordered a 'temporary freeze' on all Israeli/PA contacts, and mused that he is 'reconsidering' Israel's partial redeployment in Hebron, due to be completed by April.

PA officials condemned these measures as 'collective punishments against the Palestinian people, not against Hamas', but Arafat, in his initial response to the bombings, referred to neither. In a statement redolent with rage and frustration, he said, 'I condemn these operations completely. They are not military operations. They are terrorist operations. They are not only against civilians, but against the whole peace process.'

Such sentiments by the PLO leader are probably sincere. But they are unlikely to cut much ice with an enraged Israeli government and public. At a meeting with Arafat in Gaza on 27 February, IDF Chief of Staff, Amnon Shahak, unveiled new 'operational demands' which Israel will hold the PA to implement. These include not only the arrest and/or extradition of 15 Hamas fugitives and the disarming of all non-PA militias, but also the outlawing of Hamas and Islamic Jihad 'as political organisations'. The new consensus was summed up by US ambassador to Israel, Martyn Indyk. 'We want more stick and less carrot from Arafat', he said on 26 February. 'The process of co-opting [Hamas] has failed. What Arafat does now will affect the very future of the peace process.'

Arafat responded by dispatching his security forces to round up the usual suspects. By 1 March, PA police forces in the West Bank and Gaza had arrested 250 Palestinians for their 'suspected links' to Hamas's military arm, Izzadin el-Qassam. On 28 February, Chief of Police in Gaza City, Ghazi Jabali, gave 1 March as the deadline for Palestinians to hand over all unlicensed weapons or face 'search and raid' operations (as well as the threat of 15 years imprisonment) from the Palestinian police.

But Arafat has not, yet, hauled in Hamas's established political leadership in Gaza and the West Bank. For good reason. To launch a full-scale assault against Hamas and its infrastructure would not only risk civil war in the self-rule areas. It would undermine Arafat's central strategy *vis-à-vis* his Islamist opposition. It was a strategy – prior to the Jerusalem and Ashkelon bombings – that had been working.

From April 1995 on – when an Islamic Jihad bomber killed eight Israelis in Gaza – Arafat has applied force against Hamas. In Gaza, PA police have arrested literally hundreds of Palestinians after every suicide operation in Israel, often arbitarily and always ungoverned by any kind of due process. In the West Bank, PA intelligence forces have worked with Israeli security services to combat 'terror', a liaison that led to the destruction of Qassam cells in Jenin, Jerusalem and Hebron. And abroad PA emissaries have urged countries like Saudi Arabia and the Gulf states to slow the flow of funds to Islamist institutions in the occupied territories.

But Arafat has also dangled the carrot. Apart from the occasional closure of Hamas-backed newspapers, the PA has not just left Hamas's civic and religious institutions in the territories largely intact. It has sustained a quiet dialogue with their leaders.

This mix of hard and soft cop had the desired political effect. First, Hamas's support in the territories declined, down from a high of around 25 per cent after the Hebron massacre to just 10 per cent by the eve of the Palestinian elections in January. Second, such tactics worked to cultivate a more pragmatic Hamas leadership, especially in Gaza, whose aim was less to scupper the Oslo accords than to exist, politically, within them.

This leadership instigated and maintained a 'ceasefire with the occupation' for the last quarter of 1995, during which time only one Israeli was killed (an Arab-Israeli policeman in Qalkilya in October: no group claimed responsibility). In December, Hamas representatives met with PA officials for 'reconciliation' talks in Cairo. Hamas offered a 'truce' on condition that the PA use its offices with Israel to 'protect' Islamist fugitives. Arafat demanded an unconditional ceasefire. The talks ended without resolution, with Hamas declaring that it would not take part in the PA elections but vowing also 'not to embarrass the PLO in its commitments to Israel'. Israel's response, one month later, was to kill Ayyash in Gaza.

But even after Ayyash the rapprochement continued. In January, Qassam leaders in Gaza initiated a dialogue with PA security officials, pledging a 'freeze on all military operations' in exchange for a PA brokered Israeli amnesty for 40 Hamas fugitives. In response to the release in Gaza by the PA of 17 Hamas prisoners, Hamas spokesperson, Mahmoud Zahar, confirmed that an 'Islamist party' affiliated to Hamas would contest the PA's municipal elections to be held in June. And, in February, another Hamas leader in Gaza, Ghazi Hamad, stated publically that 'the majority of Hamas members are now ready to give up – temporarily – armed struggle against Israel and turn to political activity.'

Which is another way of saying that a minority are not. And these, say sources, are largely Qassam cells in the West Bank who view the growing PA/Hamas/Qassam reconciliation in Gaza as nothing less than their own abandonment – a jettisoning not just of Hamas's military struggle but also of its military wing as Palestinian Islamism readies itself to become an oppositional but loyal political party within the self-rule. Recent events have aggravated these intra-Hamas tensions.

First, there was the Ayyash assassination and (for some within Hamas) the PA and their own leadership's wholly inadequate response to it. Second, there has been Israel's ongoing arrest and execution campaign against Hamas activists in the West Bank. Sources estimate that of the 3,800 prisoners interned in Israeli jails, around 1,000 are Hamas, with most having been picked up since Oslo. Two Hamas activists have 'died' in prison (autopsies suggest from torture) in the last six weeks. Finally – and perhaps most seriously – on 3 February PA police shot dead two Islamic Jihad activists in Gaza's Shati refugee camp. A PA statement said the officers opened fire in self-defence. But an independent enquiry – carried out by the Israeli human rights organisation, B'tselem – found from eyewitness testimony that it was the police (and only the police) who did the shooting.

The dissensions became open in Hamas's wholly confused responses to the bombings. Statements released in Hebron and Damascus on 27 and 29 February reconfirmed that Hamas was responsible, vowing to continue *'jihad* until the occupation is removed from every part of Palestine'. But a Qassam statement issued in Gaza on 28 February announced its brigades had 'no connection' with the Jerusalem and Ashkelon attacks. A 'unified' position was restored on 1 March with a joint Hamas/Qassam statement offering a 'truce' against Israeli civilian targets on condition that Israel cease its 'state terrorism against the Islamic movement and release all Palestinian political prisoners'. The PA welcomed the move as 'a very important political statement'. Israel rejected any deal out of hand.

Hamas's return to suicide operations after a seven-month hiatus thus appears less a unified action to avenge the killing of Ayyash. It was more likely a warning – from a disaffected fraction within Hamas to Israel, the PA and its own political leadership – that any imputed 'truce' must come with conditions and must include them. The day Israel 'stops terrorism against Hamas and releases our prisoners, we will adopt a historic position ... not to shed blood in Palestine', ran the original Yahiya Ayyash Unit's leaflet.

These schisms have placed Arafat and the PA between a rock and a hard place. On the one hand, the divisions in Hamas are in many ways the fruit of Arafat's attempts to isolate their political and military arms, and then aggravate the differences between them. But the outcome could be a politics of the last atrocity with rival Hamas fractions struggling over the movement's future identity through the proxy of armed attacks on Israeli civilians. This would almost certainly lose Peres the next Israeli elections and probably bury the Oslo process once and for all. On the other, should Arafat and the PA buckle under Israel/US pressure and go after Hamas root and branch, he will reunify the Islamists, revive their flagging fortunes on the Palestinian street and strengthen the hard-liners both inside the territories and abroad.

But Hamas, too, is in crisis. Unlike the suicide operations after the Hebron massacre, the Jerusalem and Ashkelon bombings commanded very little support among Palestinians. Even before them, polls showed a consistent 80 per cent of Palestinians in the West Bank and Gaza against armed attacks on Israeli civilians. And it was telling that after the attacks the only Palestinian groups that supported them were the PLO rejectionist factions based in Damascus, but not in the occupied territories. Everything suggests that the time has come for Hamas to declare a unilateral ceasefire and reconstruct itself as a political opposition for the changed realities of Oslo. The reasons were spelled out in a communiqué issued after the Jerusalem and Ashkelon bombings by the PA's Information Ministry:

It has been proven that these kinds of operations do not end the occupation or achieve independence, but are used by Israel to impose more restrictions, increase its military presence and practice collective punishment against our people. Such operations reactivate the cycle of violence, weaken the Israeli left and strengthen the Israeli right, which thrives on and derives popular support from the bloody environment of violence.

Jerusalem, February 1996; *News from Within*, March 1996

10

The Charter and the Future of Palestinian Politics

When Palestinian students from Birzeit University recently marched on Ramallah to protest Israel's expulsion of students from Gaza studying in the West Bank, they not only defied the considerable ranks and live ammunition of the Palestinian Authority's (PA) police force. They also rejected the PLO's historic mode of conflict resolution. On route, the PA's West Bank Chief of Police, Haj Ismail, had tried to assuage the students' anger by offering their leaders a meeting with Yassir Arafat. 'But we haven't come to talk to Abu Ammar', yelled student leader, Ibrahim Kreishah. 'We've come to see our elected Legislative Council' (PLC).

The exchange reveals what is the most significant change in Palestinian political society since the guerrillaist factions took over the PLO in 1969. Its essence was summed up by the PLC's member for Jerusalem, Hanan Ashrawi. The fact of the PLC, she says, represents 'a system of accountability for the PA. It is the one address Palestinians in the West Bank and Gaza have to empower themselves, to consolidate democratic principles in their society and to have their own representatives speak out.'

With the PLC elections in January 1996, the long suppressed crisis over the issue of representation in Palestinian national politics was brought to a head. On the one hand, the elections marked the further eclipse of the PLO as an extra-territorial national liberation movement, mandated to represent Palestinians wherever they reside. On the other, Palestinians' massive participation in the poll (with an overall turnout of 80 per cent in the West Bank and Gaza) enhanced the representative status of the PA, a territorially based (but Israeli circumscribed) polity empowered to govern the civic affairs of Palestinians in the occupied territories.

The crisis consists in the PLO and PLC's contesting claims to legitimacy. For while the PLO has embodied Palestinians' historical leadership and programme, the PLC articulates the mandates of three quarters of a million real voters. It is almost certain (whatever it says in the Oslo accords) that it is going to be the PA rather the

PLO that expresses the future national aspirations of Palestinians in the occupied territories. The PLC may, as Ashrawi says, enhance their struggle for a democratic society in the West Bank and Gaza. Yet it is also an ominous development for the nearly four million Palestinians who reside outside these territories and for whom the PA and PLC are not and cannot be an 'address'.

The Role of the Legislative Council

Despite fears that the peculiar multi-constituency system governing the PLC elections would strengthen local and tribal allegiances over nationalist ones (an outcome Arafat appeared to seek, since he devised the system), Palestinians by and large voted neither out of clan nor factional interest. Rather they tended to endorse candidates with a strong record in the national struggle. These included not only 'national figures' associated with the PLO's historical leadership in exile, but also grassroots activists from inside the territories who came to the fore during the intifada.

Made up of independents, Fatah dissidents and Islamists, this latter bloc comprises around 25 per cent of the PLC's members. All ran on tickets which reaffirmed Palestinian national aims of return and self-determination. But (unlike the 'official' Fatah candidates for example) their main pitch was for greater democracy in Palestinian society, concretised in the demand that the PLC should have a direct role in Oslo's final status negotiations, due to commence in May 1996.

It is a reformist trend in keeping with the dominant political mood in the territories. Exit polls conducted during the elections found that 51 per cent of Palestinian voters believe the PLC 'should lead' the final status talks. 79 per cent believe the PLC should have 'equivalent or greater powers' than the President. 'We will no longer tolerate unilateral decisions by Arafat', says PLC member for Gaza, Haidar Abdl Shafi. 'We will insist that the PLC has a say in the final status negotiations.' Former head of the Palestinian delegation to the Washington talks, long time independent and fierce critic of the Oslo accords, Abdl Shafi gleaned more votes than any other candidate on 20 January.

Aspirations like these are deeply troubling to the PLO leader, and not only to him. First, they directly challenge what hitherto has been the basic tenet of contemporary Palestinian nationalism – that the the PLO is the Palestinians' 'sole legitimate representative'. Second, they fly in the face of the Oslo accords which state that it is the PLO, and not the PLC, that is empowered to conduct the final status talks. The PLC has rather a subsidiary role, responsible for drawing up a three year 'interim constitution' for the self-rule with limited legislative powers over such domestic matters as economic policy, local government, internal security, health and education.

The problem is the PLO, organisationally, no longer exists in the occupied territories (or, for that matter, anywhere else). 'It has passed away', says Palestinian intellectual and non-PLO member, Azmi Bishara. What has replaced it is 'Arafat and something called the PA.' And the fear, expressed by Abdl Shafi but shared by many others, is that Arafat will evoke the wholly theoretical powers invested in him by the PLO to circumvent the actual accountability demanded by the PLC. It is an anxiety aired in the current (and apparently arcane) Palestinian debates over whether or not to amend the founding document of Palestinian nationalism, the Palestinian National Covenant.

Amending the Covenant

Immediately after the PLC elections, Israeli PM Shimon Peres announced that Israel would permit the convening of the Palestinian National Council (PNC) in the self rule areas to 'annul those articles' of the Covenant 'that call for Israel's destruction'. The Covenant was adopted at the first PNC in 1964. Amended at the fourth PNC in 1969, it has stayed sacrosanct ever since.

But it is a text which reflects the circumstances of its birth rather than present Palestinian aspirations. And, in its tone and ambition, it is an anathema to mainstream Israeli opinion. Clause 19 describes the state of Israel as 'entirely illegal', while clause 22 defines Zionism as 'a political movement organically associated with international imperialism, ... racist and fanatic in its nature, aggressive and expansionist and colonial in its aims, and fascist in its methods'.

In the 1993 Oslo accords, Arafat (on behalf of the PLO) declared these clauses '*caduc*' or 'inoperative and no longer valid'. But he argued he could only formally rescind them with a two-thirds majority vote on the PNC. By the time the Palestinian/Israeli interim agreement was signed last September, the PLO leader felt confident enough to pledge this. Article 31 of the agreement states that, 'within two months of the inauguration of the PLC, the PNC will convene and formally approve the necessary changes in regard to the Palestinian Covenant'. The PLC held its inaugural session on 7 March. And Peres – rocked by suicide attacks in Israel and with elections on the horizon – is calling in the chips.

In January, the Israeli leader warned Arafat that unless the Covenant were amended there would be no progress to the final status negotiations. 'If Arafat is unable to convince the PNC to take such a decision, he must sever his links with the PLO', said Peres. 'It is impossible to belong to two organisations, one of which [the PA] calls for peace with Israel and the other [the PLO] which calls for its destruction.' After the suicide bombings in February and March, Peres went further, hingeing all movement in the peace process on the Covenant's amendment. Before ordering Israel's partial redeployment in Hebron, said Peres on 28 March, 'I want to see where we stand on the issue of the Palestinian Covenant.'

When the PNC's 21st session finally convened in Gaza on 22 April, Arafat was thus under inordinate pressure to fulfil his commitments to Israel while avoiding any debate that would aggravate the PLO/PLC schisms thrown up by the elections. He navigated these rapids in a way typical of him – less by winning a majority for the changes in the Covenant than by manufacturing a majority via patronage, procedural diktat and filibuster.

When the PNC started in Gaza, there were 448 members in attendance, including 110 recently returned from the diaspora. By the time the session closed on 25 April, there were 630 members, most of them appointed by Arafat as the PNC proceeded over its four days. The session devoted specifically to amending the Covenant (on 24 April) lasted just over two hours, with most of that time being taken up by debates over procedures for voting the changes rather than over the political meaning of the changes themselves. After an hour and a half of this, Arafat moved that the vote take place on the grounds that the Covenant 'issue had been discussed very often'.

In fact, the only occasion at the PNC when a substantive debate on the Covenant was mooted was on 23 April. PLO executive member, Jamal Sourani, and Abdl Shafi had tried to argue that the Covenant should only be amended after some sign of Israeli reciprocity, such as an unambiguous recognition of Palestinians' right to self-determination. To no avail: Arafat cut off both Sourani and Abdl Shafi in mid-speech. 'If you don't like (Oslo)', said Arafat to Abdl Shafi, 'why did you stand in the (PLC) elections?' Unable to present his case, Abdl Shafi walked out. No other PNC member followed him.

The saddest aspect of these manoeuvres is that they worked. In a show of hands, 504 members voted to amend the Covenant by making it consistent with the PNC's 1988 Declaration of Independence (which explicitly recognises Israel), the 1993 and 1995 Oslo agreements and UN resolutions relevant to the Palestinian question, especially 242 and 338. A cursory reading of those who voted in favour showed that the majority are PLO functionaries who have returned to the self rule areas over the last two and a half years for whom Oslo and the PA are less political strategies than the sole means of livelihood. 'Where do you want to be buried?' yelled Arafat during the Covenant session. 'Nowhere or in Palestine?' The returnees (or 'newcomers', as they are derogatively called in the West Bank and Gaza) chose the latter or, more precisely, the 6.6 per cent of mandate Palestine over which the PA has limited jurisdiction.

Tellingly, of the 54 members who voted against amending the Covenant, over half were PLC members. Of the 60 or so PNC members belonging to the oppositional Popular and Democratic Fronts, these again assumed the role of being extras in their own history. In a wholly irrelevant gesture, they decided to attend the PNC but not the session on amending the Covenant.

The Breakdown of National Consensus

For many of the PLC members (who are *ex-officio* PNC members) the PNC was viewed as little less than their own disenfranchisement, since their elected status still appears to carry no more weight on the PNC than that of their leader's patronage. Arafat's appointments policy is also resented among the constituencies who voted for the PLC in the occupied territories. Even before the PNC met, polls showed only 15 per cent of Palestinians in the West Bank and Gaza believed the PNC should preserve a 'key role' in Palestinian decision making. The rest feel such powers should be passed to elected bodies like the PLC.

It is a view shared by Azmi Bishara. The fundamental challenge facing the Palestinian national movement today, he says, is not to resuscitate the PLO but to reconstruct the national movement inside the territories for the changed realities brought on by Oslo. 'The PLC has three tasks before it', he says. 'It must work to ensure the highest level of openness in the [final status] negotiations, evolve democratic institutions subject to civilian control and promote as much as possible the expression of Palestinian sovereignty.'

But such an emphasis is redolent with risk. For, in shifting the centre of Palestinian politics so fundamentally from the 'outside' PLO to the 'inside' PLC, Palestinians may lose that general representative status which, via the PLO and however symbolically, bound Palestinians wherever they were. It is also a realignment wholly in keeping with long held Israeli ambitions to fragment Palestinians into their discrete geographic communities – from inside Israel, from inside the occupied territories and from the diaspora.

For this latter constituency – especially the 3.5 million among them who remain and live as refugees – debates over the morbidity or otherwise of the PLO are luxurious. Quite simply, for them it is the PLO (and not the PA/PLC) that must endure in one form or another, since without it they are bereft of a national reference or representative in any fora that decide their fate. 'The PLO has to be there as long as there are Palestinian refugees', says PLC member for Ramallah, Abdel Jawad Salah.

The debate around whether to adopt a new or preserve the old Covenant articulates this break up of Palestinian national politics. Yet it is a crisis that cannot be reduced to a facile division between 'inside' and 'outside', if only because many of the 'inside' PLC members are staunch advocates of reviving the PLO while many of the 'outside' returnees (including perhaps Arafat) appear bent on collapsing the PLO into the PA. The crisis is rather to do with how to develop strategies for a unique but enormously complex political reality. On the one hand is the popular desire to construct a new and democratic national leadership which recognises that its future juris-diction will be confined to the territories Israel occupied in 1967; on the other is the political need to activate new modes of representa-tion which ensure that such a leadership is accountable not just to these territories, but also to the bulk of the Palestinian nation that lives, still, beyond them.

Gaza–Jerusalem, April 1996; *Middle East International*, 10 May 1996

11

Closures, Cantons and the Palestinian Covenant

On 24 April 1996 – Israel's 48th Independence Day – PLO leader Yassir Arafat made good on his 1993 pledge to the late Israeli Prime Minister Yitzak Rabin to amend 'those articles of the Palestinian Covenant which deny Israel's right to exist'. In a historic decision, 504 out of the 572 members attending the 21st Palestine National Council (PNC) in the Gaza Strip voted to change the Covenant and replace it with a new version based on the 1993 and 1995 Oslo accords, the PNC's 1988 Declaration of Independence and political statement (which explicitly recognised the state of Israel) and those UN resolutions pertinent to the Palestinian question, especially 242 and 338 (which call for a resolution of the Arab–Israeli conflict on the principle of land for peace).

The decision pulled the Oslo peace process out of its worst crisis since its inauguration in September 1993. A spate of Islamist suicide attacks in Israel in late February and early March (leaving a toll of 58 dead and 200 wounded) had drawn from the Israeli government truly massive reprisals, freezing all relations with the Palestinian Authority and instituting the severest closure ever imposed on the occupied territories. Israeli Prime Minister Shimon Peres made any return to negotiations contingent on the PA rooting out Hamas's 'terrorist infrastructure in the self-rule areas' and the PNC changing the Covenant.

In the weeks after the suicide attacks, PA security forces in the West Bank and Gaza Strip arrested around 1,200 Palestinians for their 'suspected links' to Hamas's military arm, the Izzadin el-Qassam militia responsible for three of the four suicide operations, raided 30 Palestinian welfare and educational institutions and took control of 59 mosques in the Gaza Strip. On 18 April, in their first meeting since the crisis erupted, Peres met Arafat in Gaza, applauding the PLO leader for 'doing a serious job aganist Hamas'. Two weeks later, the PA's head of Preventive Security in Gaza, Mohammed Dahlan, announced that all Gaza-based members of Izzadin el-Qassam had been arrested by the Palestinian police save its military chief, Mohammed Dief. The decision to change the Covenant-capped Arafat's Israeli and international rehabilitation.

The immediate fruits for the PA are likely to be Israel's lifting of the blockade, some movement on the Israeli army's stalled redeployment in Hebron and the release of around 30 women political prisoners from Israeli jails, though all will probably occur after the Israeli elections on 29 May. More significantly from Arafat's point of view, the restitution of the peace process meant that Oslo's final status negotiations – in which the difficult issues of Jerusalem, Jewish settlements, refugees and borders are to be addressed – would commence as scheduled on 5 May.

The chief beneficiary of Arafat's labours, however, is Peres. At the time the PNC was amending the Covenant, the Israeli leader was embroiled in US-mediated negotiations with Lebanon and Syria to extract his military from their second Lebanese imbroglio in three years.

Israel had many motives for launching 'Operation Grapes of Wrath' in Lebanon on 11 April, but the least of them was to ensure the 'security' of the residents who live near its northern border. Angered by Hizbollah's increasing prowess in hitting Israeli soldiers inside occupied South Lebanon, Israel's principal objective in the operation was to compel the Lebanese and Syrian governments to deal with Hizbollah the way Arafat (under like Israeli pressure) had dealt with Hamas.

It failed. Despite the killing of over 160 Lebanese civilians and the deliberate displacement of a further 500,000, the US and French brokered 'understanding' that ended the war on 26 April is no more than a rehash of the 'understandings' reached after Israel's 1993 'Operation Accountability' in Lebanon, confining hostilities to military targets inside the occupied zone while prohibiting attacks on Lebanese and Israeli civilians outside it.

Equally galling from Israel's point of view is the fact that an operation devised largely to isolate Syria's President Assad served only to strengthen him. During the 16 days of Israel's bombardment in Lebanon, the Syrian leader played host to no fewer than six foreign ministers, including three trips to Damascus by US Secretary of State Warren Christopher. From the outset, Assad made it clear that he would not countenance any deal other than a return to the 1993 *status quo*. Despite quite conscious attacks against Lebanon's civic and economic infrastructure (and rocked by the international opprobrium heaped on Israel after the massacre of 102 Lebanese and Palestinian refugees at Kafr Qana on 18 April), Peres in the end was forced to submit to Assad's terms. Likewise, Hizbollah announced that it would adhere to the 'understanding' because it 'represents a victory for our organisation'.

Such humiliations were not lost on a largely apathetic (Jewish) Israeli public. At the close of the Lebanese debacle, Peres was no further in the polls than at its start. But among Israel's 850,000 Palestinian citizens Peres' standing plummeted. In protest demonstrations across Israel, Palestinian leaders from the Democratic Front for Peace and Equality and the Democratic Arab Party not only condemned Israel's atrocities in Lebanon and collective punishments in the occupied territories, they threatened to withdraw their support for Peres in Israel's prime ministerial elections.

If the risk of Peres losing the elections is now less than it was, this is largely due to Arafat's intervention, politically through his mauling of Hamas and symbolically through changing the Palestinian Covenant. But regardless of who wins the Israeli elections, the basic parameters of Oslo will remain. These are predicated less on 'mutual recognition of Israel and the Palestinians' legitimate and political rights' (as the 1993 Declaration of Principle states) than on the gradual realisation of US and Israeli hegemony in the region, articulated in terms of Israel's 'security'.

Yet, should this goal be achieved, it may not only foreclose any Palestinian claims to genuine self-determination and return. It may also trigger the region's next war, with Iran as the target, preferably (as Israel's Lebanese adventure showed) unallied with Syria.

Internal Closure

Oslo II, the interim agreement on the West Bank and Gaza Strip signed on 28 September 1995, was deliberately ambiguous. It allowed for two mutually exclusive contingencies. The first was that the PA's limited and disaggregated autonomy over about 58 per cent of the Gaza Strip and 27 per cent of the West Bank could become territorially contiguous and evolve, through further transfers of territory over three six-month intervals, into something resembling a Palestinian entity. Unstated in the agreement – but nevertheless shared by PA and Israeli negotiators – is the premiss that these transfers will constitute final borders since they will be instituted during the final status negotiations. But these territorial transfers are not automatic; the agreement makes clear that they are contingent on the PA meeting Israel's perceived security requirements, including the 'personal security' of some 160,000 Jewish settlers in the West Bank and Gaza Strip.

Should the PA fail to deliver on (Israeli) security, Oslo II's second contingency would come into effect. Israel has the power to effect entry, mobility and presence anywhere in the West Bank and Gaza to ensure its security, including inside the eight 'autonomous areas' where the PA currently enjoys nominal jurisdiction.

This security hegemony is maintained not only by the 130 Jewish settlements, but also by Israel's ongoing construction of 26 new bypass roads that will link settlements into a grid-like arrangement and the establishment of 62 new Israeli army bases on the peripheries of the Palestinian enclaves.

The infrastructure of settlements, roads and bases not only enables Israel to 'close' the Gaza Strip off from the West Bank and occupied East Jerusalem; it operationalises a system of 'internal closure' which allows the Israeli army to slice the Gaza Strip into two parts. In the West Bank the potential for internal isolation is even more insidious, cantonising the Palestinians into their 465 villages, seven 'autonomous' (Jericho, Jenin, Nablus, Tulkarem, Qalqilya, Ramallah and Bethlehem) and two 'occupied' cities of Hebron and Jerusalem.

The political impact of the suicide attacks has been to activate Oslo II's second contingency. On 4 March, Peres imposed an 'internal closure' on the West Bank and Gaza Strip. For the next eleven days, more than 1.3 million West Bank Palestinians were put under a wholesale curfew, with all mobility between towns and villages prohibited. In the Gaza Strip, the Israeli army 'repositioned' itself and set up checkpoints between the Strip's northern and southern halves. The toll inflicted on Palestinian economic and civic life, even temporarily, was catastrophic.

In the West Bank, Palestinian NGOs estimated that for the duration of the internal closure about 200,000 Palestinians (i.e. 80 per cent of the labour force) were prevented from reaching their workplaces. This was in addition to the 40,000 who had lost their jobs in Israel when Peres imposed the original closure on 25 February. Daily losses to the Palestinian economy were approximately $6 million. But the overall loss is 'incalculable,' says the PA's Deputy Minister of Economics, Trade and Industry, Samir Hulieleh, 'given the damage such measures cause to investments and business confidence in the autonomy'.

According to the PA Health Ministry, the internal closure shut down 245 clinics in the West Bank due to either to shortages of medical supplies or the inability of staff to get to work. The Union of Palestinian Medical Relief Committees reported that at least five people died due to being turned back or delayed at army checkpoints, including a 21-day-old baby girl who died from treatable respiratory ailments.

In the Gaza Strip, 22,000 Palestinians were denied access not only to their jobs in Israel, but also to new 'industrial zones' that straddle the Gaza–Israel 'border'. All exports and imports to and from Israel were terminated, causing severe shortages of flour, sugar, salt and dairy products as well as medical supplies and raw industrial materials. Even when the internal closure was lifted on 15 March, 'stricter security procedures' by the army at the three Palestinian crossing points cut the number of trucks crossing from a pre-closure rate of 400 to 40 a day. One result was a reduction of flour imports from 250 to 40 tonnes a day. A bread famine in Gaza was averted soley due to the emergency measures by UNRWA and the PA.

These events underscore the absolute dependency that still exists between all spheres of Palestinian society and Israeli military rule which, if anything, has become more acute since the Oslo accords were signed in 1993 as ominously, they also demonstrate the heightened military hold Israel now commands over the occupied territories.

Had the Israeli army attempted anything comparable to the internal closure in the pre-Oslo period, especially during the *intifada*, it would have produced massive civic unrest and stretched Israel's military resources to the limit. But in the post-Oslo era of joint PA–Israeli 'security coordination', within a matter of hours the Israeli army simply reoccupied Palestinian villages and refugee camps in the West Bank by instructing the PA police, in the words of Israel's Chief PA Liaison Officer, Moshe Elad, 'to step aside'. In the West Bank's seven nominally 'self-governing' cities, the PA's main security task is to keep a lid on the simmering populations incarcerated there. The only Palestinian protest to the closures was a series of tightly controlled PA–Fatah demonstrations under the banner of 'Yes to peace, No to the siege.'

Many Palestinian and Israeli analysts attest that the internal closure is the most draconian counter-insurgency measure imposed by Israel in 28 years of occupation. And it was executed without a single Israeli soldier being attacked, Israeli settler being killed or any real show of Palestinian resistance, armed or otherwise. 'It's the Gaza model applied to the West Bank', said Israeli commentator, Israel Shahak. 'And it works.'

Punishment or Policy?

The question is whether internal closure – and the cantonised future it augurs for Palestinian 'self-rule' – marks a strategic turn on the part of the Israeli government or a tactical one, brought on as colossal (and collective) punishment against Palestinians in the occupied territories for the loss of so many Israeli lives in the suicide attacks. The sole remaining hope of Arafat and the is that it is the latter. But this is by no means clear.

For the Likud-led opposition and segments of Israel's military establishment, internal closure is now perhaps the only mutant of Oslo they could live with. Even before the suicide bombings, Likud leader Binyamin Netanyahu said that a Likud government would not 'tear up' the Oslo accords, but it would not tolerate the establishment of a Palestinian state and would restrict the Palestinian autonomy to its existing 'self-rule' areas. After the bombings, Netanyahu spelled out the security measures that would underpin such an arrangement. A Likud government 'would talk to the Palestinians', he said on 19 March. 'But we will be the ones who will defend ourselves. The Oslo concept has failed. Yassir Arafat cannot and does not want to protect us. We must put our defense back in our own hands and give our security forces the freedom to hit where and when they deem right.' Polls conducted after the attacks showed that a consistent 44–46 per cent of the Israeli electorate agreed with him as do many ministers in Labour's ruling coalition government.

Is this now Peres' vision? On 10 March, he stated that Israel's re-occupation of the autonomous areas was not on his agenda so long as the PA 'disarms and arrests Hamas supporters'. But it appears that he has adopted every other aspect of Likud's version of Oslo. In the wake of the attacks, Peres reinstituted a series of punitive measures from the pre-Oslo era. In the West Bank, the army blew up five homes belonging to Hamas suicide bombers and fugitives. Twelve Palestinian welfare, school and university institutions were ordered closed for six months because of their alleged Islamist affiliations. Some 300 Palestinians were administratively detained (i.e. arrested without charge or trial) in regular and undercover army raids throughout the West Bank, including inside Palestinian villages formally under the PA's 'civic' jurisdiction. On 14 March, Peres stated that he was in favour of expelling any Palestinian connected with the recent wave of suicide attacks once Israel 'goes through the necessary military and legal checks'.

In an apparent reversal not only of policy but of deeply held personal conviction, on 3 March Peres approved the construction of a two-kilometre-wide 'buffer zone' to run along the 350-kilometre West Bank–Israel Green Line. This aims to physically segregate Palestinians from Israelis by means of fences, electronic surveillance fields, helicopter patrols and an augmented allotment of 500 soldiers and border police on hand to take out infiltrators. Palestinians henceforth will only be able to enter Israel or Jerusalem via one of the 18 official crossing points.

According to former head of the Israeli General Security Service (Shin Bet) Carmi Gillon, this does not constitute a fully-fledged 'separation' since that would cost billions of dollars (the price tag for the above measures is about $80 million) and pre-empt the final status talks on borders. But is does make a mockery of the various Oslo economic agreements. The separation line amounts to a *de facto* West Bank security border in which the transit of goods, capital and labour will be subject to Israeli veto. This transforms the proposed relationship between Israel and the Palestinians from one of 'partnership', as stated in the 1994 Paris protocol, to one of Palestinian subordination to Israel.

Finally, the series of military orders accelerating the construction of 220 kilometres of bypass roads was expedited in the aftermath of the suicide attacks. These roads have already confiscated 21 square kilometres of West Bank and Gaza Strip territory. The overall cost is $350 million. A glance at the topography of the roads reveals that they are designed not simply to serve the 'transport and housing needs of the Jewish settlements', says Palestinian geographer, Khalil Tufakji. The roads' 'primary military purpose is to surround and control the main Palestinian areas so that they can be divided one from the other'.

Opposition from Within

Whether strategic or tactical, the danger of these actions is that they will set in a process of cantonisation that may prove irreversible. This would not necessarily mean the end of the Oslo process, for Oslo, as Palestinian intellectual Azmi Bishara defines it, is 'a structureless political situation' whose content is yet to be determined. But it would foreclose the possibility of a Palestinian entity emerging in the West Bank and Gaza based on territorial contiguity and genuine political and economic sovereignty. The future Israel's measures conjure up is rather one of 'functional autonomy' in which Palestinians have power over all civic matters that concern them while Israel retains control over all territorial, resource and security matters. This solution to the 'Palestinian question' was proposed first by Israel's Defence Minister during the 1967 war, Moshe Dayan.

If this is the future, what should be the Palestinian response? After the suicide attacks, the posture of Yassir Arafat has been a mix of weak diplomatic protests at Israel's collective punishment measures and a ruthless crackdown against Islamist opponents. The latter has won him plaudits from Peres and the US State Department, but it has utterly undermined the legitimacy of Oslo among Palestinians wrought after Israel's West Bank redeployment last autumn and the Palestinian Council elections in January. Combined with the house demolitions, the mass arrests and, above all, the internal closure, the mood in the occupied territories has swung, not so much behind Hamas, but against a peace process that privileges exclusively Israeli notions of security.

Arafat's adoption of Israel's security agenda risks not only driving Hamas into an underground militia, but has started to fracture the very constituencies on which so far the PA has based its rule.

After a PA police raid on a rally at Nablus's Al-Najah University and the killing of a Palestinian by PA Intelligence agents in el-Bireh, Palestinians in both cities struck in protest. On 3 April, about 1,000 Palestinian students from Birzeit University marched on the third session of the Palestinian Council (PC), the legislative body empowered under Oslo to represent Palestinians in the occupied territories. For Arafat, the most ominous feature of these protests was that all three were led by neither the Islamist nor PLO opposition, but by the civilian wing of his own Fatah movement.

This is a constituency that has power both on the street and in the newly elected PC, a factor that contributed to the 88 member Council unanimously condemning the PA's security forces for their illegal actions at Al-Najah and in el-Bireh. It was telling that, of the 54 PNC members who voted against amending the Covenant, over half were elected PC members, including such dissident Fatah cadres as ex-prisoner leader Qaddura Fares and ex-PLO ambassador to Saudi Arabia Rafiq Natshe.

Whether these forces – together with other sectors of Palestinian civil and political society – can form the nucleus of a new democratic opposition to the PA is unclear. What is clear is that any opposition fighting on the terrain of law, human rights and democracy will not only have to challenge the PA, but also the Israeli state and army that stands behind it. The reason is self-evident. Arafat has assumed the authoritarian agenda less out of instinct or preference than because this is the only road to self-rule that Israel will allow. Should the Palestinians reject this road, however, the alternative will not be a return to the pre-Oslo *status quo* of direct occupation but to a new reality far more dangerous.

West Bank Fatah leader Marwan Barghouti paints the darkest of scenarios:

> Israel cannot re-enter Gaza, Ramallah, Nablus or anywhere else. The Israeli army left the Gaza Strip when there were less than 100 armed people there. There are now 20,000 armed Palestinians in Gaza. There are 5,000 armed in Ramallah. And they will fight reoccupation, police and people together, they will fight. They already have their orders.

Ramallah, April–May 1996; *Middle East Report*, April–June 1996

12

The Palestinians in Israel

The fact of an Israeli/Palestinian peace process has not only altered the political reality of Palestinians who reside in the West Bank and Gaza. It has had an equally profound impact on the 850,000 Palestinians who live inside Israel as 'non-Jewish' citizens of a Jewish state. One effect of the emerging political power of this constituency (representing around twelve per cent of the Israeli electorate) is predicted by Palestinian Member of Knesset (MK) and leader of Israel's Hadash (formerly Communist) Party, Hashim Mahamid. 'Without the Arab vote', he says, 'Shimon Peres cannot be elected Prime Minister.'

The Palestinian citizens of Israel (or Israeli Arabs) are the descendants of the 120,000 Palestinians who stayed on the land in 1948 after 750,000 of their compatriots fled or were driven out during the war that gave birth to the Israeli state. Subject to martial law between 1948 and 1966, Israel's Palestinians have been discriminated against in all spheres of Israeli society, most brutally in the areas of land ownership and municipal resources. To this day Palestinians in Israel are denied service in the Israeli army, a fact that bars them from many state benefits.

Since the lifting of martial law, Israel's Palestinians have mobilised around the dual aims of civic equality and national rights and are represented in the Knesset by two main political parties – the Democratic Arab Party (DAP) led by former Labour Party MK Abdul Wahab Darawshi which has two seats and the Democratic Front for Peace and Equality (DFPE) which has four.

But political apathy fed by discrimination has been the norm among Israel's Palestinians. In every Knesset election since 1966, only around 68 per cent turned out to vote (considerably less than the Jewish turnout), with, in 1992 elections, 47 per cent voting for Zionist parties rather than Arab lists (like the DAP) or Arab/Jewish lists (like DFPE). The historic beneficiary of this arrangement was Israel's Labour Party, who gained Arabs' support without having to do much to keep it.

With the Israel's 14th Knesset elections due on 29 May 1996, this could change. The influence Israel's Palestinian lobby are expected to have over the peace process is one factor. But there are also internal factors that presage greater Arab representation in Knesset. This may (as in the past) help Shimon Peres' ruling Labour coalition, but such 'help' should not be taken for granted.

In March, Israel's Islamist movement decided for the first time to contest the Knesset elections, 'not as an independent party', says Islamist movement spokesperson, Ibrahim Sarsour, 'but as an independent force within an Arab list' aligned with the DAP. The Islamists are considerable force among Israeli Arabs, controlling six municipal councils in Israel. Historically they had opposed participation in the Knesset largely over the ideological difficulty of swearing allegiance to the Jewish state. But the PLO's 1993 peace agreement with Israel followed by Israel's 1994 peace treaty with Jordan has weakened the hard-liners in the movement. Should the Islamists be able to translate the support they command locally to the national arena, then Palestinian turnout in the Knesset vote will rise to around 75 per cent.

A like development obtains with the DFPE. For the last four years Israel's ex-Communists (along with the DAP) have supported the Rabin and Peres governments 'from the outside', largely because of the peace process. But, unlike the leftist Zionist bloc, Meretz, neither had a formal coalition with Labour nor held any ministerial posts. This has enabled both DFPE and the DAP to oppose Labour when necessary.

In May 1995, the six DFPE/DAP MKs threatened to no confidence the Rabin government should it proceed with its plans to expropriate 139 acres of Palestinian land in occupied East Jerusalem. In the hope of bringing down the government, the rightist Likud opposition lined up with them. Rabin retreated, 'freezing' the expropriations until further notice. In recent weeks, too, it has been the DFPE (and not Meretz or the Jewish-dominated Peace Now movement) that has led the domestic opposition to Israel's assault on Lebanon, mounting sizeable anti-war demonstrations in Jerusalem, Tel Aviv and Nazareth.

Both interventions have enhanced the DFPE's standing, and not only among Arabs. 'I think we will double our Jewish vote in these elections', says Mahamid. 'Many Jews now see us as the only left force in Israeli politics, the only left that fights.' This could prove accurate. Damaged by its alliance with Labour in government, many analysts predict that Meretz's representation in the elections will fall from twelve seats to six or seven. Most of this support will swing behind Peres, but a sizeable minority will be picked up by the DFPE.

Combined with the Islamists decision to run, such factors are likely to increase Arab mandates in the Knesset from six to seven and possibly eight. Add to them the four Arab candidates running with the Labour Party (all of whom are expected to win) and the Palestinian bloc in the 121-member Knesset is formidable, and one Peres will have to take into account. But, warn both Mahamid and Sarsour, 'We are not in his pocket.'

On 6 May, Mahamid met with cabinet minister Yossi Beilin to discuss the DFPE's stance *vis-à-vis* advocating support for Peres in the prime ministerial race against Likud's Binyamin Netanyahu. The meeting took place in the aftermath of Israel's massacre of 102 Lebanese refugees in a UN base on 18 April as well as during the Peres government's now ten-week-old closure of the occupied territories. Under such circumstances, Mahamid told Beilin, 'We cannot ask our people to vote for Peres. Given the current mood [against Peres] among Israeli Arabs, they would ignore us anyway.'

To gain the DFPE's endorsement, Peres must lift the closure and redeploy the Israeli army from Hebron, says Mahamid. But more than this Peres 'must convince us that there is a real difference between a government led by him and one led by Netanyahu'. Such a difference is unlikely to be forthcoming – Israeli government officials have strongly implied that neither the closure nor the situation in Hebron will change much before the elections.

The Islamist/DAP bloc is similarly combative, though for different reasons. 'We are attaching no conditions about the peace process to our support for Peres', says Sarsour, 'since Hebron and the closure are issues to be negotiated between Israel and the PLO.' For the Islamists/DAP, a vote for Peres hinges on domestic matters, specifically equality of treatment and the return of Islamic Trust institutions and lands confiscated by Israel in 1948.

But the overall aim is a commitment from Peres and Labour that Israeli Arabs become recognised as an integral part of Israel's legislative system and civic society. 'Till today', says Sarsour, 'the definition of Israel is that it is a state for Jews. And what we seek are articles guaranteeing our presence as a legal national minority in Israel.' Constitutionally, this would mean Israel changing its definition from a Jewish state to 'a state for Jews and all its inhabitants'. The DFPE go further. Their ultimate objective, says Mahamid, is the transformation of Israel into 'a state for all its citizens', Jewish and Arab alike.

That such issues can be raised and will play a part in the upcoming Israeli elections attests to the political transformations 'peace' and the prospect of a Palestinian state in the West Bank and Gaza has wrought for Israel's Palestinians. It is a welcome development, says Mahamid. 'It is has created an internal balance in us. In the future we will act as a bridge between our state, Israel, and the state of our people, Palestine.'

Um el-Fahim/Kofa Kana, May 1996; *Red Pepper*, June 1996

13

Shimon Peres – a Fourth-Time Loser?

Whatever the hype surrounding Israel's 14th Knesset elections, two factors have become self-evident in the run-up to polling day. First, in terms of reaching a comprehensive peace with most of the Arab world, the vote on 29 May 1996 is probably the most critical in Israel's 48 year history. Second, the current electoral fight between Israel's two main Labour and Likud parties is the dullest in living memory.

One reason for this is the new system devised for the elections. On 29 May, Israelis will for the first time participate in two ballots, one for the 120-member Knesset or Parliament and one for the Prime Minister. The change was introduced in 1995 with the blessing of the then PM, Yitzak Rabin, who viewed it as a means of strengthening the position of Premier by limiting the disproportionate influence historically wielded by Israel's smaller (and especially religious) parties in the Knesset. But the result has been a sharp contraction in genuine political choice for Israel's nearly four million strong electorate. And this narrowing of debate has one simple cause – the polls.

Most Israeli commentators now view the outcome of the vote, especially in the prime ministerial contest between Peres and Netanyahu, as too close to call. Official Gallup surveys give Peres a steady 4–5 per cent lead over Netanyahu, but 'internal polls' conducted privately by Labour and Likud are more cautious. Labour's polls have Peres with a mere one to two point lead, while a Likud poll aired on 21 May had their man nosing ahead. All polls show the number of undecided or floating voters hovering stubbornly at between 10 and 15 per cent of the electorate. 'With the gap so narrow', conceded Netanyahu on 21 May, 'the shift of a few hundred votes could be enough to decide Israel's next Prime Minister.'

The upshot is a dash by the two main parties to the centre of Israeli politics, keeping programmatic differences between them to a minimum for fear of alienating the floating vote. On the campaign trail, Peres thus speaks like Likud, pledging 'a strong Israel with Peres' (the official Labour election slogan), reassuring all that a government led by him would keep 'Jerusalem united under Israeli sovereignty' and vowing that 'no Jewish settlement will be dismantled' in any final status deal with the Palestinians. Netanyahu, meanwhile, wears the unusual plummage of a dove ('peace with security' is the Likud campaign slogan), accepting the Oslo accords and insisting that a Likud government would 'negotiate a final status agreement' with the Palestinians 'on condition that the Palestinian Authority lives up to its undertakings'. The result, says Israeli political analyst Tanya Reinhart, is an electoral contest that is less a 'political struggle between two ideologies' than 'an imaginary battle between two different ways of implementing the same ideology'.

This is bad news for Israeli democracy. But it is even worse news for the peace process, particularly its Palestinian track, since any pull to the centre on the part of Peres means a turn to a hard-line position on matters such as Jerusalem and settlements.

Israel's floating vote is made up of three main constituencies – young first time voters, Israel's Jewish orthodox or religious parties and the 600,000 or so Russian immigrants (over half of whom are now of voting age) from the ex-Soviet Union who have settled in Israel since 1989. And none is in Peres' pocket.

Labour is investing a lot of its campaign publicity in Israel's new voter generation, drawn to Peres' idealism in the wake of Rabin's assassination but less sure of it now in the aftermath of Islamist suicide attacks inside Israel proper. Since they are an unknown quantity (and with the prayer that there are no further attacks before polling day), Labour activists believe they can be won back. They are less sanguine about the religious constituency.

There are two main religious parties in Israeli politics: Shas, an orthodox movement made up of Sephardi or non-European Jews, and United Torah Judaism (UTJ), the traditional Ashkenazi or European orthodox list. Together they had ten seats in the old Knesset and are expected to win the same in the new. Given that Labour's former coalition partner, the leftist Meretz bloc, is expected to do badly in the elections, Peres is desparate to woo the orthodox parties to forestall a Likud-led coalition dominating the next Knesset. But the orthodox are playing hard to get.

Neither Shas nor UTJ are likely to openly endorse Peres or Netanyahu for Prime Minister, though Shas, on 19 May, did strike a surplus votes deal with Likud. But analysts concur that a free vote granted to their followers means a vote for Netanyahu, since Shas and UTJ are rightist on the peace process as much as they are conservative on religious issues. Peres therefore wants them to call on their followers to abstain in the prime ministerial vote. In return, Peres is promising to maintain the religious *status quo* in Israel, granting only orthodox Rabbis the right of conversion and offering more powers to muncipalities controlled by either Shas or UTJ. Such gifts have so far had little effect. A poll carried out on 8 May among Shas and UTJ supporters found that 63 per cent would vote Netanyahu for Prime Minister; a miserly 6 per cent for Peres.

More ominously (at least as far as Palestinians are concerned), Labour in its search for coalition partners is flirting with the National Religious Party (NRP), an ultra-nationalist movement with considerable support among the 160,000 Jewish settlers in the West Bank and Gaza. Reports emerged last week of a meeting between Labour cabinet minister, Yossi Beilin, and the NRP's Rabbi Yoel Ben Nun, a settler leader in the West Bank settlement of Ofra. In return for supporting Peres, Beilin promised Ben Nun that no Jewish settlement would be uprooted in any final status deal with the Palestinians and that all settlements would stay under Israeli control. The Labour/NRP agreement has yet to be made public because, say sources, the NRP, too, is playing hard to get.

Such overtures have alarmed Israel's Palestinian minority and enraged Labour's erstwhile allies in Meretz. 'Any coalition' with parties like the NRP or Shas 'will take us back to the bad old days of no peace ... and blindness to social problems. Israel will change unrecognisably for the worse', railed Meretz leader, Yossi Sarid, on news of the putative Labour/NRP pact. But it is a mark of Peres' desperation that he is prepared to countenance such allegiances.

At the turn of the year, Peres and Labour commanded a 15–20 per cent lead over Likud. The Israeli leader then decided to bring Israel's election day up from November to May, kill Yahyia Ayyash in Gaza and launch a wholly inept war against Lebanon. The compounded result of these errors was to rescue Netanyahu from oblivion, since most Israelis figure (accurately) that if they are to have Likud policies they may as well have a Likud government.

Labour supporters, meanwhile, are starting to worry about the Peres factor. Three times Peres has led a Labour coalition against Likud in Israeli elections, and each time he has lost. As Israel approaches what Netanyahu has described as the 'most fateful elections in its history', increasing numbers of Israelis, Palestinians and Arabs are beginning to see in Peres less the architect of peace or visionary of a new Middle East, but – and entirely through his own doing – a fourth-time loser.

Jerusalem, May 1996; *Al-Ahram Weekly*, 21 May 1996

Part 3

Post-Oslo – Decline and Fall
May 1996 to December 1998

Preface

The final section covers the reign of Binyamin Netanyahu's premiership, from his election in May 1996 to the demise of his government in December 1998, four months prior to the formal deadline of the Oslo process in May 1999.

Netanyahu's initial posture to Oslo was to have no truck with Yassir Arafat's Palestinian Authority and to accelerate settlement construction throughout the occupied territories, but especially East Jerusalem. The result was the worst violence between Israel and the Palestinians in nearly 30 years of occupation, described in the opening articles 'Pictures of war' and 'Madness in Ramallah'.

The September 1996 confrontations expedited the US role in the Oslo process from one of sponsor to *de facto* broker, prodding a reluctant Netanyahu to partially redeploy from Hebron in January 1997. The Israeli leader's riposte in March was to offer the PA a miserly 2 per cent further West Bank redeployment and to authorise the construction of the Har Homa Jewish settlement in occupied East Jerusalem. For the next 18 months the peace process went into deep freeze, punctuated by sporadic violence and kept alive only by constant US rescuscitation, most notably the Wye River Memorandum signed ostensibly to put 'Oslo back on track' in Washington on 23 October 1998. Within two months – largely because of Wye's pledge of a 13 per cent further redeployment in the West Bank – Netanyahu's fractious coalition fell apart.

Apart from the two opening pieces, the articles in this section look less at this narrative than on the regional context and political consequences of Oslo's demise. 'Hizbollah, Syria and the Lebanese elections' investigates Lebanon's Shi'ite resistance movement, Hizbollah, and argues that, for all its military prowess, it remains suborned to Syrian hegemony both as a guerrilla movement fighting Israel's occupation of South Lebanon and as an oppositional party in Lebanese politics. '"All killers": Luxor, the Gama'a and Egypt's prisons' describes the brutal repression Egypt has deployed to crush its radical Islamist opponents. It concludes that while the goal of total eradication has deferred the prospect of an Islamist takeover in

West Bank – 1998

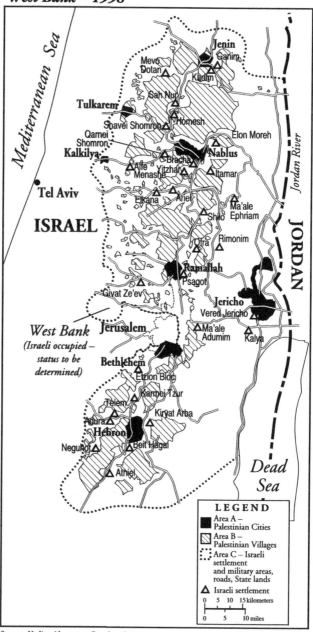

Source: Yediot Aharonot, October 6, 1995

Egypt, the cost will be atrocities akin to that visited on Luxor on 18 November 1997.

The next four pieces explore the views of four Israeli and Palestinian leaders on the probable fate of the Oslo process. In 'Fatah, Hamas and the crisis of Oslo', Fatah leader Marwan Barghouti argues only Palestinian unity at home and a coalition of international and Israeli peace forces abroad can save the Oslo process from the destructive ambitions of the Netanyahu government. Hamas spokesmen Ibrahim Ghoshah also calls for Palestinian unity, but only on the condition of an end to 'Oslo, the PA and the so called peace process'.

In 'Making peace', Israeli Labour MK Yossi Beilin describes the understandings he reached with chief PLO negotiator Mahmoud Abbass (Abu Mazen) on the shape of a final settlement between Israel and the Palestinians, a deal many would see as the maximum Palestinians can expect given the confining terms of Oslo. Beilin lays down the other conditions for a comprehensive peace in the region – Israel's unilateral withdrawal from South Lebanon and direct negotiations with Syria over the fate of the occupied Golan Heights.

These scenarios are shared by the political leader of Israel's premier Sephardi movement, Shas. In 'Believers in blue jeans', Rabbi Aryeh Deri anticipates a future where Israel will not only be at peace with its Arab neighbours but is Jewish as opposed to Zionist, religious as opposed to secular and 'Eastern' as opposed to Western.

The next two pieces looks at those Palestinians resolutely opposed to the Oslo process. 'The fire the next time' details the catastrophic plight of the Palestinians in Lebanon, made refugee with Israel's founding in 1948. Abandoned by the PLO and subject to policies of quiet deportation by the Lebanese authorities, it predicts future explosions based on poverty and discrimination rather than over the right to return. 'The meaning of Sheikh Yassin' is a profile of Hamas founder Sheikh Ahmad Yassin, and attempts to explain the appeal of his militant brand of Islamism not only in Palestine, but throughout the region.

The final two articles take as their cue the ambivalent climate surrounding Israel's 50-year anniversary as a state. 'Impossible contradictions' insists that – five years after Oslo – it is Israel's messianic right that is on the ascendant, not its secular left. It concludes that the left can only arrest its decline once it jettisons the racist assumptions at the root of Zionism. The last article, 'A Palestinian refugee at 51', returns the collection to its source – the memories of Achmed Abdallah, a Palestinian refugee who fled his home 50 years ago in the belief that he will one day return.

'Pictures of war', 'Madness in Ramallah' and '"All killers": Luxor, the Gama'a and Egypt's prisons' were published in *Middle East International*. 'Making peace' was published in *al-Ahram Weekly*. 'Hizbollah, Syria and the Lebanese elections' was published in the *Journal of Palestine Studies*. 'The fire the next time' was published in *News from Within* and the Portuguese newspaper *Publico*. 'The meaning of Sheikh Yassin' was published in the South African *Independent on Sunday*. And 'Impossible contradictions' was published in *Red Pepper*.

'Believers in blue jeans' and 'Fatah, Hamas and the crisis of Oslo' were published in shortened form in *al-Ahram Weekly* and *News from Within* repectively. This is their first complete publication.

14

Pictures of War

After three days of the worst violence in Gaza and the West Bank since Israel occupied them in 1967, Palestinians and Israelis are not only again counting their dead. As they pick over the debris of the Oslo process, the question they are pondering is whether a mutually tolerable accommodation is any longer possible between the two peoples who inhabit Israel/Palestine. The hope among perhaps most Israelis and Palestinians is that some kind of reconciliation can still be salvaged. But there is also a growing realisation that maybe it can't, at least not on the terms set down by Netanyahu.

On 29 September, the Israeli army quietly imposed an 'internal closure' on the territories' self-rule areas, isolating over two million Palestinians within seven 'autonomous' cantons. In deference to a US-engineered crisis summit between Binyamin Netanyahu, Yassir Arafat and King Hussein (due to be held 31 September), Palestinian police also reigned in their enraged people, forcibly stopping them from approaching the 'closed military areas' that seal off the enclaves.

As Palestinians await the summit's outcome – convened at a cost of 55 Palestinians and 14 Israelis dead and over 1,000 wounded – there is calm in the territories, but it should fool nobody. The calm is as much before as after the storm.

Opening the Tunnel

The storm was caused by Netanyahu's decision, on 23 September, to open a 488 metre tunnel that runs beside Jerusalem's Al-Aqsa mosque compound to exit out onto the Via Dolorosa, the very heart of the old city's Muslim quarter. The Israeli leader may have seen this as a quick fix to shore up his crumbling domestic standing. Arafat viewed it as a violation too far, decrying the tunnel as 'a crime against our religious and sacred places'.

More significantly, he used the emotionally charged issue of the sanctity of Al-Aqsa to rally his people behind the Palestinian Authority (PA) and Oslo, pitching them finally against Netanyahu and Likud. Under pressure from members from the Palestinian Legislative Council (PLC) as well as his own Fatah movement, he called on Palestinians throughout the West Bank and Gaza to protest 'the Judaisation of Jerusalem'. He didn't say how they should resist; he didn't need to.

Over the next four days, protest marches led by PLC and PLO figures such as Faisal Husseini and Hanan Ashrawi tried to converge on Al-Aqsa, culminating in major clashes with the Israeli police after prayers on Friday 27 September which left three Palestinians dead and 120 injured. But the real fuse was lit in Ramallah.

On 25 September – under instruction from the PA and Arafat's Fatah movement – several busloads of Palestinian students from Birzeit University confronted an Israeli checkpoint on route to Jerusalem. The army repulsed them using tear gas and rubber bullets. The students returned with stones and Molotov cocktails. Several hundred PA security personnel stood idly by, until, due to a incendiary mix of popular incitement and incursions by the army across the checkpoint (and so into the Palestinian controlled area), they returned fire.

It was a pattern of organised protest followed by disorganised (but armed) hostilities that spread the next day throughout the occupied territories. In Gaza, students from Al Azhar University marched on the contested Jewish settlements of Kfar Darom and Netzarim and the border-lines of Rafah and Erez, confrontations which swiftly erupted into raging firefights between Israeli and PA forces. In Bethlehem, Palestinians attacked and torched the scaffolding surrounding the Jewish enclave of Rachel Tomb, with PA police and the army exchanging fire. And, in Nablus, after Israeli troop reinforcements tried to breach through the refugee camp of Balatta, Palestinian youths and security forces laid seige to the Jewish enclave of Joseph's Tomb, a battle that left one Palestinian and six IDF soldiers dead.

By noon, Israeli Defence Minister Yitzak Mordechai declared the territories a 'state of emergency', dispatching tanks and helicopter gunships to Gaza, Ramallah and Nablus. Arafat issued orders for his forces to fire only 'in self-defence', to spare 'further civilian fatalities', in the words of West Bank PA Preventive Security (PS) chief, Jibril Rajoub. By nightfall, Gaza was relatively quiet, Bethlehem under control and Nablus under a PA imposed curfew, enabling the battered IDF unit inside Joseph's Tomb to be replaced with 54 fresh soldiers, under PA escort. 'It was a political decision agreed between the Palestinian and Israeli military chiefs', said Karmal Salamah, a PS officer from Nablus. 'We didn't take Joseph's Tomb. We just held it in our hands for a while before giving it back to the Israelis.'

At the end of bloodiest day in anyone's memory, 35 Palestinians and 11 Israeli soldiers had been killed, close on 800 Palestinians had been wounded. Netanyahu dismissed the carnage as a 'cynical manipulation of violence' by the PLO to extract Israeli concessions. Arafat called it a 'massacre'. The more accurate description was broadcast by Israeli army radio outside Netzarim in Gaza: 'a picture of war', it said.

Nationalism Resumed

In the short term, Arafat's decision to allow his forces to work in concert with the immense frustration of his people has restored his and the PA's legitimacy. But all are aware it is a wholly precarious support. 'We are not demanding anything of the Israeli government other than it implement the agreements it has signed', says West Bank Fatah leader Marwan Barghouti. 'Our protests are not intended to kill Oslo, but to restore it to life.'

It may be too late for that. The deepening consensus among Palestinians in the occupied territories is that Netanyahu, unable to proceed with Oslo without wrecking his fragile coalition, is out to kill it. On route to Washington, the Israeli leader announced that the tunnel would stay open 'for always', that redeployment in Hebron had to be renegotiated and that Arafat must 'discipline' those PA forces who fired on the Israeli army.

This is not going to happen. Having once more lifted the lid off Palestinian nationalism, Arafat can now only contain it in return for tangible progress on Oslo, principally the redeployment of Israeli troops in Hebron. He certainly cannot suppress it any longer in the name of Israel's 'security' concerns, not at least without fracturing his people, including his 40,000-strong security forces.

'If the Oslo agreement is fated to fail, better it should happen now', said Likud MK and former Shin Bet deputy chief of staff, Gideon Ezra, on 25 September. He added blithely that there was 'no danger of the *intifada* resuming' because the army was 'no longer' in the centre of Gaza and the West Bank. Ezra is one of Netanyahu's chief security advisors. The next day, Israeli tanks and helicopters were in the heart of Gaza and the West Bank because the *intifada* had 'resumed'. The signal difference – a difference that figures like Netanyahu and Ezra appear unable to grasp – is that this time it is armed not just with stones but guns in the hands of a Palestinian police force which, in defence of their people and in pursuit of their nationalism, became again a PLO militia.

Ramallah/Nablus, September 1996; *Middle East International*,
October 1996

15

Madness in Ramallah

Four Cobra helicopter gunships buzz like horseflies against a blue sky. Beneath them, apartments and office blocks, wedged into a valley of olive trees and rocky terraced hills. Now and then the Cobras fire off a spray of machine gun fire. One shifts in the sky, positions itself, propels a cannon shot into the wall of an apartment. A puff of smoke in the ether.

It could be Beirut, 1982. It's Ramallah 1996, three years after the Oslo accords, two and half years since Yassir Arafat returned to Palestine, exactly 100 days after Binyamin Netanyahu's election victory. Everything changes in the Middle East, except the targets.

On the main Ramallah–Jerusalem road, Palestinian civilians flee, gather their wounded, cower in shop fronts. Palestinian police fire uselessly from abandoned buildings. 'Yes, like Beirut', says Eyad, a 30-year-old Palestinian from Ramallah. 'They have the gunships, we have the casualties.'

For the second day running, Palestinians in the West Bank and Gaza have decided to take on the might of the Israeli army. Only the game has changed. Yesterday – in this very valley – the fight followed *intifada* rules, with Palestinian youths lobbing stones and Molotovs and the army responding (mostly) with rubber bullets. Today Ramallah has metamorphosed into Lebanon. There are 5,000-plus armed Palestinian police in Ramallah, several hundred of whom – under orders or against them, it's not clear – are firing back.

This factor alters everything, raises the stakes in this long war called Israel/Palestine. On rooftops and cliff bluffs, Israeli snipers pick off their victims with telescopic accuracy. The Cobras provide cover, then edge further into Ramallah's supposedly 'autonomous' area, pushing back hundreds of stone-throwing youths. The snipers take another rooftop. Below, people, in real terror, leave their homes, pour up sidestreets and head, instinctively, for the hospital.

Inside the hospital's compound, hundreds of Palestinians have congregated. I see young boys crying, an old man in a jabaliya groaning. But most are quiet, fazed. They simply cannot understand how a protest in Jerusalem over a tunnel has led to Israeli gunships pitching shells into Ramallah.

The quiet is broken by the wail of ambulance sirens. One screeches to a stop beside the Intensive Care Unit. A man on a stretcher is passed quickly through waiting hands, his chest a mess of blood and gut. 'The Cobras', says a doctor simply. He tells me the toll for Ramallah today (25 September) is nine dead and 65 injured, 'most of them seriously, all from live ammunition'.

The shooting stops. A rumour goes around that Arafat has instructed his police to fire only in self-defence. 'What does he think they were doing?', says Eyad. 'Trying to take Tel Aviv?' The Cobras hover and the snipers stay on their salients, but, for now, have ceased firing. At the contested checkpoint on the way to Jerusalem – where the battle for Ramallah erupted the day before – bloodied Palestinian youths begrudgingly retreat, prodded gently along by uniformed Palestinian police.

It's a ceasefire, but nobody expects it to last. It's just a reprieve. Tomorrow Palestinians will take to the streets to bury their dead and the outrage will again explode. The protests will be angrier, mightier, say the *shubab*. Tomorrow the *intifada* for Al-Aqsa will begin. Eyad isn't so sure. 'It depends on what the Israelis are up to', he says.

Nobody really knows, and that's why, mixed with the defiance, there is panic. We drive out of Ramallah, circumventing the checkpoint – now a *de facto* no-man's-land of rocks, trashed cars and burning tyres. A journalist friend calls us over.

'Have you seen the tanks?' she says.

'You mean the APCs [Armoured Personnel Carriers].'

'I mean tanks!'

We think she's crazy. But then the whole situation is crazy. We reverse and drive back, approaching the checkpoint this time from the Israeli side. After a blind curve, Eyad throws down the brakes hard. We cannot believe our eyes.

There are three Israeli tanks, khaki camouflaged, their turrets veering lazily in the direction of Ramallah. Palestinians, mainly women and children, stand on a kerb opposite. They look in disbelief.

A soldier approaches, waves us away. 'You are press. You cannot see what we have', he says. We already have.

The Israelis, too, are preparing for tomorrow.

Ramallah, September 1996; *Middle East International*, October 1996

16

Hizbollah, Syria and the Lebanese Elections

At a mass rally in August 1996, Hizbollah's General Secretary, Sheikh Hassan Nasrallah, gave notice that Lebanon's premier Shi'ite Islamist movement would field an independent list to fight the South Lebanon segment of the Lebanese elections. According to Nasrallah, attempts to agree a united list with Lebanon's other main Shi'ite party, Nabbi Berri's mainstream Amal movement, had failed.

Berri had offered Hizbollah three of the thirteen seats assigned to the Shi'ites in South Lebanon, a share that Hizbollah's cadres and most neutral observers considered manifestly unfair, given the movement's actual strength on the ground. To make things worse, Berri had made any joint list conditional on Hizbollah backing such pro-government (and anti-Hizbollah) candidates as Bahia Hariri, sister of Lebanon's prime minister, Rafik Hariri. Hizbollah's decision to run independently was 'irreversible', vowed Nasrallah, as was the movement's commitment to continue its armed resistance to Israel's 18-year occupation of the south.

One week after the rally, Nasrallah and Berri were summoned to Dasmascus. The next day, Hizbollah Radio broadcast that Hizbollah and Amal would, after all, run joint lists for the South Lebanon and Bekaa Valley elections on terms only marginally better than those rejected by Nasrallah. In the South Lebanon poll on 8 September 1996, Hizbollah returned four candidates; there was also one 'supporter' in one of the south's ten non-Shi'ite seats. A week later in the Bekaa vote, Hizbollah returned three candidates for the eight Shi'ite seats, with two non-Shi'ite supporters.

These 'victories' were received coolly by Hizbollah's supporters, and with reason. Having lost two seats in the Mount Lebanon and Beirut elections held in August, Hizbollah was now represented in the new 128-member Parliament by seven Members of Parliament (MPs) and three supporters, compared with eight MPs and four supporters in the outgoing 108-member Parliament. The combined efforts of Amal and Syria to 'cut Hizbollah down to size' in the 1996 elections appear to have worked. But to what end?

For certain Lebanese commentators, Hizbollah's 'downsizing' confirms the decline of religious extremism and a return to Lebanon's more moderate and centrist political traditions.[1] In Israel, meanwhile, commentator Joseph Mattar speculated in *The Jerusalem Report* that Syria's moves to 'delegitimise' Hizbollah in the 1996 poll could be a 'goodwill' gesture to Israel's new Likud government.[2]

Such analyses are likely to be wishful thinking. Curbing Hizbollah electorally 'is a small sign from Syria to the West and especially the US that it can contain the movement whenever it chooses', says Lebanese political analyst, Elias Khoury. 'But Hizbollah and the military resistance in the south will stay as a pressure on Israel.'[3] The real significance of the reining-in of Hizbollah is domestic. The curbing of Hizbollah, and the elections in general, consecrate a shift in the locus of policy making away from Beirut and in the direction of Damascus.

Realising Ta'if

The 1989 Ta'if accords, which formally ended Lebanon's 14-year civil war, were based on maintaining an equitable if precarious balance between Lebanon's four main confessional groups. The broker behind this equilibrium was and is Syria. As Rosemary Sayigh has shown, whatever the 'apparent shifts or hesitations' in Syria's policy toward Lebanon, its strategic objectives have been consistent and sure. 'Put negatively', she writes, 'Syria has been concerned to prevent either a Maronite rightist takeover of Lebanon in alliance with Israel, or a radical' Lebanese/Palestinian nationalist 'takeover threatening both Israeli retaliation and the destabilisation of Syria.'[4] Put positively, the objectives are in line with Syria's ideology of extending Baathist pan-Arabism to ensure its security interests and keep some sort of strategic parity with Israel. The objectives are also consistent with Syria's desire to maintain a defensive military front along the Lebanese–Syrian border with Israel, because both Damascus and the Syrian interior are vulnerable to any potential Israeli offensive through the Bekaa Valley.

Ta'if initially commanded little legitimacy among Lebanon's politically and geographically fragmented Sunni community, and evoked outright opposition from Maronite Christians allied with ex-President Amin Gemayel and Army Commander Michel Aoun. Even after Syrian aircraft bombed Aoun out of Beirut in October 1990 (the act which really drew the curtain on the war), his Maronite constituencies resisted the new dispensation. In Lebanon's first post-Ta'if general elections of 1992, a majority of Maronite Christians boycotted the poll.

In the years since, this resistance has crumbled. One reason has been the coalescing of the Sunni community behind 'their' prime minister Hariri, appointed in October 1992. Crucial sectarian forces such as Amal and Walid Jumblatt's Druze Progressive Socialist Party (PSP) have also backed Hariri's 'reconstructionist' plans for Lebanon. Another reason, however, has been the Hariri government's avowed and proactive suppression of any revival of national representation for Lebanon's 350,000 Palestinians,[5] the *bête noire* of Maronite sectarianism. The upshot has been the emergence of a more pragmatic Maronite consciousness in Lebanon, which may not like the Syrian ascendency underwritten by Ta'if but is slowly learning to live with it.

In the 1996 elections for the Christian-dominated Mount Lebanon area, 45 per cent of the electorate (a high turnout by Lebanese standards) returned 35 candidates, 32 of them allied with the pro-Syrian policies of Hariri. In Mount Lebanon also, Jumblatt and the PSP secured their tenure in the next Parliament, despite at times violent opposition from within their own Druze community. In mainly Sunni Beirut, Hariri's list won 13 of the 19 seats, although with a low voter turnout and amid serious charges of electoral fraud. Seven years after Ta'if, the formula is being realised, with civic peace between Lebanon's internally and externally divided confessions guaranteed by Syria's hegemony over all their established 'leaders'. There appeared only one snag: Hizbollah and its increasingly defiant challenge to Amal for leadership of Lebanon's 1.3 million Shi'ites.[6]

Hizbollah's challenge falls short of opposing Syria's foreign policy objectives *vis-à-vis* Israel.[7] It has more to do with Syria's domestic agenda for Lebanon, which wants the 'secularist'[8] Amal (rather than the Islamist Hizbollah) to remain the pre-eminent Shi'ite force in the country. If Hizbollah has been cut down to size in the recent elections, it is due to the threat the movement poses to Amal (and so the Ta'if formula brokered by Syria) rather than to any future Israeli/Syrian peace agreement.

Hizbollah's Entrée

Hizbollah's origins in Lebanon lie in the dispatch of around 1,000 Iranian Revolutionary Guards to the Bekaa Valley in June 1982. Iran's entrée as one more regional actor in the Lebanese theatre was approved by Syria. Prior to this, Syria had blocked any Iranian role in Lebanon. But faced with Israel's invasion – and alarmed by the possibility that the invasion might isolate Syria – Damascus turned to Iran as an ally to counter Israel's designs to force a pro-Israeli Maronite regime on Lebanon.

For its part, Iran viewed the new alignment as a means of contact with the largest Shi'ite community in the Arab world outside of Iraq and of enabling a base from which it could directly influence the Arab–Israeli conflict. Formed secretly in 1982, Hizbollah waited two years to publicly declare itself as a radical Shi'ite Islamist movement in Lebanon committed to 'continue the march for the liberation of Palestine'. It is along this axis of Syrian, Iranian and (to a lesser extent) Palestinian interests that can be measured Hizbollah's growth from an Iranian export to the most effective Arab guerrillaist force ever mounted against Israel.

For Syria, Hizbollah's greatest asset was (and is) military. Through Hizbollah, Syria can wage a proxy war against Israel in the occupied south as well as counter Israel's own proxy war waged through its Lebanese client, the South Lebanese Army (SLA). At same time, Hizbollah enables Syria to support an authentic Lebanese resistance movement. According to Nizar Hamzeh, 90 per cent of all armed actions against Israel in Lebanon since 1984 have been carried out by Hizbollah, with its suicide operations being the critical catalyst in forcing the Israeli army's 1985 retreat to its self-proclaimed 'security zone'.[9]

The military objectives of Hizbollah and Syria coincide in the south and will continue to do so as long as the occupation endures, but Syria has taken care to ensure that neither Iran nor Hizbollah gains an autonomous political role in Lebanon. The clearest expression of this subordination was over the potentially conflicting stances taken by Hizbollah and Syria toward the Palestinians in Lebanon.

Realpolitik or Solidarity? Hizbollah and the Palestinians

On 19 May 1985, Amal militias attacked Beirut's Shatilla refugee camp, triggering the 'war of the camps' between Amal and what remained of the Palestinian resistance in Lebanon. The war was to last nearly two years and claim the lives of around 2,500 Lebanese and Palestinians.

Amal's motives for ridding Lebanon of 'Arafatism'[10] were a mix of opportunism and ambition. As Sayigh convincingly argues, Amal calculated that a 'pre-emptive blow' against the Palestinian camps would not only ensure its political hegemony over West Beirut and the south, the two regions where the Palestinian resistance had been strongest. It would increase the movement's standing amongst the Shi'ite poor, whose sectarian conciousness and anti-Palstinianism had been growing since the 1982 Israeli invasion.[11]

But it is also clear that Amal could not have moved against the Palestinians without the political approval and military support of Syria. 'In Amal', writes Sayigh, 'Damascus found a local ally whose ambitions and dilemmas ... made it ripe for manipulation towards a move intended to prevent the re-emergence of the Palestinians as an independent force in Lebanon.'[12] a political rehabilitation Syria was out to deny at all costs. It was a coincidence of interests which, for political and ideological reasons, could only alarm Hizbollah and Iran.

Despite antipathy toward the PLO's secular nationalism, Hizbollah's ideological commitment to the Palestinian cause is profound. The movement officially was inaugurated on the second anniversary of the Sabra and Shatilla massacre and has always avowed the struggle against Israel and Zionism as a basic tenet of its creed. But Hizbollah also viewed the camps war as a political opportunity to widen its base among Lebanon's Shi'ites, many of whom were unconvinced that the Palestinian camps had to be disarmed (Amal's pretext for the war) and even less that a Shi'ite militia should be the party to do it.[13]

Decrying the camps war an 'international conspiracy' against the Arab and Muslim nation, Hizbollah cadres at times intervened on the Palestinian side and otherwise provided humanitarian support for the camps. Iran, too, made several diplomatic attempts to mediate a ceasefire, often in the teeth of Syrian opposition. Hizbollah and Iran also reached out to Lebanon's Sunni Islamist parties, which viewed PLO nationalism as a lesser evil to Syrian interventionism.

These resistances encountered opposition from Syria. Following the outbreak of hostilities in the camps, Amal militias armed by Syria clashed with Hizbollah, sparking a virtual civil war between Lebanon's two premier Shi'ite forces that was to last, off and on, for five years. In February 1987 – at the very height of Amal's third and final siege of the camps – Syrian troops intervened directly in Beirut to quell the growing influence of Hizbollah's militias there. After Iranian mediation, the Amal–Hizbollah clashes were ended in May 1988 with the full-scale deployment of the Syrian army throughout Beirut's Shi'ite-dominated southern suburbs. By such means, Iran and Hizbollah learned the limits of their power in Lebanon and who was going to enforce them.

Lebanonisation

Around this time Hizbollah decided, quietly, to drop its calls for a Lebanon governed by Islamic law. After a heated internal struggle[14] – resolved at the movement's 'extraordinary conclave' in Tehran in October 1989 – Hizbollah opted to throw its weight behind the multi-confessional realities laid down by Ta'if.

Since that time, Hizbollah's basic aim in Lebanon has been less emulation of the 'Iranian road' toward an Islamic Republic than the establishment of a legal party which would 'support the resistance in the south and seek to abolish all forms of political sectarianism in Lebanon'.[15] But it would pursue these ends from within the confessional mainstream of Lebanese politics rather than against it. Hizbollah's 'Lebanonisation' swiftly bore fruit.[16]

In alliance with Amal and Jumblatt's PSP – and helped by the Maronite boycott – Hizbollah returned eight MPs in the 1992 elections, forming the largest single-party bloc in the Lebanese parliament. Most observers viewed these successes as having less to do with the resistance or Hizbollah's Islamist ideology than with its prowess in establishing a network of social services for the Shi'ite poor.[17] These were especially prominent during the harsh winter of 1992 when Hizbollah's relief organisations managed to rescue many Shi'ite villages stranded in the Bekaa, while government services, conspiciously, did not.

Yet Hizbollah's new politics was no mere welfarism. During the four-year Parliament, Hizbollah deputies and their allies became Lebanon's most effective opposition, consistently assailing Hariri's multi-billion dollar 'reconstruction' policies as follies that would succeed only in miring Lebanon in foreign debt. They also charged Amal with neglecting any real social rehabilitation in the south, through its co-option within and 'clientilist' control over various government structures.[18] The popular esteem generated by this mix of radical egalitarianism and social critique – of 'politics as morality', as one Hizbollah leader put it[19] – fed into Hizbollah's ongoing military resistance in the south, as did the disproportionate Israeli retaliation it drew.

Following Israel's ferocious 'Grapes of Wrath' onslaught in April 1996, Hizbollah activists claim that they repaired '5,000 homes in 82 villages', rebuilt roads and other infrastructure and paid compensation to 2,300 farmers, and did so in the space of two months.[20]

Neutral observers concede such statistics are probably accurate. 'In south Lebanon, Hizbollah is seen primarily as a social movement, as a defender of the poor,' says Lebanese social scientist, Paul Salem.[21]

The reward for such activism was to have been greater political representation from the 1996 elections. According to Salem, by the eve of elections it was clear that, in any straight electoral contest between Amal and Hizbollah, Hizbollah would win hands down in the Bekaa and 'return around 60 per cent of the Shi'ite mandates in the south'.[22] For this reason, there was not going to be a straight contest.

Isolating Hizbollah: the 1996 Elections

In August 1996, Berri offered Hizbollah a joint slate for the elections which invited (and got) rejection. Hizbollah responded by announcing that it would stand against Amal and other pro-Hariri candidates in the Mount Lebanon and Beirut elections either singly or in alliance with leftist, independent and Sunni Islamist groups. The threat this potentially 'nationalist' coalition posed to the Ta'if consensus was bound to irk Damascus. Very soon into the electoral campaign, the gloves came off.

Berri and Amal charged Hizbollah with trying to 'fragment Lebanon and divide its people' through its advocacy of a 'Muslim state'. Hariri defined the elections as a 'battle between moderation and extremism', warning darkly that any government led by him 'would not cooperate with extremists'. Even erstwhile allies like the PSP joined the fray. Hizbollah, railed Jumblatt at a rally in Mount Lebanon, was 'damaging the nation's welfare' through its 'exclusivist' resistance to Israel.

It was the combined might of Amal, PSP and Hariri supporters which cost Hizbollah its two seats in Mount Lebanon and Beirut, whether by strength of votes or electoral fix.[23] Two weeks before the crucial south Lebanon contest, the mood from the hustings was eloquently expressed in an editorial from the Lebanese daily, *an-Nahar*: 'Hizbollah is facing a merciless war by three powerful leaders ... aimed at clipping the wings of the bird that has outgrown all others so fast that all now panic.'[24]

Hizbollah, too, was starting to panic. On 3 September, Nasrallah hit back that 'Hariri and his allies are waging an open war on us', and warned of the consequences should Amal try to rig the polls against the Islamists in the south.[25] The next day Nasrallah was called to Damascus. As far as Syria was concerned, the 'merciless war' had gone on long enough.

Conclusions

The elections – and the fraught history they encapsulate of the 'alliance' between Hizbollah/Iran and Syria – reveal certain realities about contemporary Lebanese politics. These realities have a significance way beyond Lebanon.

First, Hizbollah's eventual submission to a joint list with Amal demonstrates that it is not an autonomous political player in Lebanon. 'Hizbollah's choices are still governed by Iranian/Syrian relations', says Salim, 'and on what these powers agree should be Hizbollah's ascribed role in Lebanon.'[26] For the foreseeable future, that role is to remain what it has been in the past – less a political challenge to Amal's hegemony over the Shi'ites and more a military resistance to Israel, to be supported and restrained in line with Syrian diplomacy.

Second, the elections have demonstrated that all of Lebanon's post-Ta'if confessional leaders either actively or passively accept Syria's current hegemony over Lebanese politics. While each has different levels of support in their respective communities, all 'lead' with Syria's blessing. It is this that binds them into a fragile 'national' unity. Yet the political result, in the view of one observer, is 'the permanence of Syria's presence in Lebanon'. Each confessional leader, he says, represents a prop in a 'system where any Syrian withdrawal from Lebanon would not only precipitate civic strife between the different religious communities, but also within them'.[27] These political dependencies are of course underscored by the 35,000 Syrian troops permanently stationed in Lebanon and the nearly one million Syrian workers employed in its economy.

Finally, the elections have set the parameters for any future Syrian–Israeli peace process. Very simply, if the Netanyahu government really does wish to withdraw its soldiers from occupied south Lebanon, it is going to have to negotiate with Syria about withdrawing Israeli soldiers and settlements from the occupied Golan Heights. As President Assad said on the eve of the Lebanese elections. 'I say Lebanon and Syria first, not Lebanon first.'[28]

The denouement of the elections has shown the true weight of those words.

Beirut-Nabatiyya, August 1996; *Journal of Palestine Studies*,
Winter 1997

17

'All Killers': Luxor, the Gama'a and Egypt's Prisons

The massacre on 18 November 1997 at Luxor's Queen Hatashepsut Temple in Egypt passed swiftly from the world's headlines – its news value soon edged aside by the thousands slain in Algeria and by the prospects of even greater carnage posed by the latest Gulf stand-off. Yet, in Egypt and elsewhere, the tremors set off at Luxor still resonate, stirring private and public discussions on the source of such violence and what it augured.

This was not only because Luxor's toll of 69 dead, including 58 tourists, was the highest of any single attack in the long war between the Egyptian state and those radical Islamist movements dedicated to its destruction. The horror came as much from the manner of the atrocity.

Eyewitnesses recount how the gunmen trailed terrified civilians through the rooms of the temple and poured bullet after bullet into their bodies; how they casually stuffed leaflets into their victims' clothing; how one gunman – before departing the scene – stopped for a drink at an abandoned kiosk.

Such insolence seemed less hubris than an awareness by the attackers of their own imminent demise. During the massacre, one of the six assailants was wounded. He was immediately executed by his colleagues. On fleeing the site – pursued by soldiers and a crowd of civilians – the remaining five found refuge in a cave. A witness said he heard shots. On entering the cave, it appeared the attackers had performed a religious ceremony and committed mass suicide. Over their corpses were strewn pamphlets stating that the attack had been done by the 'Battalion of Havoc and Destruction' under the authority of the Gama'a Islamiyya (or Islamic Group), Egypt's most extreme Islamist movement.

The Gama'a Islamiyya

The Gama'a was born out of the Islamic radicalism that swept Egypt's universities in the 1970s. Initially nurtured by President

Anwar Sadat as a counterweight to Egypt's Nasserite and Communist movements, 'the Islamic groups' turned against their sponsor after Egypt's 1979 peace treaty with Israel. A handful of Islamist student activists from the southern provinces of Minya and Asyut came together to form Gama'a Islamiyya, a socio-military organisation whose aim was to establish an Islamic state via the violent overthrow of Egypt's 'infidel' one. Its first act was to assassinate Sadat in Cairo on 6 October 1981.

For the next decade, the Gama'a worked to Islamise Egyptian society 'from below', spreading out from its bases in Asyut and Minya to the urban barrios of Greater Cairo. Exploiting the lack of any real state presence in these areas, the Gama'a established itself as a *de facto* governing authority. It smuggled out fugitives to the Afghanistan front for 'military training' and provided an array of cheap welfare services in Cairo's slum districts of Giza, Ayn Shams and Imbaba, the medium through which the Gama'a's militant Islamist message was inculcated. 'We were engaged in a war of position', recalls Abu Hassan, a Gama'a activist from Imbaba. 'The aim was to create independent bases within the state.'[1]

Emboldened by the strategy's apparent success – and by the police's inability to combat it – in 1992 the Gama'a moved from a war of position to a full-scale assault on the state. Over the next five years, the Gama'a targeted senior government and police officials and 'widened the conflict' to attack Egyptian embassies abroad. It launched attacks on Egypt's Christian Coptic community, whose alleged 'Crusader proselytism' the Gama'a viewed as the 'major obstacle' in Egypt to the propagation of Islam. The Gama'a also gave covenant to attacks on tourists and tourism, 'a source of abomination' in the opinion of the currently 'disappeared' Gama'a leader, Talat Fuad Qasim.[2] Tourism is also the most important source of Egypt's hard currency.

The aim behind the 1992 turn was to reduce Egypt to chaos. Out of this disorder – predicted Qasim – the government would fall, the 'lower ranks' of the army would defect and the masses would flock to the Gama'a since 'no other political forces will survive'.[3] But the government did not collapse; nor did the masses move.

'Scientific Counter-terrorism'

If the state's strategy against the Gama'a in the 1980s had been indecisive, combating it sporadically on the military level, retreating before it on the ideological, after 1992 it was confrontational, aimed at the 'total eradication' of the Gama'a as a military, political and social force. The blueprint for this was the 'scientific counter-terrorism' concept of Egypt's former Interior Minister, Hassan al-Alfi (who was 'resigned' after the Luxor massacre). There was precious little science about it.

In its Cairo strongholds, the Gama'a's social networks were smashed, its 'street mosques' outlawed and its activists rounded up. In Asyut and Minya, Gama'a villages were put under siege, with mass arrests, curfews and 'extra-judicial killings' of real or perceived Islamists a routine part of the clampdown.[4] In desperate reprisal, the Gama'a pulled off ever more spectacular hits, such as the murder of 17 Greek tourists outside Cairo's Europa Hotel in 1996 and the massacre of 25 Copts in two southern villages last spring. But it was a terror of the last resort. Most commentators agree that by the end of 1997 the Gama'a's social and political infrastructure had been wiped out, with its leadership dead, imprisoned or dispersed to Europe, Afghanistan or the hills of southern Egypt.

Al-Alfi's counter-insurgency measures had had their effect. But also their price. Between 1992 and 1997, an estimated 1,200 people lost their lives to the conflict, most of them police officers or suspected Islamists but with a sizeable minority of civilians and Copts. Ninety alleged Islamists were sentenced to death – and 57 actually executed – by military or state emergency courts in mass trials that paid little to due process. Having uprooted the Gama'a as a force on the streets, the government saw its main task henceforth to prevent it from ever returning to them, either as an organisation or an ideology. The chosen solution was simple as it was myopic – imprisonment.

Al-Wadi al-Jadid

No one really knows how many political prisoners there are in Egypt. The Gama'a's 'unofficial' spokesperson, Montasser el-Zayat, says 35,000. The Interior Ministry gives a figure of 9,000. Egyptian human rights organisations place the number at around 20,000.

What is known is of the thousands incarcerated in Egypt most are administrative detainees, arrested on the hunch of belonging to or supporting the Gama'a or other illegal organisations. 'Since 1992, only around 700 people have been charged with specific offences by military and state emergency courts', says the Executive Director of Egypt's Centre for Human Rights Legal Aid (CHRLA), Gasser Abdel Razek.[5] The upshot of this mass detention policy is probably Egypt's largest ever prisoner population. It is a regime of containment the state appears willing to accommodate.

After the 1992 crackdown, the Interior Ministry embarked on a massive prison building programme, establishing five new jails and adding 'High Security' wings to existing ones. Access to prisons in Egypt is difficult, for prisoners' families and lawyers as much as for the press and human rights organisations. This is because Egyptian law allows the Interior Minister to 'close' prisons for 'medical or security reasons'. The ban has been justified by the Minister on the grounds that Gama'a detainees use their lawyers to relay messages to their supporters 'outside'. But there are other reasons why the Ministry would not want prisons to become 'open' to either local or international scrutiny.

Last October, the Cairo-based Human Rights Centre for the Assistance of Prisoners (HRCAP) released a report on one of these new 'bastilles'. Set in the middle of the desert some 630 kilometres from Cairo, al-Wadi al-Jadid prison consists of 216 cells divided into 12 blocks. Each cell is 24 square metres and holds between 20 and 25 detainees. Since March 1996, all recreation has been banned. One prisoner told the HRCAP that he 'had not seen the sun for over a year'. There are also 15 incommunicado cells measuring 2 by 1 metres. In these, 'delinquent' inmates have their food on the floor which serves also as their toilet.

The immediate impact of such conditions is on the detainees' health. The HRCAP assesses that there are currently 143 inmates in al-Wadi al-Jadid infected with tuberculosis. Seven prisoners have died in the prison since 1994, at least five from illness. Prisoners also complain of skin dieases, scabies, kidney inflammation and liver problems.

The aim of such appalling conditions is to break the detainees psy-chologically, believes Mohammed Zari, Director of HRCAP and the report's main author. He cites numerous other practices by the prison authorities whose purpose appears solely to instil in inmates a sense of their own human and political powerlessness. One is 'recurrent detention'.

Under Egyptian law, after 30 days of administrative detention a prisoner can appeal his arrest. If there is no charge, a Civil Court can order the prisoner's release. Except 'the Interior Ministry rarely grants these releases', says Zari.[6] The security forces will instead take the 'released' detainee to a police station and then redetain him on the claim that he has resumed his activities. 'I know prisoners who have been released in this way over 30 times', he says.[7] On return to prison, 'released' detainees are subjected to what is known as the 'reception party', an initiation rite granted to all new inmates. The prisoners are forced to crawl on all fours between a gauntlet of guards who beat them and assign them 'female' names. To spare this ordeal, prisoners and their families ask Zari not to appeal their arrest.

Havoc and Destruction

In June 1997, the Gama'a's leadership in prison offered the Egyptian government an 'unconditional ceasefire'. Despite demurral from the group's leaders in Europe and Afghanistan, most analysts saw the offer as the Gama'a's belated recognition that its naive campaign for state power had failed. For Hisham Mubarak – CHRLA's Director and one of the most authoritive sources on Egyptian Islamism* – the hope behind the Gama'a's call was that a period of grace would give way to quiet discussions with the government on prisoner releases and prison conditions. The government was not interested. 'It would be a dialogue with the deaf and blind', said President Hosni Mubarak in the aftermath of Luxor. 'They (the Gama'a) are all killers.'

It is a view shared by most ministers, many Egyptian intellectuals and large swathes of public opinion, for whom the Gama'a's indiscriminate terror – and the concomitant damage it inflicts on the Egyptian economy – has long ceased to be anything other than nihilist. It may be the consensus, says Hisham Mubarak, but it is blind. He says:

> The policy of total eradication worked only in the short term. But look at the legacy it has left. There are now thousands in Egypt who have seen their family members or friends killed, tortured or detained and for whom there will always be a sense of dormant conflict with the state. Second, because the eradication policy is indiscriminate, it rounds up everyone in prison and starts a process where the innocent become sympathisers and the sympathisers become militants. Finally, if you arrest someone when he is 18 and release him when he is 28, he has lost his education. What future does he have?[8]

The 'suicidal violence' visited on Luxor perhaps. As the dust settled on the massacre, a profile emerged of the six young men who had perpetrated it. Most were in their twenties, four were students from middle-class backgrounds and all hailed from Egypt's southern

---

* This article could not have been written without the assistance of Hisham Mubarak, who, on 12 January, died of a heart attack at the tragically young age of 35.

provinces. What bound them – and what appeared to draw them to the Gama'a – was that all had served time inside Egypt's prisons.

For the government the six were evidence enough that mass releases of others like them risks turning Egypt into another Algeria. For human rights lawyers like Mohammed Zari and Hisham Mubarak to keep 20,000 people permanently detained is 'simply to defer the explosion'. In the debate between them, Egypt is likely to be spared the establishment of a Gama'a-inspired Islamic state. But beneath the debate – amid the filth, disease and degradation of Egypt's prisons – it is the mindset of 'havoc and destruction' that is being sown.

Cairo, January 1998

18

Fatah, Hamas and the Crisis of Oslo: Interviews with Marwan Barghouti and Ibrahim Ghoshah

The spring and summer of 1997 have witnessed the most serious crisis in the Oslo peace process since its inception in September 1993. Following Israel's decisions in March 1997 to construct the Har Homa Jewish settlement at Jebel Abu Ghneim in occupied East Jerusalem and offer only a two per cent further redeployment from West Bank territory, the PLO suspended all negotiations with the Netanyahu government, including all cooperation between Israeli military and Palestinian Authority (PA) security forces.[1]

Over the next four months, public protests were organised throughout the occupied territories, with clashes breaking out between Palestinians and the Israeli army in Gaza, Bethlehem, Ramallah, Nablus, Jenin and, above all, Hebron. Many of these protests were led by Yassir Arafat's Fatah movement. The same period saw suicide bomb attacks on Israeli civilians in Tel Aviv and Jerusalem and on Jewish settlers in Gaza, claimed by the Islamist opposition of Hamas and Islamic Jihad.

The breakdown in talks as well as the revival of protests had an immediate impact on Palestinian political attitudes. Opinion polls registered a decline in Palestinian support for the Oslo process, the PA and the leadership of Yassir Arafat, and a rise in support for Hamas, including its advocacy of armed attacks on Israeli targets. Professional and student elections saw Islamist-led lists achieve victories in Gaza, Nablus, Hebron and East Jerusalem.

In February, ten PLO and Palestinian groups met to convene the Comprehensive National Dialogue, a tentative rapprochement aimed at uniting pro-Oslo and opposition Palestinian factions around 'a new national consensus' to confront the crisis. Two subsequent meetings of the National Dialogue were held in April and August.

The following interviews are with two Palestinian leaders who have played (and are likely to play) important roles in these developments. Marwan Barghouti is Fatah's General-Secretary in the West

Bank and a Palestinian Legislative Council (PLC) member for Ramallah. Ibrahim Ghoshah is Hamas's official spokesperson based in Jordan.

Fatah and the Peace Process: An Interview with Marwan Barghouti

How Serious is the Current Crisis in the Peace Process?

It is the worst crisis since the Madrid Conference. With the last Israeli government of Rabin and Peres, we certainly had our differences. But we also had negotiations. The crisis now is that we have an Israeli government that is openly uncommitted to the Oslo accords and is not interested in negotiations, but only in dictates. Worse, it is committed to increasing settlements, especially in Jerusalem and regardless of Palestinian, Arab and world opinion.

We are at the start of the crisis. Many Palestinians – including from inside Fatah – are questioning whether we were right to make the strategic choice of peace with Israel. Many Fatah cadres made this point at the Beit Sahour meeting.[2] My view is that we must distinguish between Oslo and the choice of peace and the policies of the Netanyahu government. Our protests are not directed against peace. We are committed to peace. Our protests are because there is no peace with Netanyahu. I think most of Fatah takes this view.

What is Fatah's response to the crisis?

With the confrontations in September 1996,[3] the aim was to kick-start the Oslo process, to remind Netanyahu and the world that the Palestinian masses were a factor that must be taken into account. Due to the confrontations – and the international pressure they caused – Netanyahu was forced into redeploying from Hebron. But it was clear he was adhering to the agreement against his will.

His current policies are the revenge for Hebron. He wants to destroy the peace process, build settlements and defy the Arab world, the UN and the international community. But, whereas in September 1996 the US intervened to support the Palestinians, the US now is acting against the Palestinians.

This means our tactics have to be different to those used in September. At the Beit Sahour conference, some Fatah cadres called for a return to the armed struggle. This was not the majority view – but there were voices and we cannot ignore them. The mood on the Palestinian street was not against the Tel Aviv bombing in March.

Last year, Fatah organised demonstrations in the Palestinian areas against attacks on Israeli civilians. If Fatah were to call for such protests today, we would be told, 'What about Israel's terrorism at Jebel Abu Ghneim?'

All of which puts Fatah in a dilemma, as the leading force in Palestinian society supporting the peace process. Netanyahu's policies are strengthening Hamas and the opposition on the Palestinian street, a support which widens their freedom of action. I believe Fatah's response must be to defend the peace process by organising mass popular protests – demonstrations, strikes, boycotts and so on. But we are aware such protests could easily get out of control. Most of the activists who participated in the recent clashes in Gaza and the West Bank were from Fatah rather than Hamas.

Only Netanyahu can stop this escalation, by reversing his policies on settlements and by adhering to the agreements. I am pessimistic whether Netanyahu is going to do this.

What demands is Fatah making on the Palestinian Authority?

We are demanding that the PLO cease all negotiations with Israel. We are also calling for an end to all security cooperation between Israel and the PA. We cannot and will not defend Israel's security unconditionally. We agreed to ensure Israel's security on the bases of our national security and our national rights and interests. Since Israel violates these rights and interests every day, we are no longer prepared to be bodyguards for Netanyahu's bulldozers at Jebel Abu Ghneim. If Netanyahu refuses to respect Israel's obligations under the agreement, he cannot expect us to respect ours.

Do you expect the PA's security forces to heed this call?

I don't know. But Fatah will exert pressure on them to do so – and remember Jibril Rajoub is not only the PA's head of Preventive Security in the West Bank. He is also a member of Fatah's Higher Committee, and he attended the Beit Sahour conference in that capacity.

What is Fatah's attitude to Hamas, especially after the Tel Aviv bombing?

For one year, we demonstrated we could ensure the security of Israelis. For one year, there were no terror attacks in Israel. We took the decision to stop Hamas's armed operations by force if necessary and by dialogue if possible. We had to do this, to convince Palestinian opinion that suicide operations were not the way.

Hamas is part of the Palestinian people, with real constituencies among the people. We refuse to ignore Hamas the way Netanyahu ignores the Palestinian leadership. The dialogue with Hamas lasted for a year, resulting in the National Dialogue conference in Nablus in February where Hamas accepted the PA's obligations under the Oslo agreement.

Our message to Hamas today is that we appreciate its participation in the National Dialogue and want it to continue. We say this because we want to avoid violence between Palestinians. But Fatah will not accept terror attacks inside Israel because such attacks are diametrically opposed to Palestinians' national interests. We have relations with the Israeli peace camp, many of whom are supporting our struggle, especially over Jebel Abu Ghneim. We will not act to hurt this support.

What about military attacks on soldiers and settlers inside the occupied territories?

Fatah is committed to the Oslo accords, so we are opposed to all armed attacks. But the important point is to convince Hamas not to perpetrate terror attacks inside Israel. Attacks on Israeli civilians inside Israel must be a red line for every Palestinian group, including Hamas.

The irony is that Hamas had reached this conclusion in recent months. But Netanyahu's policies have strengthened the extremist wing inside Hamas.

The Israeli government says the precondition for any resumption of negotiations is that the PA act against terrorism and the infrastructure of Hamas and Islamic Jihad. Can the PA do this?

No. It would be a very dangerous development. The PA is not an Israeli militia, working under Netanyahu's orders. It is the representative of the Palestinian people in the West Bank and Gaza. The question of 'terrorism' should be addressed to the Netanyahu government. If Israel provokes the Palestinian street, then there will be a reaction, from Hamas but not only from them – as I told you, there are some people in Fatah calling for a return to the military option.

But should the PA comply – as it complied after the suicide operations in 1996[4] – what would be Fatah's response?

We would oppose it. If the PA were to arrest the cell responsible for the Tel Aviv bombing, we would support this – because Fatah is against terror actions inside Israel. But were the PA to undertake indiscriminate arrest sweeps of all Hamas supporters like those of last year, Fatah would oppose the PA. We would not only oppose the PA; we would organise demonstrations against it.

What are your strategies vis-à-vis *the Arab world and the Israeli opposition?*

We are mobilising on all levels. Netanyahu is not only strengthening the extremists in Palestinian society, but in all Arab societies. For the last six years, we in Fatah have been saying that peace with Israel is possible. Under the last Israeli government, this became the Arab consensus, at least among the governments. But the emerging Arab consensus now is that peace with Israel is impossible.

The new consensus represents a loss to the Palestinians. But it represents a greater loss to the Israelis. This is what is so incomprehensible about the current crisis. In Netanyahu's pursuit of tactical victories for his own coalition, he is squandering the strategic victory of Israel's peace with the Arab world. This is an utterly closed mentality. For without resolving the Palestinian question, Israel and Israelis will never be welcome in Cairo, Amman or anywhere else in the Arab world. We remain the key. We understand our military weakness *vis-à-vis* Israel. But we have a passive power. The Palestinians can prevent a comprehensive peace with the Arab world and, without peace, Israel will pay the price.

Which means a major responsibility for resolving the current crisis lies with the Israeli people. Now is the time for Israel's peace forces to take to the streets, as they did following the Sabra and Shatilla massacres in 1982. This would send a message to the Arab world, signalling that not all Israelis are the same as Netanyahu and Likud.

This is the demand Fatah is making on Peace Now, Meretz and the Labour Party. These were the parties with whom we negotiated and signed the peace agreements. It is their responsibility as much as ours to determine whether peace can be rescued or whether it is to be destroyed by Netanyahu.

An Intifada of a Different Kind: An Interview with Ibrahim Ghoshah

What is Hamas's assessment of the current protests in the occupied territories?

We see the protests as the beginnings of the third *intifada*. The first *intifada* lasted from 1987 to 1993, when it was aborted by the signing of the Oslo agreement. The second *intifada* lasted four days, after Netanyahu opened the tunnel in Jerusalem last September.

Of course, the level of protests in this third *intifada* are not the same as in the first. But neither are the protests insignificant. The protests against the occupation in certain West Bank towns and villages are akin to those during the first *intifada*.

They are the first shoots of a new uprising, even though the dominant Palestinian mood after three years of Oslo is one of frustration and despair. The Palestinians are now isolated from one another, adrift on 'autonomous' islands, surrounded by a sea controlled by Israel.

This means the conditions are different from the first *intifada*. Then the battle lines were clear. You had the Israeli occupation everywhere and a people resisting it everywhere. Now you have this strange body called the Palestinian Authority and a Palestinian police force. These have a role in the third *intifada* as they had in the second.

We believe there is an understanding between the Israeli Shin Bet and the PA security forces. Both wish to keep the protests at a level of stones and rubber bullets rather than anything more. It is an understanding that benefits both sides. As long as the protests remain at this level, Israel can absorb Palestinian anger, render it ineffectual and ensure the safety of Israelis in the occupied territories. The PA, on the other hand, believes protests of this scale can be used as a tool in the coming negotiations with Israel.

Arafat wants to confront Israel's settlement policies at Jebel Abu Ghneim without weapons. But, without weapons, Hamas believes a genuine *intifada* cannot begin – I mean an *intifada* of armed or military resistance. We believe only this form of resistance will thwart Israel's settlement policies at Jebel Abu Ghneim and elsewhere.

So Palestinians are facing two countervailing pressures. The pressure of control coming from the PA. And the pressure coming from different Palestinian forces to raise the level of resistance to the Israeli occupation. The outcome of this struggle will determine the fate of the third *intifada*. If a serious escalation occurs, Arafat and the Israelis will lose control of the situation, a scenario which will favour the Palestinian opposition forces, including Hamas.

So the protests strengthen the opposition rather than the PA?

Yes. The current protests are not solely about Jebel Abu Ghneim or the settlements. They express frustration at the whole Oslo arrangement. They are protests against Oslo in practice. Three years ago, Hamas said Oslo would gain the Palestinians nothing. Palestinians are now realising this. They are realising that Oslo will grant them less than 3 per cent of Palestine, with even this 3 per cent split up into different cantons.

So there is popular anger, which Hamas intends to utilise. A recent opinion poll in the West Bank showed that 50 per cent of Palestinians were against negotiations with Israel and 50 per cent were in favour of martyrdom operations. 75 per cent said they were against any crackdown by the PA on Hamas and Islamic Jihad. In March, an Islamist list won the elections for the Engineers Association in Gaza, a body that was historically a stronghold for Fatah.

The real power of Hamas are its young cadres. They follow fighters like Ibrahim Makadmeh who, at a rally in Gaza,[5] said that negotiations and peaceful protests would lead nowhere, but armed resistance would gain the Palestinians Jerusalem. This shows the falsity of analyses which say there is a 'hard-line' Hamas outside the occupied territories and a 'moderate' Hamas inside. Makadmeh is inside, and he is expressing the consensus within Hamas.

You are saying conditions are now ripe to move to armed intifada in the occupied territories. Yet Hamas has not explicitly called for an armed uprising ...?

No. We are waiting for certain Fatah cadres to join us on this road. We know there are some in Fatah – as yet a minority – who want to resume the armed struggle against Israel. We also know there are many in the occupied territories who are dissatisfied with the current tactics of the PA. They are asking themselves why should hundreds of Palestinians be wounded every day when there are guns in the hands of the Palestinian police. If certain of these cadres were to use arms rather than stones, there would be a change in the *intifada*, turning it into a military resistance. Hamas would support this change.

This is now the only road of resistance. Protests like that of the Palestinian/Israeli 'peace camp' on Jebel Abu Ghneim are useless. No Palestinian takes them seriously.

Against whom should an armed intifada be directed?

Hamas believes the real war should be against Israeli soldiers and settlers who are occupiers on our land. As Islamists, we do not concentrate our attacks on civilians, other than in response to Israeli attacks on Palestinian civilians. We believe the real resistance should be directed against the military occupation.

But Hamas was responsible for the Tel Aviv cafe bombing ...?

I cannot answer you directly, but I understand Izzadin el-Qassam issued a statement saying it was behind the Tel Aviv operation.

Is your emphasis on armed struggle because Hamas feels the 'Oslo arrangement' has rendered redundant the mass, popular protests that characterised the first intifada?

The two forms of struggle are complementary. It is important to support any resistance, even if it is with stones. But stones will not remove the settlements. We also know armed resistance will take time to build. As long as we are on the right path, we are not in a hurry. As I said, the tide is moving toward Hamas and against Oslo, the PA and the so-called peace process.

We are waiting for the nationalist forces, especially Fatah, to also move in this direction. Once this occurs, there will be a real national unity on the ground.

Hamas has participated in the National Dialogue conferences called for by the PA and PLO factions. Is the aim to unite behind the PA during the crisis or to work on divisions within the PLO, and especially Fatah?

Hamas's ultimate aim is for the PA to disappear. The PA draws its authority from Oslo. But Hamas will never enter into conflict with any other Palestinian force, no matter what the cost to ourselves. Any fight between Palestinians is a victory for Israel.

But we believe the future will bring a new Palestinian movement. This would include not only Hamas, but Hamas would be a leading force within it. We would work with Fatah and the other PLO factions as well as with independent Palestinian forces. The new movement would transform the current autonomous areas in the occupied territories into bases of Palestinian sovereignty and independence. This would throw down a real challenge to the occupation.

And this new movement would replace the PLO ...?

Yes, because in practical terms the PA has already replaced the PLO. But, unlike the PA, the new movement would unite Palestinians from inside and outside the occupied territories and would be supported by Arabs and Muslims throughout the world.

Would it still advocate a two-state solution to the conflict?

For Hamas, there is no difference between the 1948 lands and the 1967 lands. It is possible to accept the 1967 territories in some kind of truce arrangement, so long as this truce does not entail recognition of Israel. But Hamas's goal remains the liberation of Palestine.

Ramallah, March 1997; Amman, April 1997

19

Making Peace: an Interview with Yossi Beilin

Yossi Beilin was a cabinet minister in Israel's 1992–96 Labour government. In December 1992, he initiated the 'secret channel' with the PLO which eventually led to the 1993 Oslo accords between Israel and the Palestinians. In October 1995, he reached a series of 'understandings' with PLO executive member, Mahmoud Abbass (Abu Mazen), laying out the 'red lines' that would govern any final Israel/Palestinian settlement. In January 1997, he signed a 'National Accord' with Likud's Knesset group leader, Michael Eitan, and six other Labour and Likud MKs outlining their common ideas on a permanent settlement with the Palestinians.

In the interview Beilin talks about the understandings he reached with Abu Mazen as well as the accord he signed with Eitan. He also gives his views regarding the Lebanese and Syrian tracks of peace process.

Beilin/Abu Mazen Understandings

Could you summarise the understandings you reached with Abu Mazen?

For Israel, the main issue is security. This means that any future Palestinian state must be demilitarised, that the Israeli army will stay on the Jordan River, that there will be no return to the 1967 borders, that the Palestinian refugees from 1948 will not be permitted into sovereign Israel, that Jerusalem will not be redivided, and that the Jewish settlements will not be uprooted.

I don't want to speak on behalf of the Palestinians. But, according to the 'deniable understandings' reached between Abu Mazen and myself, it was understood that there will be a Palestinian state. It will include all of Gaza and most of the West Bank, with a safe passage between them. It also understood that, generally speaking, the Palestinian area would not be compromised, would not be cut into two etc.

The Palestinian capital will be al-Quds, which will be located outside the united Jerusalem of today, but within the suburbs of Jerusalem. It will be within an area that is part of al-Quds according to the Palestinians' geographical definition. The Temple Mount [Haram el-Sharif. ed.] will be extra-territorial to Israel, which means the Palestinians will be the dominant power in the place and will determine all norms there.

The Palestinians in Jerusalem will become citizens of a Palestinian state rather than citizens of Jordan, as is the case today. They will have a borough in Jerusalem that is municipally autonomous. The issue of the final status of East Jerusalem will be deferred to later stage.

On these bases, the Palestinians will recognise Jerusalem as the capital of Israel, while we would recognise al-Quds as their capital. The 1948 refugees would not be permitted into Israel, but there would be no restrictions on their integration into the Palestinian state.

Most of the Jewish settlements would come under the sovereignty of the Palestinian state. Those settlers who wish to return to Israel would be compensated. Those who choose to stay would live under Palestinian sovereignty and obey Palestinian laws, with certain security arrangements. Most of the Jewish settlers – i.e. those who live in the areas of Gush Ezion, the Jerusalem area and Ariel – would become part of Israel. These annexed areas comprise less than 10 per cent of the West Bank. In return – as a gesture – a small part of the northern Negev would be annexed to the Gaza Strip.

Would the Palestinians be expected to recognise, as the capital of Israel, those parts of Jerusalem that were annexed to Israel after the 1967 war?

According to the understandings, these parts would be disputed areas. The Palestinians would recognise West Jerusalem as our capital. We would recognise al-Quds as theirs. Somewhere in the middle is East Jerusalem, whose status would prevail under the current arrangements. That is, it would be an area over which Israel claims its sovereignty, but which the Palestinians do not accept. There would be a joint committee set up to decide on its future.

So it is a maintenance of the *status quo* but with an agreement to change the *status quo* in the future.

What would be the fate of the 1948 refugees who do not want to live in a Palestinian state in the West Bank and Gaza?

In the understandings, there is a chapter referring to the refugees' rehabilitation, i.e. the compensation they would receive under the umbrella of a new international organisation that would replace UNRWA (United Nations Relief and Works Agency).

Does the Likud government's decision to build the Har Homa settlement contradict your understandings with Abu Mazen or is it consistent with them?

I don't see where they meet ... The understandings are about a permanent solution, not the meantime. We didn't refer to the meantime.

In relation to Har Homa, I would to say to the Israeli government, 'OK, you can build, but in the future it might be a disputed area.' I would have preferred any building to have been in the context of the final solution, when both sides know where they stand. But one cannot say Har Homa is against Oslo or against my understandings with Abu Mazen. One could say it is against the spirit of Oslo, because it is to do with Jerusalem and Jerusalem is on the agenda of the final status negotiations. But you cannot refer to a specific sentence in the Oslo accords or anywhere else which says Israel cannot build Har Homa.

To what extent did your understandings with Abu Mazen have the approval of Prime Ministers Yitzak Rabin and Shimon Peres?

They did not know about them. When the understandings became public, Rabin was dead and Peres wasn't too happy about them.

Which understandings was Shimon Peres unhappy about?

I don't know. I never discussed them with Shimon Peres.

Beilin/Eitan National Accord

Some Israeli commentators say that with the National Accord you 'were pulled rightwards' from the understandings you reached with Abu Mazen ...

The signed accord with Michael Eitan is much vaguer than the unsigned understandings with Abu Mazen. For example, in the Beilin/Eitan accord we do not say that the Temple Mount will be extra-territorial to Israel. It says there will be 'special arrangements' for the holy places in Jerusalem. It is left deliberately vague. One commentator described the understandings with Abu Mazen as the foot and the accord with Eitan as the shoe. I subscribe to this image.

But does the shoe fit the foot?

Yes. It is not always a comfortable fit. It pinches here and there, but eventually they fit. My role in both was to ensure that there was no contradiction between them.

This was achieved except for two points. The Likud MKs were against a Palestinian state but for an extended Palestinian autonomy in the West Bank and Gaza. They also demanded Israeli sovereignty over the Jordan Valley. These positions contradict the understandings with Abu Mazen. Our version is that there will be a Palestinian state and that Israel will not have sovereignty over the Jordan Valley.

What was the understanding reached with Abu Mazen over the Jordan Valley?

The Jordan Valley won't be under Israeli sovereignty. The settlements – like everywhere else in the West Bank – would be permitted to remain there and the Israeli army would be on the Jordan River.

Indefinitely?

We agreed that ten years after a permanent settlement is reached certain issues would be reviewed – the Israeli army's presence on the Jordan River is one of these issues.

Lebanon/Syria

You advocate Israel's unilateral withdrawal from south Lebanon. Is this withdrawal a fulfilment of UN resolution 425?

I believe Israel should fulfil this resolution. But I think we should also reach some informal understandings. I believe if we condition withdrawal on a peace agreement with Lebanon or Syria or both, we may be in south Lebanon for long time.

And I don't want to be there. I don't want to be a card in the hands of my enemies. I know the Syrians want us to stay in south Lebanon – its their pleasure, its not my pleasure. I think it is idiotic that we are playing into Syria's hands.

The informal understandings would be for Hizbollah to be disarmed and to establish a security fence once we redeploy our forces south of the international border with Lebanon. On the basis of these understandings, I believe we should withdraw. If, then, we are still being hit by Hizbollah or whoever else from Lebanon, we will act according to our national interests.

With whom would you reach these informal understandings?

With all the forces who play a role in south Lebanon.

Could be more specific?

No. I don't want to limit my scope. Had I been Israel's Prime Minister, I would have tried to speak to all the forces. I don't want to play the game of speaking to one but not the other, of boycotting this rather than that militia. I don't want to boycott anyone. All those willing to talk to me informally about Israel's withdrawal from south Lebanon would be welcome.

I don't think Hizbollah wants us to remain in south Lebanon. I think there are different interests between Syria and Hizbollah. I think the only common denominator is their hatred towards us, especially as long as we are in south Lebanon. I cannot be sure that once we leave the area this hatred will stop or that they won't try to act against us. But I am sure we can defend our land from within Israel rather than from without. I don't see any reason to remain in south Lebanon indefinitely.

If we could achieve withdrawal in the context of peace talks with Syria, of course I would prefer it. But I am pessimistic whether Assad wants peace with us.

The Syrians say they want negotiations to resume from the point they left off. This, they say, includes an understanding reached with Prime Minister Rabin that Israel would withdraw to the 4 June 1967 borders in exchange for agreements on normalisation and security. Is this a position you would accept to achieve peace with Syria?

No. I don't see how the Israeli government can be committed to anything that has not been signed. Why should Likud continue from the point left by us? The Syrians missed the boat. It had an Israeli Prime Minister who said that the extent of Israel's withdrawal on the Golan would be determined by the extent of the peace Syria wanted with us. Now Syria is coming to Likud and saying it wants to resume from the point we left off. How can Syria demand this? There is a new government in Israel, with its own views about the Golan Heights. I am not crazy about these views. But Likud is the legitimate government of Israel. If it wants to start talks with Syria from a new basis, it is permitted to do so.

I am anyway against any withdrawal to the 4 June lines. There is no justification for this Syrian demand. The only line is the international border. That was the line we negotiated with Egyptians, and that will be the line we negotiate with Lebanon and Syria. There is no better line than the international border. If it is illegal to conquer territory by force, then why is it permitted for Syria?

The 4 June line is not the international border. Again, were I Israel's Prime Minister, I would say to Syria, 'Please, let us end this game. You and I know the only border is the international one. You will have the Golan Heights, so let us see what we can agree regarding demilitarisation, security arrangements, normalisation, diplomatic relations. In other words, let us make peace.'

To reverse this, to start with these issues before addressing the question of borders is a mistake. But since Assad did not come when Rabin suggested everything, I doubt he will come when nothing is being suggested.

Are you saying Syria is not interested in regaining the Golan Heights?

I don't know. I am not a commentator. I've never met Assad. I've never met any of his people. I only understand what I see. And what I see is that when we were in power, we were ready to strike a deal, but Assad was not there.

If you were Prime Minister, would you be prepared to withdraw to the international border in exchange for a peace treaty with Syria?

Yes. Undoubtedly.

Jerusalem, March 1997; *Al-Ahram English Weekly*, March 1997

20

Believers in Blue Jeans: an Interview with Rabbi Aryeh Deri

The Sephardi List for Tradition (or Shas) is Israel's third largest political party and the most influential social movement amongst Israel's Sephardi community or Sephardim – Mizrahi or 'Eastern' Jews who emigrated from Arab and Islamic countries to Israel in the 1950s and 1960s.

Together with advocacy of religion and revival of the Sephardi Jewish tradition, Shas has taken a moderate stance toward the peace process and territorial compromise with the Palestinians. It was the only orthodox party to join Israel's 1992 Labour-led coalition and its spiritual leader, Rabbi Ovadia Yosef, has long granted Halachic covenant to the principle of land for peace.

Rabbi Aryeh Deri is Shas's General Secretary and, after Yosef, the movement's most powerful leader. He is viewed by many Israeli commentators as perhaps Israel's most influential politician, playing an indispensible role in the governments of Rabin and Netanyahu. He is certainly the most controversial. Currently on trial for corruption (both for his time as Israel's Interior Minister and for his role in the Bar-On affair), Deri was Israel's youngest ever cabinet minister at the age of 30. He is widely credited with masterminding Shas's rise from being a small haredi movement to a party at the very centre of Israeli politics, without which neither Labour nor Likud can govern.

In the interview, Deri talks about the origins of Shas, its attitude to Arab culture and Zionism, its views on the peace process and the Palestinians and, finally, on the distinction that should be drawn between the orthodxy of the Sephardim and that of the Ashkenazim or Jews of European descent.

Shas

What were the origins of Shas?

Since the establishment of the state, the haredi movement has been controlled by Ashkenazi Rabbis. Shas arose as a protest against this hegemony.

Shas started in 1983 as a list for municipal elections in Tiberias, Jerusalem and Bnei Brak. We had no idea we were initiating a new social movement based on the Torah. We won three seats each in the three municipalities. Then came the 1984 Knesset elections. Our original intention had been to join forces with the Agudat Yisreal [an association of mainly Ashkenazi haredim. ed.], but again there was pressure from the grassroots to stand as a separate Sephardi list. We had expected to have one or two members of Knesset (MKs) with Agudat Yisrael. In the end, we won four Knesset seats on our own.

In the early years, Shas concentrated on education. We worked in the development towns, the poor areas, the slum districts and started to build educational institutions there. The impact was incredible. It was consolidated when I was appointed a Director-General in the Ministry of Interior. I used the office to direct funds to educational institutes in areas neglected in the past. The money was used to build schools, Yeshivas and synagogues.

This was on the social level. Shas's political outlook emerged after I was made Minister of Interior. I became the link to the government for Rabbi Ovadia Yosef. Long before Shas was established, Ovadia Yosef was known for his dovish views regarding the territories. When Begin signed the peace treaty with Egypt, Ovadia Yosef went to Yamit [a settlement in the Sinai. ed.]. He told the people there that to stay in Yamit contradicted the Halacha. This outlook continued during my time at the Interior Ministry.

In 1990, Ovadia Yosef and I went to Egypt. In a speech before President Mubarak, Ovadia Yosef stated publically that life was of a higher value than land. Shas was at the forefront of the negotiations for the Madrid Conference between Israel and the US. So, from being a movement that concentrated on social and educational issues, we became a political movement. This filled a vacuum in the Sephardi community.

Some say Shas is a movement of ethnic grievance; others that it is a movement of religious pride. How would you define Shas?

Shas has never been an ethnic movement. Ethnicity alone doesn't work in Jewish politics; there must also be a political vision.

It is true that Shas is an exclusively Sephardi movement. Nor do I foresee Ashkenazi members being on our list anytime soon. But Shas does not worship ethnicity. What Shas is saying is that the Jewish people is made up of tribes and that the Sephardim are one of them. But the Sephardi community has been shunted aside ever since the foundation of the state. Shas's role is to look after the concerns of this community. I believe Shas is the only party in Israel with the credibility to do this. We are on the same level as the Sephardi community, speak their language and understand their needs. We have restored pride to this community. Through Shas, the Sephardim now have their own political and spiritual leaders, their own address. They have never had this before.

So I would define Shas as a Sephardi movement but with definite social, political and ideological views.

But what is your aim? A state based on the Halacha?

The first aim is to realise our potential. The Sephardim are a community with a high birth rate and a large number of people returning to religion. I believe this return to religion will continue. But, for Shas, this return does not mean a process where people leave their community, became isolated and start to study in black suits. This is what return to religion means for the Ashkenazi haredim. We want people to continue to wear blue jeans. For us, the return to religion means people living their normal lives while keeping their tradition, while lighting candles before the Saturday meal.

In this sense the Sephardim are like the Arabs. Both Abu Mazen and Ahmad Tibi [Palestinian leaders. ed.] are secular. But they swear to me that they fast during Ramadan. I doubt whether my friend, Haim Ramon [Labour Party MK. ed.] fasts even for Yom Kippur. We have no problem with the Sephardim who live secular lives as long as this doesn't mean their losing contact with religion and tradition. There has to be a bit of Judaism mixed in.

Politically, I believe Shas can achieve between 25 and 30 MKs, as long as we don't make a mess of things. But we don't seek to become Prime Minister or Defence or Foreign Minister. We seek influence in every sphere of life. We refuse to be sidelined or ghettoised. And, certainly, we want the state to be more Jewish.

There is currently a cultural war between Shas and parties like Meretz who embrace secularism and Western values. We are not opposed to modernity. We all want cars and computers; nobody wants a return to the well. But there is a difference between modernity and Western culture. And the problem with Western or European culture is its ideology. It has no respect for the family. It is permissive, 'free' in the sense of being irresponsible. It lives only for the present. It says make money and have fun. But these values lack meaning. We want people to live well, but also to have some meaning to their lives.

I believe the coming years will be crucial for Israel. If there were 60 MKs who demanded a state based on the Halacha, what would this mean? It means people want a real change. If this were to happen, believe me, we would look after the secular community better than it looks after itself.

Could you explain what you mean by 'a cultural war'?

I mean the war against secular Zionism – the ideology of Herzl and the Zionist Congress. This ideology wanted Israel to be a European, secular society. Secular Zionists didn't want Jewish religious people to live here. They didn't give us the choice to follow our own culture. On the contrary, they tried to force their culture on us. But the Sephardim messed up their plans. If it were not for the questions of peace, security and terrorism, the main conflict in Israel would be between the secular and the religious – a conflict that could become a war in the next few years.

So Shas is not a Zionist movement?

Secular Zionism always had a patronising attitude to the Sephardim. For me, a Zionist is someone who lives and suffers in Israel. It is someone who has his own culture, his own spiritual leadership. And Herzl is not my leader. Herzl is alien to me. His son converted to Christianity. For me, a Rabbi in Morocco is more important than Herzl. The only thing Herzl did was to create the idea of Zionism – this is his only achievement. I will not educate my children in Herzl or Nahman Bialik [Israel's 'national' poet. ed.] because both said things that go against our Torah and traditions. I have said this publicly and they (the secular Zionists) became very angry. But secular Zionism was carried on our shoulders; they tried to use us to create a 'new generation'. Shas arose to fight this phenomena.

In the future, I believe there will be a new Zionism. It will not be the Zionism that symbolises power and violence; the Zionism of being the strongest army in the region. I say power comes from God.

Shas and the Arab–Israeli Conflict

Do you see the Sephardim as part of Arab culture?

I and my colleagues feel closer to Arab culture than to Ashkenazi culture. I lived in Morocco until I was nine. My childhood was there. My colleagues were brought up in other Arab countries. Our friends were Muslims and Christians. In Morocco, we celebrated the religious holidays together. I drank the special drinks of Ramadan and we gave them *hametz* (non-Kosher food) during Passover. There was no war of cultures. They had Mohammed, we have our Prophets, but there was one God. There was no attempt to Islamise us or for us to Judaise them.

So I see the Sephardim as part of the peoples of the region, like the Arabs in Israel, Egyptians, Jordanians and Palestinians. We have no problem with them except the political conflict. And I hope this conflict will be solved through the peace process.

The conflict came with Zionism ...

Questions about the existence of Israel are not on the agenda today. The question now is what are the compromises Israel can make to solve the conflict. Everybody recognises the Palestinians are a people – maybe there are a few sick people on the right who don't. The majority see there is a Palestinian problem and a Jewish problem. The point is to resolve them and achieve coexistence. I don't want to go over old history.

Isn't there a contradiction between the views espoused by you and Rabbi Ovadia Yosef which are essentially dovish vis-à-vis the peace process and the views of your supporters which seem to be hostile to this process?

Yes. You are completely right. In Shas's early years, we were seen as Likud's shadow on political issues. Our only novelty was our concentration on religion and tradition. Even today I would say the majority of our supporters are right-wing. But you must remember that this was the generation that Begin in 1976 succeeded in mobilising against the Arabs.

It is the wisdom of Ovadia Yosef that has taken this right-wing constituency, which had tradionally voted for rightist parties, and brought it to Shas, a centre-left party. When it comes to the peace process, I would define Shas as a leftist party. The stance of Shas toward the peace process is becoming surer. And remember, without Shas's support, there would have been no Oslo agreement.

Despite this support, our constituency did not rise up against Ovadia Yosef. On the contrary, it grew. In the 1992 elections, we received 130,000 votes. In the 1996 elections, we received 260,000. A 100 per cent increase. What does this show? It shows that our constituency seeks a spiritual leadership and accepts the advice of this leadership. But change is a long process. It needs a lot of education. The younger generation being educated in our institutions is much more in tune with the politics of the Shas leadership. The older generation needs more work invested in it.

Were Shas to move to the left, do you fear you could lose this older generation of supporters?

No. We are growing, thank God. All of our supporters trust our leadership and our message. Our MKs meet regularly with Palestinian leaders without shame or fear.

But, given your comments about a 'cultural war', could Shas ever again sit in the same coalition as Meretz?

Meretz has two factions, one led by Yossi Sarid and the other by Dedi Zucker. Sarid is leading Meretz to a horrific extreme of anti-religious secularism. We will not sit with him. With Zucker's faction, we have a dialogue. It meets with Ovadia Yosef and we are seeking a common ground.

If a Labour government emerged with only Shas and Meretz in support, Shas would try to bring other parties into the coalition. We will not again form a government that is only Labour, Meretz and Shas. We would reach out to the Russian Party and the Third Way.

This is because Shas believes questions to do with the peace process require a wide national consensus. Labour wants to make peace but can't. Likud can make peace, but is unsure if it wants to. This is why we support the present coalition. Shas is encouraging Netanyahu to proceed with the peace process. If Peres had been in power and redeployed from Hebron, there would have been unrest from the settlers. With Likud in power, there was no unrest.

This is where we differ with Meretz, aside from our differences over religion. Meretz believed it could proceed with the peace process without the support of the Sephardim. It didn't understand that, without this support, Oslo was seen as an agreement of the Ashkenazim and the rich. Now Oslo is a reality for all sectors of Israeli society and not just the Ashkenazim. The Hebron agreement is durable because it carries Netanyahu's signature.

I think the last 18 months of a Likud government have not been a waste. Despite all the difficulties and problems, the period was historically very important, no less important than the years of Rabin and Peres. It has resulted in Oslo being an agreement owned by all Israelis.

Palestinians would say it has resulted in the destruction of the peace process?

I fear this could happen. But I believe the problems can be overcome. I am sure there will be an agreement.

Who does Shas regard as the better Jew – Peres or Netanyahu?

In the last elections, Shas did not tell its supporters which candidate to endorse for Prime Minister. They had a free vote. But it is no secret that Ovadia Yosef and his *hassidik* (religious students) voted for Peres. He said so openly. Ovadia Yosef respects Peres more than he respects Netanyahu. You can see this in the statements he has made since the elections.

Shas and the Palestinians

Would kind of final settlement do you envisage between Israel and the Palestinians?

This is very difficult to answer. It will be the result of negotiations. The only thing I would say is that I don't want to control a single Palestinian. I also believe the question of whether there will be a Palestinian state is now largely cosmetic. It would be wise for Israel to arrive at an understanding with the Palestinians on this matter. From my discussions with the Prime Minister, the negotiations over the further redeployment will be a lot tougher than over Palestinian statehood.

I believe we can reach an agreement with the Palestinians, but I don't know if it will be a comprehensive agreement. There is no doubt that some of the settlers will no longer live under Israeli sovereignty. They will either live under the Palestinian Authority or their settlements will be dismantled. Shas would not support dismantlement as long as the people who live in the settlements are prepared to live under the PA. If 20 families in Har Barkha (settlement) near Nablus choose to live under the PA – and the PA agrees to provide security for them – we would welcome this. Those settlers who wish to stay should be able to stay, and those who wish to leave, should leave. But it is a myth to believe that every settler will stay under Israeli control. Any person who believes this is deceiving himself and everybody else.

I foresee three main blocs of settlements remaining under Israeli sovereignty.

Which blocs?

You know which blocs [Ariel, Gush Ezion and the settlements surrounding Jerusalem. ed.]. We can find a solution to the settlements.

The real problem is Jerusalem. We will need to be very creative and wise about this problem, and agree a solution that will give respect to both sides. There is a wide consensus in Israel not to divide Jerusalem. No Israeli government could do this. But the Palestinians demand Jerusalem as their capital. And we will have to find an answer to this problem.

The other difficult issue is borders. We have a daily, routine conflict with the Palestinians. But Israel also faces threats from outside enemies. It cannot rely on pieces of paper when confronted with the threat from Iraq or Iran. We need secure borders as well as signed agreements.

As for the right of return, I really don't see a solution to this if it means all the Palestinian refugees returning. Israel is a small country with limited resources. But with goodwill and pragmatism on both sides compromises can be found. Each side will have to separate from things that are dear to him. Likud has to give up the idea of Eretz Israel and the Palestinians will have to give up the idea of returning to Haifa and Acre and of a complete withdrawal to the 1967 borders.

What is your opinion of the PA?

I have been positively impressed with the various PA officials I have met. Growing up in Israel, I was inculcated with images of Palestinians as terrorists and murderers. But now I meet Abu Mazen, Abed Rabbo, Dahlan and others and we have no problem discussing issues together.

The PA has a difficult task. Even a powerful authority would have difficulty governing Gaza. And the PA arrived with little experience in governance. It has to deal with the clash between high expectations and actual conditions. I read about corruption and internal problems inside the PA. I don't want to go into details, but it was clear to me there would always be irregularities. In the end, I am sure the PA will draw the right conclusions. The Palestinians are a people like us. We have problems we have to resolve. The Palestinians will do the same.

What is Shas's attitude to the Islamist movement?

I have very little knowledge about Hamas. But, as Interior Minister, I had to work with the Islamic movement in Israel because municipalities like Um el-Fahim and Kofa Kana were under their control. I had always been against the emergence of an Islamic movement in Israel. But, as Interior Minister, I had to have a dialogue with Islamic leaders like Shiekh Abdallah Darwish from Um el-Fahim. I refused to boycott them or work for their removal, although there were some people who wanted this, including some Arab MKs who viewed the Islamists as rivals.

In the end, I grew closer to the Arab and Druze municipalities, supported them and tried to correct some of the discrimination they suffered. I raised their concerns on the national level. Nobody denies this. With the Arab councils, I felt their word was their word, there was a sense of loyalty and a respect for religion. To be honest, as mayors, the Islamists were the best. They were dedicated to their communities, provided good services and had clean hands.

My only problem with Islamism is when it is used ideologically to justify political extremism, as a licence for terrorism against Jews. I believe the moment a religious leader uses a holy book, any holy book, to justify killing, he ceases to be a religious leader.

Shas and the Haredim

Is the haredi movement becoming more Zionist?

The Zionist project was realised with the establishment of the state. The war between Zionism and religious Jews as it was 50 years ago is now over. There are today no longer Zionists among the secular Jewish leadership, no longer an idealised Zionist leadership. Look at the Kibbutzim; today these are movements of money, selling land to set up shopping malls.

At the same time, the haredi community has grown substantially in recent years and has had to deal with modernity. It understands that this growth will not continue unless it is integrated into the life of the state. The haredim require jobs, training, political leaders, which require them to be part of the system. There are now only a few groups, like Natora Karta, who refuse any contact with the state. But this group is becoming extinct.

The Zionisation of the haredim is due to the fact that the Ashkenazi haredim have lost its leadership. When there are no clear, cystallised leaders among the haredim, the movement moves to the right. The Sephardi haredim have this leadership. This is why the National Religious Party (NRP) is so jealous of Ovadia Yosef and declared war on Shas, especially after we joined the Labour coalition in 1992. The NRP's main flag now are the settlements, its leadership has been taken over by the settlers and the street. The result is that the Ashkenazi haredim who follow the NRP have become more right-wing and nationalistic.

If, as you say, there is a clear difference between the Ashkenazi and Sephardi haredim, why is it that the latter still mimics the former in appearance and dress?

You must remember that Shas is only twelve years old. We were all brought up by the Ashkenazi haredi establishment. And, obviously, we have been influenced by this. The Ashkenazi Rabbis were our leaders; 'they looked after us'. The real question is how we will look in 20 years, when the generation Shas is now educating comes of age.

I agree there is imitation of the Ashkenazi haredim. In Morocco, there wasn't this hassidic separation from society. We had Rabbis and a Jewish community, with some members who were more religious and some who were less. But there was no segregation into 'religious' and 'non-religious' Jews. This segregation is the legacy of Europe, a product of the European Enlightenment. It was a segregation that preceded Zionism.

Yet, despite this forced assimilation, you cannot deny that Shas is different from the other haredi groups. Look at the behaviour of Rabbi Ovadia Yosef and our other Rabbis. He does not imitate the isolation and exclusivity of the Ashkenazi Rabbis, who focus only on religious study. He is directly involved in people's daily life and concerns. The Ashkenazi Rabbis are concerned with neither the world nor the state; they are concerned with their followers in Jerusalem or Brei Bnak. Ovadia Yosef meets members of the US Congress and with Palestinian leaders. An Ashkenazi Rabbi would view such meetings as unimportant.

Can Shas survive after Ovadia Yosef?

Thank God he is healthy and well and we hope we will live until he is 120. But, yes, there will be difficulties. Every generation has its own leaders, and leaders must change. This is life. You may as well ask me what will happen to the PA after Arafat or to Syria after Assad.

Shas's idea and vision is not the property of one man. They have evolved out of our people's needs. It is of course easier when there is a clear spiritual leadership. I don't think anyone can replace Ovadia Yosef. Maybe there will be a collective leadership, but for sure it will be a less powerful leadership. We will climb that hill when we come to it.

Jerusalem, December 1997

21

The Fire the Next Time? Palestinians in Lebanon

'1997 will be the year of surprises', said Munir Makdeh on New Year's Eve. Makdeh is a Palestinian from 'Ain Helweh refugee camp near Sidon which, with around 60,000 refugees, is the largest of the twelve remaining Palestinian refugee camps in Lebanon.

Makdeh is also the leader of Yassir Arafat's Fatah movement in 'Ain Helweh. In 1993, he threatened to kill the PLO leader for signing the Oslo accords with Israel, an agreement many of Lebanon's Palestinian refugees saw as the PLO's final abandonment of their right to return to their homes in what was, pre-1948, Mandate Palestine and is now Israel.

With his trim beard and empty gun holster, Makdeh and his followers are the legatees of Fatah's revolutionary era, when national liberation was a matter of armed struggle rather than negotiations. They rule 'Ain Helweh 'by force', says a camp resident. But the force is buoyed by popular discontent.

In November 1994 and June 1995, gun battles erupted between Makdeh's dissidents and Arafat loyalists in 'Ain Helweh, and Makdeh won. As for 'surprises', the first occurred on 6 January when the 175,000 Palestinians living in Lebanon's camps staged a one day general strike in protest at the deterioration of camp services run by the UN agency for Palestinian refugees, UNRWA (United Nations Relief and Works Agency). In 'Ain Helweh, Palestinian youths brandished rifles and lit burning tyres. It was a warning. 'This place will explode', says a camp resident. 'But the cause will not be Oslo or the right of return – it will be poverty.'

Towteen

Of all the estimated 3.1 million registered Palestinian refugees living in the occupied territories and the diaspora, the status of those in Lebanon is the most precarious. Once the bastion of the PLO, over the last 15 years Lebanon's Palestinians have suffered a series of near-mortal blows, testing their capacities of resistance and survival to the limit.

Following Israel's 1982 invasion, the PLO was forced to evacuate Lebanon, taking many of the camps' ablest leaders to Tunis and thence to the West Bank and Gaza. Between 1985 and 87, Lebanon's Shi'ite Amal movement (backed by Syria) attacked Palestinian refugee camps to prevent the PLO's political rehabilitation in Lebanon, causing the deaths of around 2,500 Palestinians and Lebanese and the estimated destruction of 60 per cent of the camps' infrastructure. The 1990/91 Gulf war resulted in a mass expulsion of Palestinians employed in Kuwait to Lebanon and, with them, the final drying up of all PLO-funded services, leaving an average unemployment rate in the camps of at least 40 per cent. Finally, the Oslo accords triggered a shift in aid priorities in UNRWA and international NGOs away from Lebanon and the diaspora in favour of the Palestinian 'self-rule' areas of Gaza and the West Bank.

The sum political impact of these defeats is expressed by a Palestinian woman from 'Ain Helwah. 'It's *towteen* they're cooking up for us. Next year they'll start implementing it', she says. '*Towteen*' is Arabic for implantation and, in Lebanon, means the Israeli/US-driven solution to the refugee problem where Palestinians outside of Palestine are given permanent residency in their countries of abode.

Getting Rid of the Palestinians

Polls show a solid 70 per cent of Palestinians in Lebanon against *towteen*, with most holding out for their right to return to Palestine as enshrined in UN resolution 194. Nor is the Lebanese government prepared to accept the permanent resettlement of Palestinian refugees on its turf. If there is one issue that unites all of Lebanon's confessional groups, it is opposition to *towteen* in particular and to the Palestinian presence in Lebanon in general. This is not just expressed in attitudes like that of Lebanon's Foreign Minister, Faris Buwayz, who, in April 1994, said Lebanon's ultimate goal was to 'rid itself' of all its Palestinian residents. It is written into Lebanese law.

Unlike refugees in Syria and Jordan, Palestinians in Lebanon are not allowed to work in their host economy. In the past, they got by working in the camps, for the PLO or, illegally, as cheap labour for whichever Lebanese employer would take them. But even this door is closing. The last decade has seen the Syrian migrant workforce in Lebanon swell to between 500,000 and one million, taking the menial jobs the Lebanese refuse but the Palestinians used to do.

But the gravest threat to the Palestinians is the Lebanese government's September 1995 decree forcing all resident Palestinians living or studying abroad to obtain visas to re-enter the country. Most Lebanese embassies since have simply refused to issue visas for Lebanon's Palestinians. The result, says Palestinian lawyer, Suheil Natour, is that 'almost 100,000 Palestinians have lost their residency rights in Lebanon in the last year', reducing the overall Palestinian population in the country from around 350,000 to 250,000. UNRWA officials say such figures are probably accurate.

Palestinians say the problem is compounded by their lack of any political representation in Lebanon. Angered by Arafat's acceptance of Oslo without winning from Israel at least the principle of their right to return, most Palestinians in Lebanon feel abandoned by the PLO and view the Palestinian Authority (PA) in the West Bank and Gaza as little more than an Israeli agent. But they also chide the PLO opposition for its lack of any credible alternative to Oslo. Nor does their secular nationalism square with Palestinian Islamist opposition groups like Hamas and Islamic Jihad.

A New Unity?

Is there any hope on the horizon? Two months ago, Makdeh's dissidents were reconciled with Arafat's main loyalist in Lebanon, the Fatah leader, Sultan Abu Anaim. This was followed by meetings between PLO executive members Farouk Qaddumi and Faisal Husseini and the leaderships of PLO's Popular and Democratic Fronts (PFLP/DFLP). Since then, say sources, Arafat has renewed some funding to the PLO's Red Crescent hospitals in Lebanon and to the families of Palestinian martyrs. This seems to have bought peace with the Fatah dissidents. 'The PLO leadership made a mistake with Oslo', says Makdeh today. 'But there is no longer a fight between us.'

But dissension remains, and not only over Oslo. For DFLP activists like Natour, the critical issue facing Palestinians in Lebanon is the struggle for civic rights. 'We don't seek the same rights as the Lebanese because we believe we will achieve our right of return', he says. 'But we want the right to work freely in the Lebanese private sector.'

To this end, the PF and DF have been lobbying for elections inside the camps to select Palestinian representatives authorised to negotiate with the Lebanese government. The pro-Syrian Palestinian factions of Saiqa and Abu Musa are opposed. 'They know they would lose if there were a straight electoral contest in the camps', says Natour. But, since Oslo, Fatah has also been against elections. 'I don't think

Arafat wants to negate the refugee question', says Natour. 'But he doesn't want it raised ahead of Oslo's final status negotiations.'

This stance, however, could be changing. Following the reconciliation in Fatah, elections were held for UNRWA's Palestinian staff association in Lebanon. Out of 82 positions, the PFLP emerged as the strongest faction with 16 seats. But Fatah came second with 15, suggesting a revival of Arafat's fortunes in the camps. Should Fatah decide to throw its weight behind the idea of refugee elections, 'things could move', says Natour.

For a community that has been bloodied by inter-Arab and intra-Palestinian feuds almost as much as by its resistance to Israel, national unity counts for a lot. It is a rapprochement Israel and the Lebanese government should also heed. It was the reunification of the PLO factions in 1987 that laid the political bases for the *intifada* in the occupied territories. And, as shown by the protests on 6 January (which enjoyed the support of all Palestinian factions, pro- and anti-Oslo alike), a new unity could spark a similar fire among the Palestinians in Lebanon.

'Ain Helweh, Sidon and Mar Elias, Beirut, January 1997;
News From Within, February 1997

22

The Meaning of Sheikh Yassin

To visit Sheikh Ahmad Yassin's home in Gaza is to understand the pull he has among Palestinians.

Driving over the bumpy, improvised roads that lead to his house in Gaza's impoverished Sabra district, the inescapable impression is of the enduring misery of Palestinian refugee life. Thousands live here for no other reason than this is where they landed up after being driven from their homes in Mandate Palestine during the 1948 war that delivered the state of Israel to the Jews and exile to the majority of Palestinians.

Yassin is one of them. Not for him the luxurious villas where now reside the many ministers and commanders of Yassir Arafat's Palestinian Authority (PA). His house has neither an armed guard nor a forbidding wall, but a welcome sign and a heap of wrecked cars that lie, in a sprawl, on the other side of the road. It is from such flotsam – human and material – that Yassin and his philosophy were forged.

Ever since he established the Mujamma Islami (the Islamic Centre) in Gaza in 1973, Yassin has acquired the mantle of 'spiritual leader' of Palestinan Islamism. A founder of the militant Hamas movement in 1988, he was twice imprisoned by the Israelis – once in 1984 on charges of weapons possession and again in 1989 for his alleged involvement in the kidnap and killing of two Israeli soldiers. In October last year, Israel was forced to release him after a botched Mossad assassination attempt on another Hamas leader, Khalid Mishal, in Amman. King Hussein demanded Yassin's freedom as the 'price' for maintaining diplomatic relations with the Jewish state. But an ulterior motive was the King's cognizance of the political and moral weight Yassin commands among Palestinians, in Jordan as in Gaza.

It is a weight that lies heavily on the Sheikh's ailing shoulders. A quadriplegic due to a sports accident in his teens, Yassin is wheeled into his home's modest reception room by two male youths. The slighest jar of the wheelchair causes him pain. He looks older and frailer than his 61 years. Yet – throughout our talk – he receives visitors seeking his counsel and reads communiqués held up before him by one or other of the youths. He also betrays a boyish sense of humour. On discovering that a new listening device has made his hearing worse, his severe features fold into a mischievous grin. 'So that it why the *shubab* [the youths] brought it to me. They don't want me to answer your questions.'

Treatment for a potentially deadly ear infection was the reason Israel and the PA permitted Yassin to leave Gaza in February this year. He made full use of the chance. Over the next four months, he was received regally in Saudi Arabia, Kuwait, Iran, Qatar, Abu Dhabi, Syria and Sudan (he was barred entry to Jordan, Lebanon and South Africa). He reportedly raised over $50 million for his movement and relayed to all and sundry that Jihad 'rather than negotiations' would liberate Palestine. The tour massively enhanced Yassin and Hamas's stature and, for precisely this reason, went down sourly with the PA and activists from Yassir Arafat's Fatah movement. Was that the intention?

'Everyone has an opinion about the tour', says Yassin. 'But it was not at the PA's expense. Nor was I opposing the PA. I spoke only of the Palestinian–Israeli confict. And my aim was to strengthen the Palestinians and the PA in that conflict.'

There is an element of waffle in such answers, but there are other elements too. Since he was freed from prison, Yassin has said many things. But his most insistent message has been that of Palestinian unity, 'because we are one people, with one cause and one future'. Among many Fatah leaders (including perhaps Arafat) there is the belief that Yassin represents the most pragmatic wing of Hamas, the only figure who could underwrite a 'proper relationship' between Hamas and the PA.

The debate is over the terms of that relationship. According to sources in Fatah, Arafat has two made demands of Yassin. One is that Hamas recognise the PA as the 'only' national authority in the self-rule areas. The second is that Hamas accept the stricture that, while there may be 'a plurality of opinions' among Palestinians, there cannot be 'a plurality of militias'. These are conditions Yassin and Hamas have found difficult to swallow, at least publicly.

On his return to Gaza last month, Yassin scotched all rumours that Hamas was about to join a reshuffled PA cabinet. The PA draws its legitimacy from the Oslo agreements which 'were and are a failure', he says. 'Since Hamas rejects these agreements, how could we join a cabinet that is obliged to implement them?'

On Hamas's armed actions against Israeli targets (including the suicide or, as he prefers, 'martyrdom' operations) Yassin is more ambiguous. 'Hamas will let the PA pursue the Oslo process without fighting it', he says. 'But Hamas reserves the right to resist the occupation.' He adds, however, 'there are two kinds of resistance'.

'First, there is the military struggle against the occupation and settlements. This is a struggle that will not be stopped. Second, there are military actions which are in response to Israeli attacks on our civilians. Hamas has long made it clear that it will stop attacking Israeli civilians once Israel stops attacking Palestinian civilians.'

The question is whether 'Israeli attacks' mean civilian killings or include policies such as the demolition of Palestinian homes, settlement construction and land confiscation.

'Of course these are attacks on Palestinian civilians', answers Yassin. 'But, for the moment, Hamas is not responding to them. In the future, it might. In the meantime', he adds with a withering glance, 'it would be wise for the world to pressure Israel to halt these kinds of attacks.'

How much authority Yassin commands over Hamas's military policy is a moot point. He is adamant it is not he, but Hamas's military arm, Izzadin el-Qassam, that determines the armed struggle 'according to its own plans and circumstances'.

Yet it remains a fact that there have been no military operations claimed by Hamas in either Israel or the occupied territories in the nine months since Yassin was released from prison. And there is speculation that an 'understanding' may have been reached in which Yassin has exerted his influence to maintain quiet on the military front to enable Arafat the chance (in the words of one Fatah leader) 'to achieve something from Oslo'.

The expectation of Yassin and Hamas is that Arafat will achieve nothing, especially with Binyamin Netanyahu in power. 'He doesn't even respect agreements he has signed', snorts Yassin, contemptuously. At that point, runs the argument, Arafat and Fatah will be forced to abandon the olive branch and go back to the gun. Yassin will welcome this. The moment 'the Palestinian leadership decides to resist the occupation and free the land, we would support it', he says. 'These are Hamas's aims and we are with anyone who shares them.'

With the Oslo process collapsing on all points such a scenario is hardly far-fetched. It is also redolent with warning. Should Oslo fail, it would convey to Palestinians that Yassin was right to reject it on the grounds that resistance is the only language Israel understands. For the Israelis, the message is simpler yet: peace now or Hamas later.

Gaza, July 1998
Independent on Sunday (South Africa), July 1998

23

Impossible Contradictions – Israel at 50

Sitting in his small study at Haifa University – perched on the summit of the Mount Carmel mountain range that dominates Haifa port and the Lower Galilee – Israeli historian Ilan Pappe muses on where Israel is at, 50 years on.

'I don't think we have Zionists in Israel any more', he says. 'What we have are neo-Zionists and post-Zionists, or rather Zionists who have yet to understand that the founding myths of Zionism are no longer functional.' These potential post-Zionists include political forces like Israel's leftist Meretz bloc, the Peace Now movement and Pappe's own party, the Democratic Front for Peace and Equality. The neo-Zionists are settler and other nationalist-religious groups who have gone back to Zionism and extracted from it a 'most extreme, most fanatical' essence.

'The neo-Zionists are Israel's new right', says Pappe. 'For them values like democracy and liberalism are dispensable. The only value that counts is the Jewish nation. If preserving this nation means another war with the Arabs, so be it. If it means occupying more Arab land, so be it. This is the ideology that assassinated Rabin – it knows no inhibitions.'

Pappe's taxonomy was illustrated on 30 April, Israel's Independence Day. While the Jewish state observed its 50th year, Palestinians observed a festival at Jebel Abu Ghneim in the 'closed' and occupied West Bank.

Settler and other rightist groups had called on their followers to gather there to 'lay a symbolic cornerstone' at the site of the Har Homa Jewish settlement, whose authorisation last year by Israel's Likud-led government caused the collapse of the Oslo peace process.

And gather they did. From morning to dusk, thousands streamed through what remains of the hill's pine forest and walked along the new dirt roads that now ring the mountain. On the crest of the hill, families laid out picnics amid the ruins of an ancient Arab fort. On a makeshift dias covered with Israeli flags, 'Jewish nationalist' rock music blared out while men and women danced themselves into a religious fervour.

Most of the estimated 10,000 who attended the festival were wearing black kippurs and, for the women, medium-length dresses, the emblem of Israel's pro-settler National Religious Party. But there was a considerable number in jeans and Nike T-shirts, draped in the blue and gold colours of the Likud Party's Betar youth movement. Whatever their affiliation, all were there to assert the sovereignty of Israel over the West Bank and effect, symbolically now but for the future actually, the demographic and territorial transformation of Jebel Abu Ghneim into Har Homa. They were – in Pappe's parlance – 'neo-Zionists'.

Those he hopes will become 'post-Zionists' were assembled at the foot of the hill. Around 300 Meretz and Peace Now supporters were staging a 'counter-demonstration' against the settlers' takeover of Jebel Abu Ghneim. To make up for their small numbers, the protestors tried to inflate a massive white dove. But it stubbornly refused to leave the ground. They then lined the road leading to the mountain, picketing each one who attended the festival. One women in a headscarf and pushing a pram raised her eyebrows in contempt. 'Why do you listen to them?', she asked, referring to Peace Now. 'They're a minority.' Given that those on the hill out-numbered those at its foot by around fifteen to one, the question needed an answer.

Why was the turnout of Israel's Peace Camp at Jebel Abu Ghneim so derisory? No one with any sense of proportion can dispute that groups like Peace Now are committed to peace and against settlements like Har Homa. But a clue to the left's current torpor in Israel was given in the slogans its followers took to Jebel Abu Ghneim. Amid the usual 'Har Homa = the end of peace' and 'Bibi [Netanyahu] is bad for everyone', one banner stood out. 'Har Homa is not Zionism', it read. For the Palestinians who lost their lands 50 years ago – and who live under Israeli occupation today – Har Homa has always been Zionism. And, for Israelis like Ilan Pappe, Har Homa is Zionism now.

'The Zionist left in Israel wants to square the circle', he says. 'It wants Israel to be a democratic state, but denies that it can be a state for all its citizens. It says that Jews – who do not live here – can be equal citizens of Israel, but Palestinians – who live or did live here – cannot. It pretends that Zionism has somehow had nothing to do with the oppression of Palestinians. These are impossible contradictions.'

Until they are resolved, suggests Pappe, the left is likely to stay marginal in Israeli society. Once they are resolved – and probably 'after further violent upheavals' – the left may not only be for peace but ready for it on the basis of a post-Zionist ideology. But this is for the long term. In the short term, the left will continue pumping up a dove that refuses to fly. And the right will have the mountain.

Haifa, April 1998; *Red Pepper*, May 1998

24

A Palestinian Refugee at 51

This week Palestinians are commemorating the 50th anniversary of the al-Nakba or the catastrophe of Israel's establishment as a state in 1948. For the four million or so Palestinians who are today refugees because of that event the catastrophe remains as poignant and bitter now as it was then. A Palestinian refugee from Gaza explains why.

Achmed Abdallah is a 51-year-old Palestinian refugee from Jabalyia camp in Gaza. We sit in the little yard in front of his shelter. There are two trees in the yard, hung with his family's washing. Here is his story:

> I was born in a village called Khaliyat, eight miles north-east of Jabalyia. There were 300 people in the village. It was a quiet, close-knit community. My mother still sings the songs my father sang to celebrate the harvest. My father died in 1947, when I was nine months old.
>
> I don't know the exact date when the Jewish troops attacked the village. We had no notion of Israelis at that time – there were only Jews and Arabs. They surrounded the village on three sides, leaving the west free. The people fled. This was after Deir Yassin, so people were afraid there would be another massacre.
>
> During our flight, a Jewish fighter threw a bomb at us. It killed my two brothers and five sisters. My mother and I were the only survivors. I was the youngest. I had been saved by my mother placing me under her chest. To this day, her hand, arm and shoulder are covered in scars. She remembers standing up and calling out to her sons and daughters to help her. Then she saw their bodies, covered in blood.
>
> The news spread and my uncles came looking for us. They put my mother on a donkey to an Egyptian military hospital in Magdal [Ashkelon]. They assumed I was dead. They dug two graves at a holy shrine near the village – one for the boys and one for the girls. Someone touched me on the legs, where I had been hit. I cried out and they saw I was alive. Then they were attacked again. They fled. I was left in a field.

The next morning an old woman from the village passed by the field. She took me to my uncles. All the people from the villages were trying to reach the seashore, because this was the only route to Gaza. Thousands flooded into Gaza City. But we had no relatives there. The village of Khaliyat gathered in one field and slept under the grape vines. This was my first home in Gaza.

For the next few years, Achmed and his mother lived 'an animal existence'. His mother earned money by picking and selling animal manure from the fields. In the early 1950s – once UNRWA (the UN agency reponsible for providing welfare to Palestinian refugees) was established – they were provided with a tent. In 1954, they were one of the first families to move to Jabalyia camp. 'It was a one room shelter – nine metres square', says Achmed. 'It served as our living room, bedroom, bathroom and kitchen. This was my third home in Gaza.'

Despite such hardship, Achmed was a good student. In 1967, he graduated and took a teaching training course at an UNRWA centre in Ramallah. He eventually landed a job as an UNRWA English teacher in Gaza. He remembers his first pay packet.

I danced all the way home, clutching the money in my hand and threw it before my mother. 'Mother!' I said, 'Be proud!' But she didn't want the money. She said, 'Achmed, I want the first fruit from the tree in my village. I want my children back.' I understood what she meant. It was time for me to get married.

Thirty-one years on, Achmed has a wife and three sons and five daughters. 'I gave them different names to my dead brothers and sisters', he says. 'But my mother calls them the same names. So Munif, my eldest son, is Mohammed, Mohammed is Ahmad, Mahmoud is Achmed, Manar, Fatma and so on.'

Achmed likens his mother to the character in Maxim Gorky's novel, *The Mother*. If that figure personified the struggle of the poor, his mother embodies the cycle of loss and regeneration of the Palestinians. She also expresses every refugee's dream of the future. 'She has a treasure', says Achmed. 'Every night she places a special chest beneath her pillow. Inside it is a strip of cloth from my father's *galabiya* and the title deeds to his land in the village. She always says to me, "Achmed, one day you will need these. Never give them to anyone and never sell them to anyone."'

Achmed sees his own life contained within other cycles of hope and disillusion. He remembers the enthusiasm with which the Palestinians in Gaza greeted Gamal Abdul Nasser's revolution in Egypt and, through it, the promise of the liberation of Palestine through the unity of the Arab nation. After the 'devastation' of the 1967 defeat, he identified with the PLO and its advocacy of armed struggle as the 'only way' to recover Palestine. The *intifada* (which erupted outside his door in 1987) he saw as a 'message' to the world that Palestinians were ready to accept a two-state solution on condition that Israel withdrew from the West Bank and Gaza. And, like most refugees, he is utterly scathing about the Oslo accords which brought the Palestinian Authority to Gaza and the uprising to an end.

> I think the period of PLO nationalism faded with Oslo. The PLO decided to put aside the gun and make the strategic choice for peace when it had nothing in its hands. But this means it has no way to pressure Israel in the negotiations. Israel can say, 'Accept what we are offering or else'. But it is offering us nothing. Maybe the authority can accept this. But we will not accept it.

After such a life, what forgiveness? Achmed is surprisingly forgiving. 'Even though I lost my home and my family at the hands of the Israelis, I don't hate them', he says. He explains his acceptance of Israel as partly due to his own personal loss. 'Anyone who has burned by the fire of dispossession would not wish to inflict it on another', he says. He also believes there is 'something in us as Arabs' that cannot view another people eternally as the enemy. But, above all, it is the experience of being a refugee that enhances his need for reconciliation with those who forced this condition on him.

> A refugee is never really treated as human being. If I want to travel to Israel and visit the site of my village, I can't. I have no passport. For refugees, the basic demand is to be allowed to live as others live. Since this is my demand, we must let others live, including the Israelis. And we can live together, either in two states or, as I would prefer, in one.

But such forgiveness should not be mistaken for surrender. Whatever the eventual solution – and however long it takes – Achmed insists it must include the right to return to his village. 'My father owned 100 dunams of land in Khaliyat', he says. 'And, for the sake of peace, I am prepared to give up 99 of them. But I must have one dunam – so that I can build a house on the land where my mother lived, my brothers and sisters were born and my father is buried.'

Jabalyia, April 1998

References

Chapter 2: What Kind of Nation? The Rise of Hamas in the Occupied Territories

1. Hamas is not the only manifestation of political Islam in the occupied territories. An important, catalyst role has been played by Islamic Jihad, particularly in the years preceding the *intifada* in 1987. For analyses of Islamic Jihad, including its continuities and discontinuities with Hamas, see Jean-Francois Legrain, 'The Islamic Movement and the intifada' in *Intifada: Palestine at the crossroads*, ed. Jamal R. Nasser and Roger Heacock (Birzeit University & Praeger Publishers, 1991) pp. 175–91; and Ziad Abu Amr, *Islamic fundamentalism in the West Bank and Gaza* (Indiana University Press 1994).

2. Between February and May 1993, 1,522 Palestinians were injured and 67 killed in the Gaza Strip alone, including 29 in May, making it the bloodiest month of the uprising. For an account of the unprecedented scale of Israeli repression, see my 'Why Gaza says yes, mostly' in this volume.

3. Islamists claim that Hamas was founded in Gaza on 8 December 1987, the very eve of the uprising. The first leaflet signed by the Islamic Resistance Movement, however, was issued on 11 February 1988. See Jean-Francois Legrain, 'The Islamic Movement'.

4. Before the Israeli occupation in 1967, the MB in Gaza was a branch of the Egyptian MB, and in the West Bank, of the Jordanian MB. In the mid-1970s the MB was reorganised, with Gaza and West Bank branches forming one body with the Jordanian MB. But, as Ziad Abu Amr points out, 'reliance on external [Jordanian] guidance did not mean complete compliance or coincidence of views. The MB believed that each Islamic movement must enjoy some freedom in its own country in order to meet its own needs and to address its peculiar circumstances.' See his *Islamic fundamentalism*, pp. 10–11.

5. Ibid., pp. 15–17.

6. Quoted in *A special report on religious fundamentalism* (Damascus, Palestine Studies Centre, August 1988).

7. The hesitation was due to the MB's, and especially Yassin's, doubts as to the durability of the uprising. See Abu Amr, *Islamic fundamentalism*, pp. 66–8.

8. The sacriligious nature of any endorsement of territorial nationalism was eloquently expressed by a West Bank Muslim Brother, Sabri Abu Diab, in the early 1980s. 'The land ... is either a land of atheism or of Islam; there is no such thing as Arab, Palestinian or Jewish land ... Land cannot be considered holy, because holiness is only characteristic of Allah, so how can we sanctify and even worship a very small geographical area [Palestine] rather than Allah, as the so-called nationalists do?' Quoted in Abdel Kareem Yaseen, *The Islamic Resistance Movement in Palestine (Hamas)* (Cairo, Sina Publications, 1990), pp. 32–3.

9. 'The PLO', commented Hamas leader Khalil Koka acidly in 1988, 'is the sole legitimate representative of its constituent organisations.' Quoted in Ze'ev Schiff and Ehud Ya'ari, *Intifada: the Palestinian Uprising – Israel's third front* (New York, Simon and Schuster, 1990), p. 235.

10. A popular wall slogan of the time read, 'Hamas considers the unveiled to be collaborators of a kind.'

11. See Rema Hammami, 'Women, the hijab and the intifada', *Middle East Report*, May–August 1990.

12. Schiff and Ya'ari, *Intifada*, p. 234.

13. The purpose of these meetings was to politically undermine the PLO's claim to being sole legitimate representative of the Palestinian people. On Israel's ongoing liaison with the MB and Hamas, both prior to the uprising and during it, see Mouin Rabbani, 'Israel and the Palestinian fundamentalists', *Middle East International*, 18 November 1994.

14. This was the first acknowledged operation by Hamas's military wing, Izzadin el-Qassim. Israel's outlawing of Hamas followed the arrest of Yassin who, until then (May 1989), had been left largely unmolested by Israel's security forces during the intifada. See Lisa Taraki, 'The Islamic Resistance Movement in the Palestinian uprising', in Zachery Lockman and Joel Beinin, eds, *Intifada: the Palestinian uprising against Israeli occupation* (London, I.B. Tauris, 1989), pp. 171–82.

15. The Israeli occupation authorities thus misread Islamism as a 'traditional' political structure rather than an 'ideological' (i.e. nationalist/modernist) one. See Rema Hammami and Islah Jad, 'Women and fundamentalist movements', *News from Within*, October–November 1992.

16. 'The PLO is never directly attacked by the Islamic Resistance Movement; never quoted, it does not exist', says Jean-Francois Legrain of Hamas in this period. See his 'The Islamic Movement'.

17. Hamas, of course, was not alone in this assessment. Its public defiance of the PLO leadership worked to aggravate dissensions within the PLO.

18. In a meeting with Hamas representatives in Khartoum in 1992, Arafat said that were he to concede to their demands he would have to resign as PLO Chairman. See Danny Rubinstein, *The Mystery of Arafat* (Steerforth Press, 1995), p. 131.

19. Quoted in Jean-Francois Legrain, 'A defining moment: Palestinian Islamic fundamentalism' in James Piscatori, ed., *Islamic fundamentalism and the Gulf crisis*: The Fundamentalism Project (American Academy of Arts and Sciences, USA, 1991), pp. 70–88.

20. The specific charge was Yassin's involvement in the 1989 kidnapping and assassination of two Israeli soldiers. See note 14 above.

21. This was also the conclusion drawn by Hamas's leadership in the occupied territories. 'I am certain that the Islamic Movement is not interested in having any conflicts with Fatah. I'll go even further ... the Islamic Movement will lose in any confrontation', said Hamas leader Aziz Rantisi immediately after the July clashes.

22. For a critique of this degeneration of the *intifada*, see Ghazi Abu Jiab's articles, 'The killing of collaborators' and 'Reflections on the present state of the *intifada*: achievements and failures', *News from Within*, July 1992.

23. Jerusalem Media and Communications Centre: opinion poll (Jerusalem, January 1993).

24. 'Although the Islamic movement rejects the DOP, it has no interest in defeating it by force. It sees its role as one of trying convince Palestinians of the agreements's shortcomings, and of dealing with its negative aspects on both the Arab and Islamic levels. It does not seek confrontation with the transitional [Palestinian] authority, because confrontation will not promote these objectives', says Islamist intellectual Bassam Jarrar. See my interview with him, 'The Islamist Movement and the Palestinian Authority', *Middle East Report*, July–August 1994.

25. Quoted in Andrew Gowers and Tony Walker, *Arafat: the Biography* (Virgin, 1994), p. 129.

26. Israel Shahak, 'Hamas and Arafat: the balance of power', *Middle East International*, 4 February 1994.

27. 'Revived' because Hamas's first attacks on Israeli civilian targets came after the Al-Aqsa mosque massacre in Jerusalem in 1990, when Israeli Border Police shot dead 18 Palestinians. This 'war of the knives' consisted of random stabbings by isolated individuals. The suicide/martyrdom missions in the wake of the Hebron massacre were altogether more planned, professional and deadly.

28. Such attacks on civilian targets inside the Green Line assigned what Jean-Francois Legrain has called a 'new geography' to the Palestinian/Israeli struggle. They undermined a tacit consensus, held by all the PLO factions since around the mid-1970s, that military operations inside Israel and the occupied territories should be confined to military targets. See Jean-Francois Legrain, 'Hamas, legitimate heir of Palestinian nationalism?', *Political Islam in the Middle East* (Washington, United States Institute of Peace, March, 1994). Also, Lamis Andoni, 'Palestinian opposition dominated by the right', *Middle East International*, 2 December 1994.

29. Bassam Jarrar, 'The Islamist Movement'.

30. In June 1995, an army spokesperson confirmed that 3,215 Palestinians had been arrested in the preceding seven months, 'most of them members of Islamic groups'.

31. See Ehud Ya'ari, 'Can Arafat govern?' *Jerusalem Report*, 13 January 1994.

32. *Ha'aretz*, 21 December 1993.

33. See my 'The PLO opposition: rebels without a constituency', *Middle East International*, 7 October 1994.

34. Hamas's share of the vote at Birzeit was virtually the same as, the previous year. It achieved victory through its unprecedented alliance with the Fronts.

35. Interview with Yassin in Yizhar Be'er and Saleh Abdl Jawad in *Collaborators in the occupied territories: human rights abuses and violations*, (B'tselem, Jerusalem, January 1994) pp. 219–28.

36. *An-Nahar*, 18 May 1994.

37. Bassam Jarrar, 'The Islamist Movement'.

38. Quoted in Graham Usher, 'Hamas' shifting fortunes', *Middle East International*, 24 September 1993.

39. Ibid.

40. *Al-Wasat*, London, 1 November 1993.

41. *An-Nahar*, Jerusalem, 10 January 1994.

42. Bassam Jarrar, 'The Islamist Movement'.

43. In such polls Hamas-backed slates consistently score between 35 and 45 per cent of the vote. This should be compared with national opinion polls which show Hamas with 12–14 per cent support compared to Fatah's 40–49 per cent.

44. Bassam Jarrar, 'The Islamist Movement'.

45. This was not the first meeting between the army and Hamas representatives after Oslo. In December 1993, Almog met with Hamas's leaders inside Israeli prisons. Initially denied by Hamas, these meetings were subsequently confirmed by Zahar, who had 'no objection to such meetings'.

46. These include, of course, the PLO.

47. Bassam Jarrar, 'The Islamist Movement'.

48. Rema Hammami and Islah Jad, 'Women and fundamentalist movements'.

49. Bassam Jarrar, 'The Islamist Movement'.

50. A recent survey of social attitudes among Palestinians in the occupied territories revealed a consistently more religious consciousness on the part of women aged 15–19 than women aged 20–29. See Marianne Heiberg and Geir Ovensen, *Palestinian society: a survey of living conditions* (FAFO, 1993).

51. The change in emphasis can be gauged in Hamas's shifting policy towards Palestinian collaborators. Prior to 1989, Hamas's actions against suspected collaborators were determined by its Majad unit, the MB's 'intelligence' wing established by Yassin in 1986 to 'collect information about suspected security and morality collaborators' (e.g. those who 'poison the soul of society by disseminating filth and vices, such as licentiousness, drug and alcohol trafficking, distribution of pornographic films' etc). Between the start of the *intifada* and 1989 – when Yassin and many of Majad cadres were arrested – Hamas killed around ten collaborators, mostly of the 'moral' variety. After this, collaborator policy fell to the Izzadin el-Qassam cells, 'young activists with an extremely hard-line approach to collaborators'. The impact was dramatic. Between 1989 and the end of 1993, Hamas killed 150 suspected collaborators, most for allegedly security or nationalist offences (such as working for the GSS) rather than moral offences. See Yizhar Be'er and Salah Abdel Jawwad, '*Collaborators in the occupied territories*', p. 107 and pp. 176–80.

52. Imad Akel was a leader of Izzadin el-Qassim in Gaza killed by the army in November 1993. He had been 'wanted' for three years and was responsible, say the army, for killing eleven Israelis and collaborators. His assassination led to widespread protests up and down the Strip.

53. I owe the phrase to Amira Hess. See her 'What if an Israeli Jew I knew had been in Hadera?', *Ha'aretz*, 26 April 1994.

54. I owe this conceptualisation of Hamas as an 'invented tradition' to Rema Hammami. See her 'Women, the hijab and the intifada'. On the general concept, see Eric Hobsbawn and Terence Ranger, *The Invention of Tradition* (Cambridge University Press, 1983).

55. The Marxist factions in the PLO (PFLP, DFLP, Fida and the People's – formerly Communist – Party) are organised on broadly democratic centralist lines. Fatah is more loosely organised around clan-like as well as political structures based on one or more local leaders. The ultimate source of authority lies less in the formal decision-making structures of the organisation than in the political and economic dispensations of the leaders and, of course, leader (i.e. Yassir Arafat).

56. For Bassam Jarrar, *hodna* cannot be translated as a peace treaty, since this assumes some sort of recognition of the enemy. Rather, it is a temporary cessation of hostilities with the enemy until power once more resides with the forces of Islam. The cessation may last for months, years or even centuries.

57. If anything, it marks a bow to nationalist orthodoxy, particularly the 'theory of stages' formulated by the PLO in the 1970s, where a 'national authority' could be established in an area of liberated territory as a prelude to the recovery of Palestine as a whole.

58. Khalid Amayreh, 'Hamas debates its next move', *Middle East International*, 27 May 1994.

59. Quoted in Yossi Torfstein, 'Despite the sword', *Ha'aretz*, 26 April 1994.

60. Bassam Jarrar, 'The Islamist Movement'.

61. One Islamist – who spoke on condition of anonymity – summed up the pragmatists' position (and dilemma) thus: 'We want to give the PA a chance to realise that Israel is not serious about Oslo. We will demonstrate through unilateral actions – such as a temporary ceasefire agreement – that we are not responsible for Israel's procrastination. But the PA must understand that we, too, have a constituency: many of our younger cadres are pressing for physical retaliation. If the PA doesn't allow the moderates to operate, then the extremists will prevail and move to underground forms of struggle.'

62. For example, on 18 November 1994 confrontations between Palestinian demonstrators and PA security forces in Gaza left 13 dead and over 200 injured, the highest daily toll of fatalities in Gaza in 27 years of occupation. See my 'Black Friday and its aftermath', *Middle East International*, 2 December 1994.

    These events revealed dissensions within Hamas not only between its younger, more militant cadres and its older, more established leadership in Gaza; but also between the 'inside' Gaza leadership, who generally counselled conciliation in the wake of 'Black Friday', and outside Hamas leaders such as Ibrahim Ghoshah in Jordan and Musa Abu Marzuq in Syria, who urged reprisals. Hamas is thus starting to mirror those same generational and geographical divisions that have plagued the PLO leadership.

63. Quoted in *Jerusalem Post*, 29 October 1994.

64. Quoted in Graham Usher, 'Hamas after the Tel Aviv bombing', *Middle East International*, 4 November 1994.

65. Ibid.

66. Lamis Andoni, 'Islamist group signals shift in strategy', *Christian Science Monitor*, 13 September 1994.

67. See the comments of the Palestinian secularist, George Giacaman. 'The opposition will be unable to stay alive except under a PA that

guarantees freedom of association and political activity, defends civil liberties, allows public decision making and governs by rule of law instead of the random choice of an individual or party. The pillar of Palestinian civil society is going to be the presence of opposition parties.'

68. See my 'Women, Islam and the law in Palestine', *Middle East International*, 23 September 1994.
69. One that often stands in marked contrast to the PLO's institutions.
70. Islamist precepts for the economy veer between such wholly unoriginal remedies as social-democratic market interventionism or neo-liberal scenarios tempered by welfarist (*zakat*) provisions. As for political and social reform, this is reduced to an ultimately coercive advocacy of 'virtuous' (as defined by Islamists) personal behaviour. See Oliver Roy, *The failure of Political Islam* (London, I.B. Tauris 1994).
71. In a statement issued by Izzadin el-Qassam on 18 April 1994 Jews are described as 'God's enemy'.
72. Jamil Hilal, 'PLO institutions: the challenge ahead', *Journal of Palestine Studies*, Autumn 1993.
73. Ibid.
74. See Gilles Kepel, *The Prophet and the Pharoah: Muslim Extremism in Egypt* (al-Saqi Books, London, 1985), pp. 223–6.
75. A slogan in Gaza daubed on walls after the Hebron massacre.

Chapter 4: Palestine: the Economic Fist in the Political Glove

1. 'Border conflict', *Ha'aretz*, 16 December 1993.
2. Quoted in *Ha'aretz*, 15 December 1993.
3. 'Peres: Israel, PLO agree on open market', *Jerusalem Post*, 17 December 1993.
4. 'The breakthrough: waiting for the word "withdraw"', *Jerusalem Post*, 3 September 1993.
5. Ibid.
6. Mark Taylor, Research Officer, UNRWA, Gaza Strip. Interview with author.
7. Mouin Rabbani, 'Gaza-Jericho first: the Palestinian debate', *Middle East International*, 24 September 1993.
8. Interview with author. All quotations from Abd al-Shafi are from an interview I held with him in October 1993. The full text is published in *Middle East Report*, January–February 1994.
9. 'Investing in peace', *Jerusalem Post*, 14 May 1993. The reports referred to are Sadan's *A policy for immediate economic-industrial development in the Gaza Strip* (Ben-Ezra Consultants, August 1991)

and *Durable employment for the refugee-populated region of Gaza* (April 1993).

10. According to Edward Said, 'over 80 per cent of the West Bank and Gaza economy is dependent on Israel'. See his 'The morning after', *London Review of Books*, 21 October 1993.

11. Adel Samara, 'Israel swallowing the economy of Palestinian cantons', *News from Within*, 5 October 1993.

12. Hisham Shawa, 'Letter to the Arab League', *al-Quds*, 6 January 1994.

13. Ezra Sadan, *A policy for economic-industrial development*.

14. 'Peres: Israel, PLO agree on an open market'.

15. For a theoretical analysis of the role of 'industrial parks' in the 'new imperialism', see A. Sivanandan, 'New circuits of imperialism' in *Communities of Resistance: writings on black struggles for socialism* (Verso, London, 1990).

16. 'PLO wary of Israel's economic plans', *Jerusalem Post*, 23 September 1993.

17. Asher Davidi, 'Israel's economy strategy for Palestinian independence', *Middle East Report*, September–October 1993.

18. Ibid.

19. Ibid.

20. Edward Said, 'The morning after'.

21. For the political background to Israel's closure of the occupied territories, see my 'Why Gaza says yes mostly' in this volume.

22. Mark Taylor, interview.

23. Adel Samara, 'Israel swallowing the economy of the Palestinian cantons'.

24. Edward Said, 'The morning after'.

Chapter 7: The Policies of Internal Security: the PA's New Intelligence Services

1. *The Interim Agreement* (Israeli Press Office, 21 September 1995).

2. Specifically UN Security Council Resolutions 242 and 338 which emphasised 'the inadmissibility of the acquisition of territory by war' and called for 'the withdrawal of Israeli armed forces from territories occupied in the recent [1967] conflict'. On the abandonment of international legality entailed by Oslo, see Naseer Aruri, 'Challenges facing Palestinian society', *Middle East International*, 25 August 1995.

3. Under Oslo II, the PA has agreed to protect Israeli citizens within Israel's pre-1967 borders as well as 'the personal security of its citizens in the West Bank'.

4. Israel's massive infrastructural investment (see note 7 below) to assure security during the interim period has led some observers to

conclude that the ultimate shape of the Palestinian entity will not be dissimilar to that foreshadowed in Oslo II. As for the pace of redeployment, the six-month intervals established in the agreement are conditional on the PA protecting Israel's 'security interests'. See *The Interim Agreement*, pp. 2–4.

5. For a 'tactical' interpretation, see the interview with Arafat published by *an-Nahar*, 19 September 1995. For a 'strategic' interpretation, see Edward Said, 'The Mirage of Peace', *The Nation*, 16 October 1995.

6. *The Interim Agreement* – Main Points, p. 5.

7. To implement redeployment, Israel is currently establishing 62 new military installations and constructing 116 kilometres of new settler-only bypass roads in the West Bank.

8. The phrase is Khalil Shikaki's, Policy Director of the Centre of Palestinian Research and Studies, Nablus. See his comments in Naomi Weinberger, 'The Palestinian national security debate', *Journal of Palestine Studies*, Spring 1995, p. 18.

9. Ibid.

10. *Declaration of Principles on Interim Self-Governing Arrangements* (Jerusalem Media & Communication Centre, November 1994, p. 5.

11. Peace Watch, *Survey of the six Palestinian Security Forces, totalling 5,000 men, which currently operate in Jericho and the West Bank (Background paper*, 17 July 1995, p. 4.

12. There are currently PSF offices in Ramallah, Hebron, Nablus, Bethlehem, Tulkarem, Jenin and a-Ram.

13. Quoted in Graham Usher, *Palestine in Crisis: the struggle for peace and political independence after Oslo* (Pluto Press, 1995), p. 71.

14. Interview with al-Haq lawyer, Khalid Bitrawi, September 1995.

15. Ibid. See also the interview with Rajoub in *al-Quds*, 2 February 1995, in which he states the PSF is the 'practical expression of Fatah since all its officers and personnel are Fatah members ...'.

16. See B'tselem, *Neither Law nor Justice: extra-judicial punishment, abduction, unlawful arrest, and torture of Palestinian residents of the West Bank by the Palestinian Preventive Security Service* (Jerusalem, August 1995); Amnesty International, *Trial at Midnight: secret, summary, unfair trials in Gaza* (June 1995); and numerous press statements issued in the last year by *al-Haq* and the Gaza Centre for Rights and Law, especially the latter's *Mass arrest campaign in the Gaza Strip* (9 February 1995) and *Appeal to Chairman Arafat to reverse the decree establishing a state security court* (12 February 1995).

17. On the law and order vacuum created by the intifada, see Yizhar Be'er and Salah Abdel Jawad, *Collaborators in the occupied territories: human rights abuses and violations* (B'tselem, Jerusalem, 1994), pp. 29–31.

18. For examples of such cases, see B'tselem, *Neither Law nor Justice*, pp. 13–14.

19. For an example of an alleged collaborator being 'turned', see the case of Barakat Mohammed Jarar in Steve Roden and Bill Hutman, 'Order in Jericho', *Jerusalem Post Magazine*, 19 May 1995.

20. Despite their political differences, members of both the PLO and Islamist opposition to Oslo tend to view Rajoub and Dahlan as 'authentic nationalists'. On the differing assessments Hamas has of 'Fatah of the inside' and 'Fatah of the national authority', see the interview with Mahmoud Zahar, 'Hamas: waiting for secular nationalism to self-destruct,' *Journal of Palestine Studies*, Spring 1995, pp. 81–9.

21. Steve Roden and Bill Hutman, 'Order in Jericho'.

22. Israeli journalist, Ehud Ya'ari, summarised the IDF and GSS's 'understanding' of the Rome meeting in the following way. 'Fatah-armed bands whose members were wanted by the Israeli security services, like the Hawks, will have special tasks. They will be charged with putting down any sign of opposition [to Oslo]; the intent is for them to administer show-punishments at the earliest possible stage, aimed at creating proper respect for the new regime.' See his 'Can Arafat Govern?', *Jerusalem Report*, 13 January 1994.

23. See *Ha'aretz, Yediot Aharonot* and *Mariv*, 19 September 1994.

24. Steve Roden and Bill Hutman, 'Order in Jericho'. Palestinian sources also stated that PSF/IDF collusion took place during the Wachshon imbroglio. This was certainly the view of Hamas, who issued a statement at the time warning the PA to 'cease supplying information ... on our *mujahedin* [holy fighters] ... to the Zionist intelligence and occupation authorities.' See 'What kind of nation? Chapter 2 in this volume.

25. Graham Usher, 'Oslo 2 – frenzied efforts falter', *Middle East International*, 22 September 1995.

26. Ibid.

27. Rabin's statement to the Knesset, 30 August 1993.

28. *Ha'aretz, Yediot Aharonot*, 7 September 1993.

29. Ehud Ya'ari, 'Can Arafat Govern?'

30. For accounts of these often bloody inter-agency clashes see 'Presidential Guard Killed', *Palestine Report* (Jerusalem Media and Communications Centre, 4 September 1994) and Khalid Amayreh's 'Fatah's House Divided', *Middle East International*, 14 April 1995.

31. Shback was a leader of the Fatah Hawks in Gaza, and Samhandana was for a brief period head of the PLO's Gaza office post-Oslo but prior to the arrival of the PA.

32. In September 1995, a major gun battle over this issue erupted in Gaza between Samhandana's Force 17 units and Jabali's Gaza City civil police. See Graham Usher, 'Oslo 2 – frenzied efforts falter'.

33. Hamas is also easily the largest political force in the occupied territories after Fatah, with polls showing Hamas receiving a consistent 15 per cent level of support as against Fatah's 40–45 per cent support. See the regular surveys published by the Centre of Palestine Research and Studies, Nablus.
34. Graham Usher, 'What kind of nation?'
35. For Rajoub, Hamas are 'nationalists. They care about Palestinian interests no less than I do'. Quoted in Steve Roden and Bill Hutman, 'Order in Jericho'.
36. Jabali's view of Hamas can be gauged by comments he made three days after Black Friday. 'Hamas knows only how to speak with weapons, so the Fatah Hawks will be in the street like Hamas. If Hamas goes somewhere to make trouble, it will be finished.' See Graham Usher, 'Black Friday in Gaza and its aftermath', *Middle East International*, 2 December 1994.
37. Graham Usher, *Palestine in Crisis*, p. 69.
38. 'Seemingly' because Arafat may have been utilising such divisions between his forces to put Hamas on the defensive, working thereby to aggravate dissensions between Hamas's more moderate political leadership in Gaza and its more militant military cadres abroad.
39. For the full text of the PA/Hamas Draft Agreement see *Al-Ahram Weekly* (English), 14–20 September 1995.
40. Yezid Sayigh, 'Sovereignty and security of the Palestinian state', *Journal of Palestine Studies*, Summer 1995, p. 10.
41. Gaza Centre for Rights and Law, *Mass arrest campaign in the Gaza Strip*.
42. Gaza Centre for Rights and Law, *An appeal to Chairman Arafat to reverse the decree establishing a state security court*.
43. B'tselem, *Neither Law nor Justice*.
44. Interview with al-Haq lawyer, Khalid Bitrawi.
45. Jamil Hilal, 'PLO: crisis in legitimacy' and Azmi Bishara, 'Bantus-tanisation or binationalism?' in *Race & Class*, October–December 1995 and Chapter 6, this volume.

Chapter 16: Hizbollah, Syria and the Lebanese Elections

1. This the opinion of Mohammed Mashmoushi, deputy editor of Lebanon's *As-Safir* newspaper. Interview, Beirut, August 1996.
2. 'Out of favour: a test of strength in Lebanon's elections', *The Jerusalem Report*, 19 September 1996.
3. Interview, Beirut, August 1996.
4. Rosemary Sayigh, *Too Many Enemies: the Palestinian experience in Lebanon* (London and New Jersey, Zed Books, 1994), p. 142.

5. For an account of the severity of this suppression, see Rosemary Sayigh's 'Palestinians in Lebanon: (dis)solution of the refugee problem', *Race & Class*, vol. 37, no. 2, October–December 1995.
6. There has been no official census in Lebanon since 1932, so the cited figure is an estimate. But it is generally conceded that the Shi'ites now form the largest single confession in Lebanon.
7. Hizbollah's head of Political Council and MP for south Lebanon, Mohammed Ra'ad, concurs that 'Lebanon's strong ties with Syria serve to counter American political and economic pressures in the region.' Interview, Beirut, August 1996.
8. Amal's 'secularism' is a moot point. While the movement's charter denounces 'loathsome sectarianism', its membership is almost entirely Shi'ite. Nor has Amal ever supported any initiative to deconfessionalise Lebanese politics. Rather, Amal's 'preference' for post-Ta'if Lebanon appears to be at one with Syria's – 'a reconstructed central state and a replastering of sectarian coexistence'. See Sayigh, *Too Many Enemies*, pp. 142 and 175–6.
9. Nizar Hamzeh, 'Lebanon's Hizbollah: from Islamic revolution to parliamentary accommodation', *Third World Quarterly*, vol. 14, no. 2, 1993, p. 322. On the causes of Shi'te anti-Palestinianism, see Sayigh *Too Many Enemies*, pp. 178–82.
10. For Syria and Amal, 'Arafatism' denotes a political opposition not just to the policies of Yassir Arafat and his Fatah movement, but to any independent Palestinian organisation in Lebanon.
11. Sayigh, *Too Many Enemies,* pp. 184 and 188.
12. Ibid., p. 143.
13. Hussein Agha, 'The Syrian-Iranian axis in Lebanon' in *Lebanon on Hold: implications for Middle East peace* (The Royal Institute of International Affairs/Centre for Lebanese Studies, London, 1996).
14. According to Hamzeh, one faction, led by Nasrallah, 'sought to keep Hizbollah in a state of perpetual jihad against all those opposed to their vision of an Islamic Lebanon', urging the continuation of the hostilities against Amal. The second, and ultimately victorious, faction called for Hizbollah's 'rapprochement with other fundamentalist and non-fundamentalist groups in Lebanon', including Amal. This second line enjoyed the support of Iran's President, Hashimi Rafsanjani. See Hamzeh, 'Lebanon's Hizbollah', pp. 323–24.
15. Mohammed Ra'ad. Interview, Beirut, August 1996.
16. For Hizbollah's 'spiritual guide', Sheikh Mohammed Hussein Fadlallah, 'Lebanonisation' refers to a political approach where:

> the Islamic movement ... examines the prevailing circumstances in Lebanon and formulates its strategy within that framework, making allowances for Lebanon's particular circumstances, its

confessional sensitivities, its perception of its environment. In other words, in spreading the faith, the Muslims in Lebanon should not follow procedures that would be inappropriate to Lebanon.

See 'Islamic Unity and Political Change: interview with Sheikh Mohammed Hussein Fadlallah', *Journal of Palestine Studies*, 97, Autumn 1995, p. 67.

17. Mohammed Mashmoushi. Interview, Beirut, August 1996.
18. One example is Amal's control over the government's Council of the South, ostensibly responsible for rehabilitation and welfare in south Lebanon.
19. Hizbollah's Information officer, Ibrahim Mussawi. Interview, Beirut, August 1996.
20. Head of Hizbollah's Jihad el-Bina (Holy Reconstruction)–civil engineering branch, Malik Sa'ad. Interview, Nabatiya, August 1996.
21. Paul Salem, Interview, Beirut, August 1996.
22. Ibid. Salem bases these projections on surveys carried out by his own Lebanese Centre for Policy Studies in Beirut. Other sources say similar figures were the estimate of Syria's Military Intelligence in Lebanon.
23. Hizbollah claims that it won 80 per cent of the Shi'ite vote in Ba'abda (the area within Mount Lebanon which includes Beirut's Shi'ite dominated southern suburbs) but that its candidate was ousted by Christian and Sunni voters allied with Amal. In Beirut, Hizbollah's candidate brandished before the press dozens of fake ballot papers – evidence, he said, of electoral fraud by supporters of Hariri.
24. *Al-Nahar*, 21 August 1996.
25. Many Amal and Hizbollah members implied, had it not been for the last-minute pact, there would have been a real possibility of armed hostilities between the two movements, especially in south Lebanon.
26. Interview, Beirut, August 1996.
27. Given the sensitivity of these comments, the (Lebanese) observer refused to be attributed.
28. Press conference, Cairo, 3 August 1996.

Chapter 17: 'All Killers': Luxor, the Gama'a and Egypt's Prisons

1. Interview with the author, Cairo, July 1996.
2. 'What does the Gama'a Islamiyya want?' Talat Fu'ad Qasim, interview with Hisham Mubarak in *Political Islam: essays from*

Middle East Report (University of California Press, 1997), p. 321.
Qasim was arrested in Croatia in September 1995. He has since
'disappeared'.
3. Ibid., p. 323.
4. For a graphic account of the repression, see Karim el-Gawhary,
'Report from a war zone: Gama'a vs. Government in Upper Egypt',
Middle East Report, May–June/July–August 1995.
5. Interview with the author, Cairo, January 1998.
6. Interview with the author, Cairo, January 1998.
7. Ibid.
8. Interview with the author, Cairo, January 1998.

Chapter 18: Fatah, Hamas and the Crisis of Oslo: Interviews with Marwan Barghouti and Ibrahim Ghoshah

1. The security cooperation was formally restored, with American
   mediation, following the visit to Israel and the occupied territories
   of US special Middle East envoy Dennis Ross in August 1997.
2. On 23 March 1997, an emergency session of Fatah's Higher
   Committee was held in the West Bank village of Beit Sahour, near
   Jebel Abu Ghneim. The meeting recommended that the PA suspend
   all political and security cooperation with Israel and called on
   Palestinians to 'engage in direct struggle with Jewish settlements'
   and 'boycott Israeli goods' in the PA self-rule areas.
3. The popular and military confrontations erupted in the occupied
   territories in September 1996 following Netanyahu's decision to
   open a tourist tunnel beside the Al-Aqsa mosque compound in
   Jerusalem's old city. Eighty Palestinians and 15 Israelis lost their
   lives in the clashes. See *The clashes of September 1996: investigation
   into the causes and use of force* (Gaza, Palestinian Centre for Human
   rights (January 1997).
4. Following suicide bombings in Israel in February and March 1996,
   PA security forces arrested over 1,200 Palestinians on suspicion of
   belonging to Hamas and Islamic Jihad, took over 450 mosques in
   Gaza and outlawed all non-PA militias. On the illegality of these
   measures, see Amnesty International, *Palestinian Authority:
   Prolonged political detention, torture and unfair trials* (London,
   December 1996).
5. Makadmeh is a leader of Hamas's military arm, Izzadin el-Qassam.
   Arrested by the PA after the 1996 suicide bombings, he was released
   without charge one year later. On 21 March 1997 – the same day
   as a Hamas bomber killed three Israeli women in a cafe in Tel Aviv

– Makadmeh addressed a 10,000-strong rally in Gaza. Calling on Palestinians to engage in 'an *intifada* of different kind', he said 'the bulldozers of the enemy' would not be stopped by 'an unarmed people, but only through holy warriors carrying explosives on their shoulders'. On news of the speech, the PA issued a warrant for Makadmeh's arrest for making statements 'harmful to Palestinian security'. Makadmeh has since gone into hiding.

Index

Compiled by Auriol Griffith-Jones

191

Printed and bound by CPI Group (UK) Ltd, Croydon, CR0 4YY

13/04/2025

14656487-0001